UNDER COVER OF SCIENCE

UNDER COVER OF SCIENCE ➢ AMERICAN

LEGAL-ECONOMIC THEORY AND THE QUEST

FOR OBJECTIVITY ➢ James R. Hackney Jr.

Duke University Press ■ Durham and London 2007

© 2006 Duke University Press
All rights reserved.
Printed in the United States of America
on acid-free paper ∞
Designed by Katy Clove
Typeset in Minion by Keystone Typesetting, Inc.
Library of Congress Cataloging-in-Publication Data
appear on the last printed page of this book.

CONTENTS

To my wife (Ann McCarthy Hackney), my son (Adrian Hackney), and my mother (Vernia Hackney)—the three people who have shaped my past, present, and future.

ACKNOWLEDGMENTS

■ My venture into intellectual history was in many ways accidental. I majored in economics as an undergraduate, and did just enough graduate work in the subject to realize I did not want to pursue a doctorate. However, I was fortunate to be able to continue my interest in economics at Yale Law School, which had a wide array of scholars devoted to the field. The list of my professors who served as mentors and tutored me in law and economics included Guido Calabresi, Jules Coleman, Henry Hansman, George Priest, Susan Rose-Ackerman, Roberta Romano, and Alan Schwartz. Each in his or her own way contributed to my understanding of economics and its intersection with law. However, I have to lay my interest in the intellectual history of what I refer to as "legal-economic theory" at the feet of Calabresi and Priest. Dean Calabresi (whom we all referred to as Guido, even as students) fascinated me during my first-year torts class. It was during those initial days in law school that my mind began to tussle over how lawyers think about economics and law. My first encounter with the intellectual history of legal-economic thought was an article by Priest on the intellectual origins of strict products liability. What struck me as a student most about the article, aside from the discerning scholarship, was that the narrative spun out by Priest seemed to miss some of the texture I associated with strict liability arguments from having sat in Guido's class.

Time passed, and after a brief respite as a corporate lawyer I made my way into the legal academy. Soon my attention was directed at resolving my student angst. The result was an article entitled "The Intellectual Origins of American Strict Products Liability: A Case Study in American Pragmatic Instrumentalism." There was quite a distance between my initial reaction to Priest's work and the pragmatic instrumentalism piece. Not having studied intellectual history formally, I relied upon "informal" tutelage from Morton Horwitz ("Mort"), Duncan Kennedy, and G. Edward White. Because they were nearby (across the Charles River in Cambridge) and intellectually simpatico, my relationship with Horwitz and Kennedy was particularly close. One moment is crystal clear and made an immeasurable impact on my career. I was lunching with Mort and discussing my tentative thoughts regarding the intellectual origins of strict products liability when I expressed my insecurity about entering the intellectual history thicket. His response was that you become an intellectual historian by doing intellectual history. That bit of advice sent me on the intellectual journey leading to this book.

This work was produced with help from several institutional sources. I benefited from several provost grants from Northeastern University and research stipends from its law school. I also received a John M. Olin fellowship from the University of Southern California School of Law during my sabbatical year in 1997. It was after that year of reflection that I began seriously thinking about the overarching themes animating this book.

Three scholars read my first full draft: Steven Reucroft, Andre Mirabelli, and Daniel Schaffer. All of their comments were extremely valuable. Steven Reucroft and Andre Mirabelli, both trained physicists, tutored me on my description of scientific developments. Needless to say, not having been formally trained as a scientist, I found that their guidance served me well. Dan helped me understand concerns that a general (but extremely literate) reader would have with my discussion. Dan, a colleague at Northeastern, is representative of the collegial support I have received throughout my career from my friends on the faculty. I would be remiss in not mentioning the numerous insights that I received from my colleagues John Flym, Steve Subrin, and Karl Klare over the years. John, while a Bostonian for much of his life, is my prototype for the Parisian intellectual. Together we spent many a late night having the sorts of deep intellectual conversations that so often occur after just the right combination of food and drink. These were not conversations about text. They were foundational discussions on knowledge and human existence. For these I owe John a tremendous debt. Steve shared an interest in pragmatism with me. Karl has been a consistent sounding board for my thoughts on legal theory. I also want to thank my colleague Hope Lewis, who has always encouraged me in my endeavors. My thoughts regarding philosophical movements were often crystallized after discussions with Steve Nathanson, a colleague in the philosophy department.

Pieces of this book are loosely based on work I have previously published: "The Intellectual Origins of American Strict Products Liability: A Case Study in American Pragmatic Instrumentalism" (*American Journal of Legal History* 39, no. 4, 1995), "Law and Neoclassical Economics: Science Politics, and the Reconfiguration of American Tort Law Theory" (*Law and History Review* 15, no. 2, 1997); "Law and Neoclassical Economics Theory: A Critical History of the Distribution/Efficiency Debate" (*Journal of Socio-Economics* 32 (2003): 361–90); and "The 'End' of: Science, Philosophy, and Legal Theory" (*University of Miami Law Review* 57, no. 3, 2003). I am indebted to the editors and to the external reviewers of these journals for their editorial guidance. The editorial staff at Duke University Press has helped shepherd this project along. Raphael Allen was my initial editor and assisted me in properly framing the book. Reynolds Smith coached me through the final stages.

This book has taken up a lot of my professional and personal space. I thank everyone who has indulged me, as well as aided and abetted me, in my pursuits (sometimes unknowingly). Professionally, there is no one more responsible for aiding me in producing this book than my assistant, Elsie Chan, who has devoted more time and attention to the project than either of us probably cares to admit. Personally, my wife, Ann McCarthy Hackney, has sustained me in undertaking this endeavor in countless ways —be it with cheerful encouragement or by pressing me about when I would "finally get the book done."

The reader may note that the end of the book is much more prescriptive than the historical narrative that makes up the vast bulk of it. As I wound down this project and thought about what it all meant, I felt a desire to convey how the lessons of the historical tale relate to our current situation. It is my belief that we have reached a stage in human civilization in which the ability to engage in dialogue across cultures is imperative to our continued existence as a species. While I had always been concerned about such issues, the birth of my son, Adrian Hackney, has made them even more personal and urgent. My principal reason for doing intellectual history and focusing on the topics I choose is that I believe they have much to say regarding who we are and how we arrived at our present state of affairs. The ideas that unfold in this text, while often articulated in abstract terms, really go to the heart of the human condition. I trust that you will find them as interesting and rewarding as I have.

THE STRUCTURE OF AMERICAN LEGAL-ECONOMIC THEORY

■ Legal theory provides the intellectual underpinning for law. It is the constellation of ideas that shape our conception of law: how it should be formed, the purposes of its deployment, and its meaning. Legal theory has often been taken to be a scientific enterprise (and thus "objective"). However, the philosophy and practice of science and its relationship to legal theory have scarcely been discussed. Indeed, the term "science" is often deployed in legal theory with little discussion regarding its meaning.

This work focuses on economic theory as the discipline at the confluence of science, philosophy, and American legal theory. This is a study on "legal-economic" theory. While intellectual forces that shaped legal-economic theory have undoubtedly affected legal theory generally (if only in a need to respond to the claims of legal-economic theory), the quest for objectivity and scientific pretensions has been particularly manifest in legal-economic theory.

The principal function of legal-economic theory is to explicate the interplay of the legal system and the economic order. Its implications are wide. Our beliefs regarding legal-economic theory have a lot to say about our economic system, particularly the distribution of wealth. Economic theory has been a crucial foundation for policy arguments laid out by legal theorists. Indeed, many arguments claiming that legal-economic theory is an objective enterprise reflect arguments concerning economic theory and its scientific status. Moreover, those debates mirror more general scientific and philosophical debates.

Objectivity in legal theory implies the existence of non-controversial, consensus-based norms that determine law and can be articulated by neutral observers, be they jurists or theorists. While the belief that law is a scientific enterprise has not been widely shared in legal academe since the Second World War (with the notable exception of some powerful voices in the law and neoclassical economics movement, commonly referred to as "law and economics"), "objectivity" as a rallying cry still has much currency. The claim to scientific status is a powerful argument for objectivity, but it is not a necessary one. Objectivity can be juxtaposed to an avowedly political conception of legal theory (and by extension adjudication), because the foundations for legal prescriptions are by their very nature controversial. The idea that legal theory is political (nonobjective) does not necessarily mean that adjudication imposes no constraints on judging. There are "rules of the road." The claim is that neither the rules (often based on legal theory) nor their interpretation is non-controversial.

American law, particularly the common (or judge-made) law, has always relied on claims of "objectivity" (nonpolitical adjudication). This is necessary because the common law is for the most part handed down by judges who are subject to limited democratic accountability, if any. In the battle over which intellectual impulses should guide common law construction based on claims to objectivity, American legal-economic theorists (principally élite judges and legal academics) have been engaging in a pitched battle to maintain law's legitimacy while promoting their preferred economic vision. Historically, the most powerful weapon in this battle, and the one most frequently called upon by legal-economic theorists, has been science rhetoric. Thus, the debates concerning legal-economic theory reflect a dominant strand in western intellectual thought—scientism (privileging knowledge forms deemed scientific).

Examining legal-economic theory sheds light not only on American law but on more general debates as well. Science, and more particularly the idea that scientific modes of inquiry reign supreme, plays a crucial role in shaping western collective thought. Science has not necessarily had a direct influence on legal theory. However, since American legal-economic theory is part of, and is influenced by, our collective thought, conceptions of science profoundly affect legal-economic theory even if the force is only manifested indirectly. It is important to appreciate not only the role that scientism has historically played in American legal-economic theory but how scientific developments have influenced the definition of what may legitimately be claimed to fall under the rubric of science. While scientism has largely remained unabated as a dominant ideology since the seventeenth century, there have of course been significant developments in science. Shifts in American legal-economic theory have been influenced by the impact that scientific developments have had on the philosophical implications of science and on how scientism is deployed.

My focus is on private common law and most particularly accident (tort) law in America. Accident law makes up a large part of the social ordering placed in the hands of judges. In addition, it has been the subject of much popular and political debate. Recent media coverage of such topics as a "$2.7 million" lawsuit for hot coffee spilled at a McDonald's, medical malpractice, and conservative efforts to "reform" the tort system all illustrate the importance of, and interest in, accident law. The reason for the intense contestation is that accident law is deeply interrelated with the distribution of wealth in America. Tort law forces us to wrestle over issues of fundamental justice, such as under what circumstances someone who unintentionally harms another should be made to pay compensation for the related injuries.

The principal legal-economic theories explored in this historical account are classical legal thought, legal realism, law and neoclassical economics, and critical legal studies. These legal-economic theories are linked respectively to classical economics, institutional economics, neoclassical economics, and Keynesian or socialist economics in economic theory; to formalism, pragmatism, the analytic turn, and neopragmatism or postmodernism in philosophy; and to Newtonian physics, Darwin's theory of evolution, Einstein's theories of relativity, and quantum mechanics in science. The scientific discoveries are unique because they have far-reaching philosophical implications. They pose a basic question about the universe and our makeup that presses the bounds between science and philosophy: Is our physical world deterministic (capable of being discussed in certain or absolute terms) or probabilistic (destined to at least have pockets where uncertainty reigns)? In sum, the vision conjured up by Newton and Einstein is deterministic, while that of Darwinism and quantum mechanics is probabilistic. The implications are so broad that it is often not clear whether scientists in these areas are doing science, philosophy, or both. The theories have forced intellectuals in a wide array of fields to fundamentally reconsider deep-seated (but often unspoken) beliefs about the way the world works. My concern is principally over philosophical interpretations, because they carry larger social significance. However, to truly understand the motivations and shifts in philosophical trends it is necessary to keep track of scientific discovery.

This work encompasses American and European intellectual history. The ideas are presented at a level that is accessible to the general reader while doing justice to complexities. Therefore, this historical account of science, philosophy, economics, and legal theory is selective, the criterion being a connection to legal-economic theory and its evolution. In particular, the focus regarding the various legal theories discussed is on strands within those theories that are most relevant to legal-economic theory. While the discussion is segmented by epochs demarcating distinct intellectual climates, there is often significant chronological overlap between movements. Therefore, the periodization should be taken as a convenient heuristic as opposed to a rigid demarcation. A concerted effort has been made to place ideas in social context where relevant. However, this is not a social history. The social milieu is discussed when relevant in crystallizing theoretical connections.

This history is not linear, chronicling inevitable advance, or linear progression, in legal-economic science. A central thesis is that the "quest for objectivity" in legal-economic theory might more aptly be described as the "praxis of objectivity." Multiple forces play roles in constructing legal-economic theory, including its history, culture, and ideology. That legal-economic theory is shaped by many factors, particularly ideology, has been to a great extent masked under "cover of science."

Legal-economic theory, because of its direct intervention into our social ordering, is qualitatively distinct from basic science. In this regard, my skepticism regarding the quest for objectivity in legal-economic theory should not be viewed as an indictment of science qua science. However, the need to call upon science to meet cultural aspirations will be chronicled, because it is crucial to understanding scientism as a tool for sustaining objectivity claims in legal-economic theory.

Legal-economic theory has historically been enthralled by scientism. By cloaking legal-economic theory (an enterprise that is shot through with wealth distribution politics) in science, theorists act to legitimate their preferred political-economic systems. This is scientism's ideological role. Philosophical theories seeking to mimic the sciences play a crucial part because they provide a link between scientific discovery and the larger culture (which also is enthralled by scientism). Modern American legal-economic theory reflects this infatuation.

In the end, the hope is that by looking back on American legal-economic theory and the infatuation with scientism, we may more fruitfully reflect on what American legal theory generally looks like in our current (postmodern) times. This final reflection is a contemporary commentary, marking (please excuse the phrase) the "end of," or perhaps a pause in, our quest for objectivity based on scientific pretensions. If so, in the future legal-economic theory will be undertaken as an exercise in practical politics and intellectual dialogue rather than an approach to reaching apolitical universal truth. Commentary on "contemporary events" risks lacking temporal perspective. In this regard, the discussion might be best classified as informed speculation.

Chapter 1 lays out the seventeenth-century scientific views that shaped the modern consciousness. Scientific certitude arose in the seventeenth century as an intellectual counterpoint to Renaissance skepticism. It planted the seeds for modernity. Two distinct visions of the scientific enterprise arose from this period—Francis Bacon's empirical inductivism and René Descartes's hypothetical deductivism. However, it was Sir Isaac Newton's grand achievement in physics, blending Baconian and Cartesian methods to construct an elegant mathematical model of the universe, that laid the foundation for science's preeminence in modernity. The goal is to survey the intellectual landscape, particularly the bent toward scientism, that would shape debates in American legal-economic theory from its inception until well into the twentieth century.

American legal-economic theory was initially informed by scientific debates. Classical legal theorists, from the Republic's inception and continuing into the post–Civil War era, made claims that the common law was objective and that judges were not engaged in politics. A large part of their appeal was that common law judges remained true to a deductive (formalist) methodology, deriving legal rules from certain a priori principles (natural laws). This outlook was viewed as conforming to scientific dictates, and thence at least approximating scientific certitude. As such, it was argued that law was an objective enterprise. A bedrock principle was individual liberty to own and use property (the foundation of classical economics), highlighting the interplay between economic theory and law.

This initial fusing of legal and economic theory had inevitable political consequences. The existing distribution of wealth was legitimized and future inequalities legally sanctioned.

The classical position was initially challenged philosophically by legal positivists who questioned classical claims to scientific validity. This philosophical challenge was fused with a call for redistributing wealth (contra classical laissez-faire dictates) under the utilitarian banner. Importantly, the challenge did not call scientism into question but claimed to be more scientific. While this interchange between classicals and positivists largely took place in Great Britain, it would cast a large shadow over American legal-economic theory.

Chapter 2 discusses how American legal theorists after the Civil War began to question formalist foundations and classical claims to certitude, marking the first rupture in American legal-economic theory. This interrogation did not take place in a vacuum. In fact, American intellectual thought generally, exemplified in philosophical pragmatism, assailed formalism. The scientific impulse for this criticism was Darwin's theory of evolution, which questioned whether a priori principles and certitude were attainable. The critique was centered on a competing claim to objectivity. The true path to scientific objectivity lay in empirical-inductive methodology and explicit recognition that knowledge acquisition is a probabilistic enterprise. Again, scientism remained in place as a centerpiece. In the early twentieth century legal realists began arguing that classical formalism was a disguise for laissez-faire ideology. Institutional economists leveled a similar critique against classical economics, proposing that there should be more government intervention in the economy in an effort to redistribute wealth from the "haves" to the "have-nots" (echoing the utilitarian position). Like arguments were made by the legal realists in pushing for judicial intervention to assist economically marginalized groups.

Chapter 3 chronicles the shift in American legal-economic theory after the Second World War. Much like the prior rupture in American legal-economic theory, this too reflected larger trends. Early in the twentieth century Newtonian physics was displaced by Einstein's relativity theories and mathematical physics reasserted supremacy over evolutionary biology and its inductivist impulses: determinism again trumped probabilism. In philosophy, pragmatism was displaced by analytic philosophy. Neoclassical economics replaced institutional economics in microeconomic theory, and Keynesian economics established its dominion in the macroeconomic sphere. In legal-economic theory, law and neoclassical economics displaced legal realism. Again, the shift was based on a claim to objectivity—only this time the argument was that the previous era's indeterminism should be replaced by a new formalism and its corresponding exactness. Also echoing prior displacements, there was an argument that legal realism was more about the redistribution of wealth than about science: the work of well-meaning, but theoretically unsophisticated, progressives pushing their personal political agenda in an inappropriate arena (common law courts). This political agenda would be supplanted by the "objective" goal of maximizing wealth. Law and neoclassical economics represents an attempt to reconstitute a formalist structure and advocates (in significant part) a political posture harkening back to the classical era. While in many ways law and neoclassical economics proponents were outside the mainstream (in terms of their small numbers in the legal academy and the political conservatism of some of the more prominent among them), they exerted tremendous force both within law schools and elsewhere because of their claim to scientific superiority (amid the continued influence of scientism) and an increasingly pro-market political environment outside of academe. Their dominance was particularly manifest in legal-economic theory.

Chapter 4 addresses contemporary American legal-economic theory at a time when certitude and scientism have come under heavy assault. Physicists have developed quantum theory and are now peering into an indeterminate subatomic world, exposing the limits of the quest for certainty. Analytic philosophy's scientific pretensions have been heavily criticized as neopragmatist and postmodern waves have swept through academe. Scientism seems to be on the wane. In American legal-economic theory, critical legal studies theorists have leveled analogous criticisms against the alliance of law and neoclassical economics. The argument put forth by those in the critical legal studies movement is that law and legal-economic theory are by their very nature political (as defined earlier), and cannot avoid implicating the distribution of wealth and its political consequences. For the first time in the history of American legal-economic theory, we face the specter of theory that does not claim scientific objectivity. This explains why debates concerning legal-economic theory seem particularly heated. The distribution of wealth cannot be submerged within science. The policy terrain for the debate over distributional concerns is shaped by a Keynesian economic order that fuses laissez-faire ideology with the practical imperatives of government intervention.

The Epilogue is in many ways speculative in nature. It discusses trends in the philosophy of science and philosophy, and how they might shape legal theory in the future. Today all claims to scientific truth (as a universal, totalizing concept), whether in the "hard" sciences or the social sciences, are called into question. This is reflected in legal academe. Multiple perspectives inform contemporary American legal thought, ranging from law and neoclassical economics, socioeconomics, law and religion, critical legal studies, critical race theory, feminist theory, and queer theory—to provide only a partial list. This perspectivist approach is reflected in philosophy as well. The increasing pluralism in American legal theory (including legal-economic theory) raises the question whether a genuine dialogue can take place among legal theorists.

ONE

MODERN SCIENCE, CLASSICAL THOUGHT, AND

THE BIRTH OF AMERICAN LEGAL-ECONOMIC THEORY

■ Modernity is a complex concept. Stephen Toulmin has characterized it as having two distinct branches—literary and scientific.[1] Initially sixteenth-century Renaissance literature, and its humanistic
impulses, significantly shaped modernity. While literary musing
strongly influenced modern intellectual thought in the West, our
principal focus will be on the scientific contributions to modernity.
In America, the prototypical modern state, the scientific ethos dominated legal discourse until recently. Classical legal theory highlights
the point. Classical legal theory derives from classical thought (or
the classical era)—seventeenth-century through early-nineteenth-
century ideas concerning science, philosophy, economics, and law.[2]

Scientific modernism, or modern science, originates in the seventeenth century. Francis Bacon and René Descartes epitomize philosophical speculation on scientific method. They both promoted
modern science as a powerful, all-encompassing worldview standing
against religious zealotry, relativism (skepticism), and other perceived societal ills. Indeed, their influence on the modern mind can
scarcely be underestimated. While they both held distinct views regarding scientific method, it is useful, before turning to their specific
philosophical visions, to explore their similarities. It is only then that
Sir Isaac Newton's grand contribution can be understood as reflecting Baconian and Cartesian ideas. Newtonian physics established
science as the preeminent intellectual field and the discipline for all
other fields to mimic, including law.

A summary of the cultural and historical background to the seventeenth century is necessary to fully appreciate the tectonic shift represented by the rise of science. In the seventeenth century Europe was embroiled in political, cultural, and intellectual crises. The Thirty Years' War (1618–48) had brought to a head festering religious crises, which were manifested in the Reformation and led to brutal combat. Without the Roman Catholic Church as a touchstone for social cohesion (instead it was being invoked as a call to arms), there was cultural crisis. Catholic partisans, Erasmus of Rotterdam most prominently, set the intellectual foundation for the counter-Reformation, arguing that Protestant theology fell short because there was no way to mediate varying conceptions of religious truth. Individual interpretation necessarily led to religious nihilism. This religious skepticism was infectious.

Philosophical skepticism reflected the general cultural crisis. Skepticism is widely recognized as setting in relief modern thought.[3] If we mark the seventeenth century as modernity's starting point, the succeeding four centuries may be looked upon as an extended effort to respond to the skeptical impulse. To understand its import as the departure point for modernity, we first must sketch out the contours of skepticism.

Sixteenth-century scholars were deeply interested in antiquity and Greek skepticism, particularly the writings of Sextus Empiricus. Empiricus and the later skeptics argued that human limitations with regard to knowledge acquisition through the senses made it impossible to divine universal truths. In attacking the quest for certainty, skeptics leveled an extensive critique against Aristotelian science. (Post Reformation, Aristotelian philosophy was also suspect because it had been adopted as Roman Catholicism's unofficial philosophy.) This critique extended the skeptical crisis to science—the very heart of the western intellectual tradition.

Michel de Montaigne, the most influential sixteenth-century skeptic, was deeply influenced by Sextus Empiricus's writings. He took particular aim at claims to scientific certainty in his essay "Apology of Raymond Sebond."[4] In stressing that sense-knowledge was uncertain, Montaigne struck at the burgeoning scientific revolution's core. His critique took on specific significance in a climate where Aristotelian science had been roundly criticized. Montaigne exemplified the sixteenth-century skeptical crisis, setting the stage for efforts to resurrect the quest for certainty and for modernity. Make no mistake—the stakes are high. Are we to accept the notion that claims to knowledge are tentative or will we assume the stance that we can conquer all doubt? It is the latter path that marks the initial trajectory of modernity, including American legal-economic theory.

The path was laid out by two towering seventeenth-century figures in western intellectual history, Francis Bacon and René Descartes. They both begin by granting skeptics their initial suspicion that the senses are not infallible. However, they arrived, through different paths, at the conclusion that scientific certainty is indeed obtainable. The different styles make up the two dominant scientific conceptions in western thought: rationalism (represented by Descartes) and empiricism (represented by Bacon). Varying terminology may be used to express their ideas. For example, deductivism or reductionism will be used as a proxy for rationalism, and inductivism or experimentalism for empiricism. The central point is that two distinct scientific strands were developed to counter skepticism. Of course, this is a gross generalization that will be given a more nuanced treatment as we progress. Indeed, Descartes and Bacon each had room in his scientific method for tools championed by the other. However, there is a distinct emphasis in both Descartes's and Bacon's philosophies of science. More important than differences in their individual methods, both Descartes and Bacon took it as their grand quest to rescue western civilization from skepticism. In its place, they installed science as the antidote to cultural crisis.

Descartes is, to say the least, an enigmatic figure in western intellectual history. While he is best known for his metaphysical stance, as articulated in his *Meditations*, it is arguable that his deepest influence lay in his views on scientific method.[5] *Meditations* is based on a fictional character's intellectual musings or meditations over six days (there is one meditation for each day). Descartes's metaphysics, constructed through the meditations, were to underpin his previously devised method. The method placed science on the firm terrain of certitude. However, to establish this sure footing Descartes would first have to rebut the skeptical challenge. He had to have a metaphysics—a philosophical grounding for knowledge.

Descartes is ingenious in his approach to slaying the skeptical dragon. In the *Meditations* he begins by having his fictional intellectual adopt an extreme skeptical stance. The strategy is to embrace the skeptical premise and nevertheless derive universal truth. Descartes begins in the First Meditation by calling into doubt all truths. Indeed, suspending belief even in

God, he supposed that there might be a "great deceiver" who had wickedly tricked Descartes into believing falsehoods. Descartes could not even trust his senses, because they too might lead him astray. In keeping with a skeptical stance, all was called into question. This position was in direct opposition to Aristotelian philosophy, which depended on the external senses to underpin analysis.[6] Nevertheless, Descartes realized that his own existence was the one thing that could not be doubted: thence the famous: "I am thinking, therefore I am." Descartes took this insight to the extreme, positing that he existed as a mind (a thing which thinks), not necessarily connected to a body (since he could be deceived as to its existence). The problem is that the mind is prone to error and thus cannot be trusted to direct Descartes to any other truths aside from his existence.

Descartes knew that he must devise a truth criterion that would allow him to trust his thoughts. In the Third Meditation he reasons that he can take as true that which appears to him to be both clear and distinct. However, the "great deceiver" still poses a problem, which Descartes surmounts by reasoning that there must be a God and that God would not deceive his own creation. Although to the contemporary reader it may seem odd to invoke God to shore up a philosophical discussion, Descartes was a product and a captive of his times, a Catholic who had received a Jesuit education. The religious jousting of the seventeenth century was over different religious practices, not over whether God existed. Moreover, because of widespread religious persecution, it was prudent for a prominent intellectual to be considered a believer. And to some Descartes did not go far enough: even though he placed God prominently in the *Meditations*, theologians criticized him, arguing that his writings were inconsistent with church doctrine.[7] Descartes's concern over these matters is manifested by his frequent attempts to gain approval from his former Jesuit teachers and other theologians.

With God in place, the possibility for truth exists. However, God does not assure human infallibility. We are all still prone to error. To guard against false ideas, we have to strive for the same clarity and distinctness, later referred to as intuition in *Rules for the Direction of our Native Intelligence*, which had brought Descartes to a belief in God's existence. Descartes's method helps us discern what is clear and distinct. The world may be deceitful, but there is hope for truth. We may even, under certain conditions, rely on our senses to a limited degree. But it is the mind that holds the key to certainty. If we organize our thoughts well, we will be able to counteract our tendency toward error, but that requires much discipline. The discipline would be acquired through Descartes's method.

Descartes had gone about setting out his method as early as 1628, when he drafted his methodological treatise *Rules for the Direction of our Native Intelligence*,[8] predating *Meditations* by some thirteen years. However, instead of publishing *Rules* Descartes anonymously published his *Discourse on Method* in 1637, which proved to be one of the most important philosophical statements in the western tradition.[9] Although a work dealing with science, *Discourse on Method*, which Descartes called a "fable," like *Meditations* is penned in a style more suited toward literary modernists such as Montaigne (demonstrating the blurred lines between literature and science), and in the popular language of French rather than the more scholastic Latin. Descartes also employs an autobiographical approach that invites the reader to take part in the process by which he derived his *Rules for the Direction of our Native Intelligence*.

In *Discourse on Method* Descartes takes as his starting point the same doubt that animated *Meditations*. He must hold up his beliefs to the cold light of reason. Also foreshadowing *Meditations*, Descartes comes to the realization that he cannot doubt his own existence and accepts it as the first principle in his philosophy. From this first principle and other intuitions, Descartes goes on to examine "what were the first and most ordinary effects that could be deduced."[10] Cartesian method is based on intuition and deduction. One might discern a naïve circularity in his argument. He states that his "reasonings follow each other in such a way that, as the last are demonstrated by the first, which are their causes, the first are proved, reciprocally, by the last, which are their effects."[11] Nevertheless, Descartes attempts to safeguard himself from claims of circularity by recognizing that hypotheses must be tested against reality.

While *Discourse on Method* is Descartes's most famous methodological statement, Descartes readily admits that it is sparse in detail. One must look to the *Rules for the Direction of our Native Intelligence* to flesh out his method. Descartes's purpose in writing the *Rules* was to demonstrate that science could be unified under one method—the Cartesian method. In this sense, his efforts exemplify the modernist scientific quest. Descartes is careful, in Rule II, to circumscribe the scientific enterprise by warning against attempts to do science in areas for which our knowledge-capacity is inadequate. It should not be undertaken in areas in which absolute certainty cannot be attained. Cartesian science leaves no room for probabilistic inquiry. Mathematics, a quintessential example of a Cartesian science, wholly embraces deductive reasoning. The deduction that Descartes accepts is not limited to abstract logic: mathematics also relies upon contemplation (or, as Descartes phrased it, enumeration), which in turn relies on something other than pure logic (specifically, memory) and therefore resembles inductive reasoning.[12] Thus Descartes recognizes that the other knowledge base, experience, may uncover truths. However, induction is too susceptible to error (remember his opinion of sense data) to be much relied upon. This does not mean that mathematics is the only mode of scientific inquiry, but that all other sciences must attain its level of certitude—through deductivism or "universal mathematics."

The foundation for Cartesian deductivism is the very same intuitionism alluded to in *Discourse on Method*. However, in *Rules for the Direction of our Native Intelligence* Descartes goes a lot further in explaining intuition. Most importantly, it is not derived by the senses or even imagination. It is arrived at through a "conception which an unclouded and attentive mind gives us so readily and distinctly that we are wholly freed from doubt about that which we can understand."[13] Indeed this intuition is "more certain than deduction itself."[14] It is also more fundamental to the method because it is the basis for first principles.

Descartes represents the height of abstract thinking—championing the mathematics-centered science. His method stands in stark contrast to that proposed by the other towering seventeenth-century philosopher of science, Sir Francis Bacon. Thomas Kuhn maps out a useful dichotomy in thinking about the relationship between Descartes and Bacon, and their relative places in science historiography.[15] Kuhn argues that on the one hand Descartes represents the mathematical tradition in science—taking the mantle from studies in antiquity of astronomy, harmonics, mathematics, optics, and statics. Bacon on the other hand represents the experimental tradition, stemming primarily from experimental activities that had long been incorporated into the western intellectual tradition (including Aristotelian philosophy). Descartes is reacting in great part to philosophical skepticism; Bacon's focus is on scientific practice. Descartes devises a new science to quiet the skeptical storm; Bacon's hope is so to discredit false scientific precepts—and hence rescue mankind. However, Bacon is fully aware that skepticism is "[by] far the greatest obstacle to the progress of the sciences."[16]

While Descartes wrote in a quasi-autobiographical style, Bacon wrote, in his most famous methodological treatise, *Novum Organum*, using aphorisms. Bacon understood the implications: "the first and earliest seekers after truth, with greater frankness and better success, were in the habit of casting the knowledge which they intended to keep for use, into *aphorisms*."[17] The aphoristic style highlighted that Baconian method was a work in progress and not a fully completed theory. In fact, it was Bacon's fondest hope that others would use his method to initiate investigations. The *Novum Organum* is separated into two books. Book I discusses, in large part, the problems with existing methods and the need for Bacon's new science. Book II, which will only be briefly taken up later, lays out the new method.

All science, according to Bacon, had adopted in one form or another the wrong method in obtaining truth: "[T]he sciences we now have are nothing more than nice arrangements of things already discovered, not methods of discovery or pointers to new works."[18] Bacon looks disparagingly at the axiomatic logic championed by the schoolmen as well as "ordinary" induction.[19] However, his greatest scorn is left for the logicians who attempt to arrive at knowledge through deductively reasoning from first principles—the Cartesian method.

The problem with "ordinary" induction, which Bacon contrasted to his "exclusionary" deduction, was that it did not take into account sense limitations. So while skepticism regarding sense perception was not as central to the way Bacon derived his method as it was for Descartes, it did play a role. Aristotle advocated ordinary induction, and Aristotelian induction drew broad generalizations from limited observations. Once theories had been derived from these observations, they would be shielded from contrary evidence by ad hoc distinctions.[20] The problems with ordinary induction resembled other stumbling blocks to truth, which Bacon broadly described as idols.

Four idols afflict the human mind: idols of the tribe, idols of the cave, idols of the marketplace, and idols of the theatre. Idols of the tribe are those shortcomings in human understanding that grip us all. They are part and parcel of the human condition. We inherently distort truth and bend it to suit our own preconceived notions. Data contrary to our beliefs are discounted while those which confirm our beliefs are relied upon too heavily. Moreover, echoing Descartes, Bacon argued that a basic defect in the human sensory system leaves it open to deception.[21] In particular, we suffer from the tendency to perceive things that are in flux as being constant.

This tendency can be contrasted to the idols of the cave: individual peculiarities (of mind, body, education, environment) which hamper understanding. As we depart from the tribe and retreat into our individual caves (minds), these idols, or individual prejudices, creep in. Bacon believed that Aristotle perpetuated this idol: "The most striking example of this is seen in Aristotle, who utterly enslaved his natural philosophy to his logic, rendering it more or less useless and contentious."[22] Idols of the marketplace are those errors that are manifested in human understanding because of defects in language. Words are used to correspond with common understanding that may have no relationship to the real world. These defects are transmitted and thence spread through conversations and interactions with others in the tribe.

Idols of the theatre are the faulty philosophies that have been handed down over the ages. The philosophies constitute tribal (human) stage plays that create fictional worlds having little to do with reality. Here Bacon takes direct aim at existing philosophies and lays the basis for his new method. He divides philosophical schools into three broad camps: sophistical, empirical, and superstitious. Again, Aristotle is a major target: "The most striking example of [*sophistical* philosophy] is in Aristotle, who corrupted natural philosophy with his dialectic."[23] Sophistical philosophy relied solely on dialectic (logic and deductive reasoning) to arrive at truth.

Empirical philosophy, though potentially the most beneficial route because it might be based on real-world experience, in practice was the most dangerous. The danger derived from the exclusive reliance of empiricism, as then practiced, on isolated and often bizarre experiments. Empiricism fostered alchemy and the occult arts. Bacon worried that those who wished to follow his inductivism would, given the natural tendency to error, fall into the old empirical philosophy habits.

Bacon has little to say regarding superstitious philosophy, except that it can be detected in the tendency to inflate and deform thought. This is evident in many philosophies (including theology). While the idols seem to create a formidable barrier to human understanding, Bacon believed that by identifying the idols he had cleared the way for the first useful science in human history. In this regard, his ambitions were no less lofty than those of Descartes. Bacon, like Descartes, sought to redefine philosophy of science and save humanity.[24]

Unlike the skeptics who took limits on the senses as barriers to human understanding, Bacon argued that if the senses were channeled using the proper method, meaningful knowledge could be acquired. In contrast to Descartes, who through his thought experiment sought to evade sense data altogether, Bacon aimed to incorporate and discipline sense data. With this accomplished, entire new vistas would be open for human understanding: "[T]he entry into the kingdom of man, which is founded on the sciences, may be like the entry into the kingdom of heaven."[25] And what is the kingdom of heaven to bring? Bacon envisioned that scientific pursuits would lead to practical works benefiting humanity. This betterment was the ultimate measuring rod for science. Thus there is a utilitarian element to Baconian science that is wholly missing in Descartes.

The following quote gives a good synopsis of what Bacon was trying to accomplish with his method: "Those who have handled the sciences have been either Empiricists or Rationalists Empiricists, like ants, merely collect things and use them. The Rationalists, like spiders, spin webs out of themselves. The middle [(Baconian)] way is that of the bee, which gathers its materials from the flowers of the garden and field, but then transforms and digests it by a power of its own."[26] Bacon's "middle way" was principally inductive. Whereas Descartes arrived at axioms through introspection, Bacon argued that axioms must be devised and tested against evidence. However, unlike prior empiricists' efforts, it was not enough to merely make observations. One must also take into account instances where there is evidence against the proposition under consideration. Bacon applied his inductive method in *Novum Organum*, book II. The actual application is, to say the least, quirky. He discusses topics ranging from heat to the tides. It is little surprise that Bacon is so readily dismissed as a scientist. His arguments leave much to be desired, even to one not trained as a scientist.

Yet Bacon is rightly referred to as a philosopher of science. In setting forth his ideas about scientific methodology and scientific purpose, Bacon can be viewed as having demystified science for the broader intellectual community. Bacon effectively carved out an alternative to the methodological polar opposites: on the one hand magic, which was associated with experimental arts and the production of knowledge toward practical ends;[27] and on the other natural philosophy, which passed itself off as science but was stunted by its fixation with deductive reasoning.

Bacon's vision was to all but wholly reject natural philosophy as then constituted and replace it with his revised experimentalism. In line with his rejecting the natural philosophy emphasis on knowledge based on individual intuition and deduction, Bacon proposed that knowledge would best be produced on an institutional level. He envisioned a scientific learning institute in which knowledge would be produced (and verified) as a group process as opposed to being left to the lone genius. Knowledge could be manufactured for the common good, just like any other human product. Bacon's belief that this form of knowledge production was inevitable, and that it was his calling to show the way, is tied in with his (and many contemporaries') millenarianism. Bacon's belief in inevitable progress was tinged with deep religious devotion. God had preordained a better society and Bacon's role in creating it.[28] Contrary to the modern conception of science as secular, its beginning was inextricably religious. It is Bacon's messianic mission and drive to propagandize, more than any original thinking on his part, that explain his significance to modern intellectual thought and scientism. However, neither Descartes's nor Bacon's philosophy of science would be enough to overthrow Aristotelian philosophy, which was grounded in physics. It was only with the advent of a "new" physics that the Aristotelian edifice would crumble.

Nothing did as much to foster the seventeenth century's infatuation with science as Sir Isaac Newton's discoveries and their practical applications. In *Philosophiae Naturalis Principia Mathematica* (1687) Newton envisioned that the universe operated like a machine, and this mechanistic paradigm became the model for science and reason. Newtonian physics stood as a beacon for the proposition that the world works in a predictable and determinate fashion, framing western thinking. *Principia* brilliantly fused Cartesian deductivism and Baconian inductivism. Newton began by observing facts about the world. These observations led him to a theory about the way the world works. He would then deduce conclusions from his theory concerning other phenomena. The theory could then be tested by further observations.

Seventeenth-century scientists had been struggling to devise a universal gravitation theory that would replace ancient conceptions. At issue was the need to explain how heavenly bodies moved. Galileo Galilei had already described earthly gravitational phenomena, and Johannes Kepler had for the first time accurately described planetary motion. Newton discovered the physical laws governing both motion and gravity, which explained what his predecessors had only described.[29] He began by defining certain crucial concepts such as mass and inertia. Newton then set forth his three laws of motion: the law of inertia, the law of acceleration, and the law of action and reaction. Newton's mechanics were built on these laws. Newton also formulated his two conservation laws (conservation of mass and conservation of momentum) and the universal law of gravitation.

While Kepler, Nicolaus Copernicus, and Galileo had described the motions of the universe, displacing the Aristotelian conception that the solar system revolved around the earth, Newton had succeeded in describing why the universe behaves as it does. The mechanical laws of gravity applied to both heaven and earth. The entire universe could be analogized to a machine (in particular, a clock) and its workings uncovered through reason.

Newton had made an astounding breakthrough in physics. While other scientists had been working on similar problems, Newton's *Principia* was the first systematic account. In this regard, Newton is a scientific giant. His mechanistic vision would go largely untouched until another scientific colossus, Albert Einstein, completely revolutionized physics more than two centuries later.

As evident in its title, translated as ' Mathematical Principles of Natural Philosophy," Newtonian physics was presented as being governed by mathematical laws. It thus benefited from Cartesian elegance and certitude. The mathematical form exemplified scientific reasoning, which would influence the larger intellectual milieu. It is important to distinguish how the larger public perceived Newtonian physics from its practice. While Newton was a great believer in experimentalism and empirical verification, the final product of his works, *Principia*, was received as a set of axioms delivered from upon high. John Dewey went so far as to remark, "Newton foisted a fundamental 'rationalism' upon the scientific world all the more effectually because he did it in the name of empirical observation."[30]

This rendition of Newtonian physics, as describing how the universe hangs together and its mathematical form, no doubt sounds familiar enough. Why the world acts as it does, which is separate from (and not essential to) Newton's laws of physics, often gets lost in the rendition. However, the presumptions supporting Newton's physics are important in understanding his larger worldview and its reception in the greater intellectual community beyond physics.[31]

It is natural for us not only to want to know how the world works, but also to wonder why it works a certain way. In Newtonian physics this meant that one fundamental question had to be answered: What accounted for gravitational phenomena? Newton, engaging in speculative philosophy (as opposed to the experimental philosophy that accounted for the laws of gravity), ascribed gravitational force to a stationary ethereal substance pervading the universe. This substance influenced bodies in such a way as to account for gravitational pull. God, or to borrow the phrase coined by Newton, "the Deity," acted as the puppetmaster orchestrating this phenomenon. The Deity was omnipresent and fixed—the one constant in time and space. This fairly occult explanation was unsatisfactory to some, including the German philosopher and rationalist Gottfried Wilhelm von Leibniz. However, Newton refused to give a physical explanation based on speculation (hypothesis), true to his view that science must be driven by evidence. This stance was interpreted as an endorsement of a Baconian worldview, further enhancing Bacon's stature.[32]

Newton postulated that time and space could be measured as absolute entities and were fixed. Stephen Mason sums up why this theory is significant: "Such a view that time, space and motion were absolute quantities persisted right down to the twentieth century, for in all subsequent theories involving an etherial medium . . . there was one set of systems and observers in the universe who could measure in principle absolute velocities, namely those that were at rest in the cosmic order."[33] Absolute time and space can be contrasted to the relational view put forward by Leibniz, who believed that space and time were not independent but tied to other things and events. The scientific debate between the absolutist view (Newtonian) and the relational (Leibniz) spilled over into philosophy because it was linked to general speculation regarding space, time, and human perception. Absolutism triumphed, supported the geometric vision, and allowed determinism to prevail.

Newton's deterministic natural world, combined with Descartes's absolute knowledge and Bacon's view that science should serve humanity, framed modernity and the quest for certainty. The visions remained a constant, but at times hotly contested, theme in western intellectual thought through the twentieth century.

■

The scientific revolution and cultural upheaval shook up European civilization as it emerged from the seventeenth century. Science began serving a legitimating function.[34] It was the key to social cohesion, and its cultural status as an "objective" forum eclipsed other forms of argumentation—literary, for example—as most legitimate. Ever since, modern culture has required that any enterprise with pretensions to stature claim to be scientific. However, short of doing science, à la Newton, how can one claim to be engaging in the scientific enterprise? The answer is that by following a methodological course that adheres to scientific dictates one can lay claim to the prestige of science—even if the actual enterprise engaged in has very little to do with the activity we commonly identify as science. Modern western intellectual activity has been remarkably centered on the effort, oftentimes misguided, to mimic science.

Descartes and Bacon originally respond to cultural crisis and offer up science as an antidote. Thence, in no small part they bear responsibility for scientism in the modern era. Second, they provide templates for what it means to do science. As such, the methods offered up by Descartes and Bacon constitute valuable assets to be appropriated by those who wish to cloak themselves in the garb of science. Their cloaking may bear little resemblance to the actual method that either Descartes or Bacon expounded (let alone actual scientific practice), but the discourse can still serve the legitimating function.

The dilemma is that Descartes and Bacon view science differently. Of course, for those who really do science this is not very important, because the point is not to adopt a pure method but to further scientific discovery—that is the bottom line. In fact, while my portrayal has emphasized Descartes's deductive thought and Bacon's inductivism, each allows some room for the other's method in his system. What is commonly referred to as the "scientific method" combines both approaches. However, those who do not in fact do science but attempt to cloak themselves in science have a harder time of it. Both deductivism and inductivism can be made to fit a particular agenda, but that leaves the door open for critiques that the approach was chosen to obtain a desired result. Unlike in the sciences, these criticisms cannot be rebutted through experimentation or empirical evidence, because of the ephemeral nature of nonscientific enterprises.

Debates over method do not occur in a vacuum. What it means to do science is largely contingent upon cultural perceptions. These perceptions are driven not only by the way scientists go about doing what they do (method), but also by how they describe our world. Method aside, Newton's conclusion that the universe operated as a mechanical clock influenced how the larger culture perceived science. Newton's physics implies that the physical world is on a fixed, predetermined path susceptible to mathematical representation, analysis, and prediction. The cultural perception was that through science we could comprehend the physical universe with certainty. This scientific vision, which had been championed by Descartes and Bacon, shaped western collective thought.[35] Thus, after the seventeenth century the quest to be scientific in many areas outside the physical sciences, including law, was in effect a quest for certainty.

Legal theory is the stage on which actors—be they scholars, jurists, or practicing lawyers—engage in their efforts to justify or reshape law. Legal theorizing is distinct from the practice of law, just as formulating scientific method is distinct from engineering. While legal theorizing is primarily done in academe, others in the legal profession are informed by it, and at times contribute to it.

We do not have to look very far to begin tracing the connection between legal theory and science. Francis Bacon was an influential contributor to English legal theory and by extension legal theory in America. Bacon had an illustrious legal career—serving both as attorney general and as lord chancellor. He argued that his scientific method should be applied to the law. In this regard, his major contributions to legal theory are twofold: arguing for empiricism in deriving the law and casting it in a scientific light.

In seventeenth-century Europe, law would indeed take on a scientific veneer. M. H. Hoeflich has done an admirable job laying out the argument that seventeenth-century European legal theory developed by following primarily the deductive, or, as Hoeflich frames it, geometric model.[36] Despite Bacon's general admonition that the scientific study of law should be inductive in nature, western legal theory often did not comport with

Baconian inductivism. As for applying the deductive method to legal theory, the principal proponent was Descartes's fellow rationalist Leibniz, who was trained as a lawyer and wrote several legal texts. He argued that legal science must mimic mathematics and follow the deductive method. Hoeflich chronicles how the geometric method spread across Europe, originating on the Continent but also having a great effect in England.[37] This movement was profoundly influenced by ideas associated with Newtonian physics. While legal theory was decidedly deductive, there was some room for inductivism where politically expedient.

In order for the deductive machinery to be deployed there must be principles from which particulars may be derived. It is at this point that the law ceases to be solely about method and crosses over to the political. In the Anglo-American tradition, as well as to a significant degree on the Continent, these principles were derived from the "natural" law. Natural law has been defined as a "system of rules and principles for the guidance of conduct which, independently of enacted law or of the systems peculiar to any one people, might be discovered by the rational intelligence of man, and would be found to grow out of and conform to his nature."[38] Thus it was unsurpassed as an objective basis for law.

Roger Berkowitz has thoughtfully tied together Liebniz's rationalist philosophy, its impact on his legal theory, and the crucial link that natural law provides between the two.[39] Berkowitz first argues that while Leibniz is rightly associated with the geometric paradigm, he did not believe that geometry alone could provide a scientific basis for law. Law is a real-world phenomenon, and thus requires reliance upon natural scientific methods. In this regard, Berkowitz argues that Liebniz "was the first jurist to think about law as a product of modern science."[40] Just as the natural sciences had to have first principles (foundational laws), legal science must be grounded on an immutable foundation. Liebniz chose natural law to be that foundation. With natural law as the first principle, all lesser laws could be derived. This system had the quality that Liebniz ultimately strived for— certainty. That same certainty (or objectivity) would later animate American legal-economic theory.

A key text in understanding American legal-economic theory and its natural law underpinnings is Sir William Blackstone's *Commentaries*. In the *Commentaries* we see an Anglo-American application of Liebniz's legal scientific method. The *Commentaries* are a four-volume set of legal treatises written by Blackstone between 1765 and 1769 in an effort to systematize English common law.[41] Their scientistic thrust makes Newton's influence in British intellectual life readily apparent. As stated by Daniel Boorstin in his meticulous essay on Blackstone's *Commentaries*, Blackstone was "doing for the English legal system what Newton had done for the physical world."[42] Blackstone's was the first attempt to distill English common law in a comprehensive way, and he did so with the desire to make it accessible to a broad audience (as Blackstone phrased it, "gentlemen of independent estates and fortune") and introduce his readers to legal science.[43] The *Commentaries* proved to be of incalculable importance to eighteenth-century English legal theory and would eventually become highly influential in America as well.

Blackstone took the natural law as an inevitable starting point. The "Supreme Being" or "Maker" imparted the natural law to the world when "He," according to Blackstone, created the universe. There are natural laws that dictate human affairs, just as there are such laws governing the physical universe: "Upon these two foundations, the law of nature and the law of revelation, depend all human laws; that is to say no human laws should be suffered to contradict these."[44] There is a striking parallel between the axiomatic structure of the *Commentaries* and Newton's physical laws. Natural law principles are analogous to Newton's laws of motion. From these principles, particular legal rules are deduced. The natural law originates with the "Maker," physical laws with the "Deity."

Of course, man should adhere to the natural law, because "as man depends absolutely upon his [M]aker for every thing, it is necessary that he should, in all points, conform to his [M]aker's will."[45] Not only are we obligated to conform to our Maker's will, but it is inevitable that we do so. And what is our Maker's will? It is the natural law. Fortunately, we have the moral intuition to discover the foundational principles that constitute natural law. In particular, the good citizens of England were blessed with a legal system that comported perfectly with the natural law. In effect, English law and natural law were synonymous. This equation, combined with its scientistic pretensions, legitimated English law.[46] Nevertheless, Blackstone's claim to science is patently false.

Newton derived his physical laws from observation. Those observations were "objective" in the sense that they constituted physical phenomena (such as gravity or the location of planets in the universe) that were not socially constructed and for the most part were non-controversial. The corollary for Blackstone was English law, observed but socially constructed and politically charged. Thus while the *Commentaries* were fashioned after the Newtonian scientific method, their core was profoundly political. The scientific gloss was key to putting forth the appearance of objectivity for the *Commentaries* and the claims to legitimacy for English law.

In discussing legal study, Blackstone urged students not to undertake apprenticeship without university training, an admonition that would later be echoed by American legalists. Importantly, university training familiarized the perspective lawyer with natural law foundations: "If practice be the whole he is taught, practice must also be the whole he will ever know: if he be uninstructed in the elements and first principles upon which the rule of practice is founded, the least variation from established precedents will totally distract and bewilder him . . . he must never aspire to form, and seldom expect to comprehend, any arguments drawn, *a priori*, from the spirit of the laws and the natural foundations of justice."[47] Once legal foundations were understood, the law student could then "reason with precision [(certainty)], and separate argument from fallacy, by the clear, simple rules of pure, unsophisticated logic" and "fix his attention, and steadily pursue truth through any [*sic*] the most intricate deduction, by the use of mathematical demonstrations." Again, this was all dependent on the student having "impressed on his mind the sound maxims of the law of nature, the best and most authentic foundation of human laws."[48]

A university education was necessary for future lawyers to understand the scientific method. Practicing lawyers were not only to be legal practitioners but also legal scientists (theorists). It was important to claim the mantle, the cover, of science because in the modern world science provided a basis for legitimacy. Scientism was used to reify and legitimate existing social relationships. Boorstin has argued that behind Blackstone's natural law reasoning lies the one core value that Blackstone holds sacrosanct over all others—particularly the values of humanity and liberty that he also extolled—property.[49]

Blackstone devised a legal theory that preserved existing property relationships and the existing distribution of wealth—and then urged that this theory should be central to legal education. While I have painted a relatively neat picture, there are intricate wrinkles and creases in Blackstone's view. However, all conveniently falls into place to bolster English law and thus property. In summarizing natural law, Blackstone pithily asserts that the Maker has "graciously reduced the rule of obedience to this one paternal precept, 'that man should pursue his own true and substantial happiness.' This is the foundation of what we call ethics, or natural law."[50] The status quo property and wealth distributions are naturalized because they result from self-interest, or, as Blackstone more pleasantly phrased it, "that universal principle of action"—"self-love."[51] This principle fits nicely with a laissez-faire ideology and presages Adam Smith's soon-to-be-written *The Wealth of Nations*. Blackstone was expounding a legal-economic theory that supported a legal vision conforming to the prevailing economic order. The connection between Newtonian physics, natural laws, and laissez-faire economics was aptly summarized by John Dewey: "Laissez-faire was the logical conclusion [of natural law theory]. . . . This doctrine is demonstrably the offspring of that conception of universal laws that phenomena must observe which was a heritage of the Newtonian philosophy."[52] If the world is inherently rational and unchanging, then any attempt to intervene, including in the socioeconomic sphere, was necessarily doomed to failure. Crucially, while the *Commentaries* were packaged as merely reporting on English common law, they actually served as a commentary on an ideal social structure. Blackstone was doing political-economic theory under the guise of legal science.[53]

Thus was legal science called upon to protect property and champion limited government intervention. Blackstone's legal-economic theory may be summed up in his own words: "The law of nature [(self-interest)], being coeval with mankind, and dictated by God himself, is of course superior in obligation to any other. . . . But in order to apply this to the particular exigencies of each individual, it is still necessary to have recourse to [(deductive)] reason, whose office it is to discover, as was before observed, what the law of nature directs in every circumstance of life, by considering what method will tend the most effectively to our own substantial happiness [(self-interest)]."[54] This is a political manifesto. Its enthusiastic reception on American soil reflects the need that American élites had to appropriate modern tools in crafting a society with qualities similar to those of Blackstone's England, particularly the treatment of private property. Stephen Toulmin has noted that the "more confident one was about 'subordination and authority' in Nature, the less anxious one need accordingly be about social inequalities." In this regard, the "world view of modern science—*as it actually came into existence*—won public support around 1700 for the legitimacy it apparently gave to the political system of nation states as much as for its power to explain the motions of planets, or the rise and fall of the tides."[55]

Given America's revolutionary beginnings, the questions of legitimacy were even more pressing than in Blackstone's England. The legitimacy of law itself was called into question because of two fundamental facts concerning America: its thoroughgoing anti-authoritarianism and its religious underpinnings. In the new republic the American legal establishment was not held in high regard. Perry Miller has described the "widespread hostility of ordinary Americans to the very concept of law and more specifically their bitter antagonism to the Common Law."[56] One significant problem with the common law was that it originated in England, from which America had just won its freedom. Compliance with it ran against Americans' nativist spirit. This sentiment is clear from Thomas Jefferson's observation: "Of all the doctrines which have ever been broached by the Federal government this novel one, of the Common Law being in force and cognizable as an existing law in their courts, is to me the most formidable."[57] The view was also reflected in popular culture. Miller argues that the portrayal of law in James Fenimore Cooper's *The Pioneers* in 1823 captures a widespread antagonism toward legal élites.[58] A central theme throughout the popular series is the various legal transgressions of the protagonist, Natty Bumppo, who opposes legal restrictions in his frontier domain. He is led into militant skirmishes with the law, which is personified by the fictional Judge Marmaduke Temple. Judge Temple is portrayed as evil incarnate, imposing a repressive legal regime against the spirited Bumppo.

Reservations concerning legalism were also based on fears that the law was a heathen creation and a threat to religious teachings. The backlash might be fully expected in a country swept up in revivalist fervor. In America the Great Revival marked the first half of the nineteenth century. Revivalists from various Protestant sects spread across the country in an effort to rescue the country from secularism.[59] Legal élites responded by arguing that their legal principles were moral and even based on scripture. In constructing a legal theory to sustain their argument, they relied heavily on Blackstone.

In antebellum America, Blackstone's *Commentaries* were akin to a legal bible. Along with other treatises (such as Chancellor James Kent's *Com-*

mentaries and Justice Joseph Story's *Laws of Bailments, The Conflict of Laws,* and *Equity Jurisprudence*), the *Commentaries* played a vital role in educating the American lawyer.[60] They were an instant success, with at least a thousand sets sold in the Unites States by 1771. The popularity of the *Commentaries* inspired "Americanized" versions in which American precedents were inserted and Blackstone's monarchist sentiments were replaced by republican anecdotes.[61] Among other notable jurists and commentators, Kent and Story acknowledged their intellectual debt to Blackstone and modeled their own treatises after the *Commentaries*.[62]

The nineteenth century "treatise movement" was marked by commentaries devoted to systematizing the common law.[63] Therefore it is easy to understand the fascination with Blackstone, despite his English pedigree. He outlined a legal system and a model for commentary that were tailormade for American legal theorists. However, the impact was not solely on élites. Despite the popular reaction against legalism, Blackstonian thought spread with American expansion. It was not unheard of for laymen in newly settled territories to act as legal counsel with little more than the *Commentaries* or another treatise as their guide.[64]

Blackstone's belief that the law's moral foundation lay with the "Great Creator" made it possible for legal theorists to argue that the law merely reflected divine will. There was no conflict between religious principles and law. Nowhere was this more evident than in David Hoffman's influential *A Course of Legal Study* (1836). Hoffman intended his work as a guide for both lawyers and students of the burgeoning "legal science." In his tribute to Joseph Story, which prefaces the book, Hoffman takes note that "[t]he life of all study is method" and that "it is the main object of the following pages, not to teach, but to point out the method of acquiring."[65] The method has aptly been described by Howard Schweber as "bounded inductivism."[66] Hoffman begins by directing the reader to master a corpus of literature so as to familiarize himself with legal first principles. The student of law is then directed to search out and catalogue its rules. Inductive search should always be connected to religious or natural law. This is a decided twist on Blackstone's natural law theory. Legal rules are not deduced from natural law. However, they must adhere to natural law as a matter of faith. Law is "dictated to us by the light of nature, or by revelation" and constitutes the "system of rules to which intellectual and physical worlds are subjected."[67]

The first and ultimate source of principles is the Bible. The Bible is inspired by the "great Legislator of the universe" and lays out the "dictates of nature." As such, it sets forth the "foundation of the laws." Indeed, the Bible constitutes the "foundation of the common law for every Christian nation."[68] While Hoffman discusses selected secular texts, including the works of Cicero, Aristotle, Locke, Bentham, and Adam Smith, none is meant to supersede the Bible as ultimate arbiter. Hoffman also made a strenuous argument for relying upon Roman law in searching for first-order legal principles. The Roman imperial code was admired because, as Leibniz had noted, it mimics geometry.[69] Roman law is held up as exemplifying "divine science."[70] It is a universal, natural law, and satisfies the need to have law based on "pure reason" and "eternal principles of justice."[71]

This affinity toward moral philosophy, with a distinct emphasis on natural law principles and religious doctrine, was not limited to training legal élites. Indeed, it was central to general university education in antebellum America.[72] It was seen as essential for every law student to be exposed to the basic moral teachings, so as to impart them to others and better understand the rules that had developed over time. Hoffman provided a guide to moral education for those who were not university trained, reflecting Blackstone's admonition that potential lawyers be university trained or at least widely read.

Despite the emphasis by some on "bounded inductivism," deductive methodology greatly influenced the treatise movement and American legal theory generally.[73] With principles in tow, the student could use deductive analysis and derive particular rules. Why is this significant? Again, we return to the issue of legitimization. One way to elide criticisms that the law is an élitist tool was to argue that it is objective. Legal theorists of the late eighteenth century and the early nineteenth were preoccupied with legitimizing law as a science. As early as 1794 James Kent, perhaps the preeminent legal theorist at the time, argued in a lecture at Columbia that law must be "stripped of its delusive refinements, and restored to the plain Principles of Reason."[74] It would have to be a mighty reason to overcome the twin American skepticisms (toward law): anti-authoritarianism and religiosity.

The treatise movement was a big step toward establishing legal science. Legal treatises marked a fresh start for American legal theorists. Obviously, much American legal doctrine derived from English common law. However, for those who kept the Revolution close to their hearts, relying on English legal relics was antithetical. Legal theorists argued that this was a nonissue, because they accepted Blackstone's approbation that English law was synonymous with universal natural law. In particular, Kent argued that in the common law lay a reservoir of wisdom never before witnessed by mankind.

Kent made his grand contribution to the treatise movement with his *Commentaries on American Law* in the 1820s. In them Kent systematically laid out American law principles. Like other treatises of the period, Kent's was designed to illustrate law's logical consistency. Inspired by Blackstone, they scientifically distilled law. Even the uncultivated American citizenry would have to bow to the altar of legal science.

Perry Miller makes an insightful point regarding early American legal theorists: "They could easily assert that an inherent rationality ran through the epochs of the Common Law, but once they announced to the Republic that the body of law which they administered was a science, they had to avow—not so much to their critics as to themselves—whether they constructed their wisdom by induction out of particulars into generalities or by deduction form the basic principles into the specific instances."[75] There is no question that the legal theory of the times was decidedly deductive. Deductivism's elegance and seeming certainty were unmatched by inductivism, making it that much more simple to argue for its objectivity. In addition, once first principles were established, law's basic direction was preordained: no appeal to experience could alter the ultimate result. Just as Blackstone had made protecting property the ultimate value in his legal-economic theory, American theorists viewed protecting property rights and individual liberty as paramount. The American republic was founded by landed gentry who had every intention to maintain their status against redistributionist impulses. James Madison in the *Federalist* 10 (1787) warned against class war—"the most common and durable source of factions, has been the various and unequal distribution of property." Factions were based on economic class: "A landed interest, a manufacturing interest, a mercantile interest, . . . with many lesser interests, grow up of necessity in civilized nations, and divide them into different classes, actuated by different sentiments and view." Legal-economic theory served to regulate the "various and interfering interests" and protect against the "rage for the equal division of property" and other "wicked projects." The redistribution of wealth would not take place under the existing economic order.[76]

Law's function in protecting the existing distribution of property was manifested in many legal opinions invoking natural law theory in the classical era. Beginning in the early 1800s and intensifying after the Civil War, America experienced protracted and significant economic upheaval. The turmoil frequently revolved around workers' increasing demands for fair wages and working conditions. State legislatures responded with legislation designed to grant workers certain rights, such as the right to strike and to receive workers' compensation. Courts responded by striking down progressive measures, on the basis that they unlawfully interfered with business owners' property rights. Using the natural law framework, various state courts as well as the U.S. Supreme Court reasoned that since property was sacra sancta as a first principle, any government regulation that violated the right to dominion over property violated natural law and must be rendered null and void.

The analysis disregarded context. Workers were not viewed as underdogs struggling to obtain a fair share of the ever-expanding economic pie, but as the bargaining equals of business owners. With this worldview, courts saw no need to favor labor. Workers had the ability to bargain with management just as in any other contractual relationship. Government intervention was therefore unfair to business owners. No attention was paid to power or group dynamics. Under the natural law view, the focus was on the individual, not the group.

Perhaps the most infamous application of the natural law worldview is the U.S. Supreme Court opinion in *Lochner v. New York* (1905). The *Lochner* court had to determine whether a New York state law limiting bakers' working hours was constitutional. The law was an attempt to apply the state's police powers to regulate safety, health, and general welfare. The court struck down the legislation as violating the parties' contract freedom. In doing so, Justice Peckham, writing for the majority, reasoned that "there is no contention that bakers as a class are not equal in intelligence and capacity to men in other trades or manual occupations."[77] Allowing state intervention would upset the prevailing property order.

As noted by Duncan Kennedy, the majority opinion in *Lochner* incorporates a classical worldview, which Kennedy describes as synthesizing "positivist science of law, natural rights constitutionalism and Classical Economics."[78] Justice Harlan deployed the same scientistic analysis in his dissent. Although Peckham and Harlan reached different results, the logic deployed was identical, reflecting a Newtonian view that the world can be analyzed with certainty and determinate conclusions reached deductively. Just as Newton's laws of motion could be used to precisely measure how billiard balls collided on a pool table, legal science could be used to reconcile conflicting economic interests. Once economic relations were atomized they could be analogized to billiard balls colliding in the "game" of social conflict. This scientism, which reemerges in legal-economic theory throughout its historical development, was blended with a distinct conception of property and the role of the state in the classical era.

While *Lochner* dealt with labor issues concerning wage rates, it also illustrates, along with subsequent anti-statist opinions by what came to be called the "*Lochner* Court," a pro-business orientation with direct implications for accident law. A pressing issue in accident law, which will be taken up in chapter 2, is workers' compensation for accidents in the workplace. The classical view regarding government efforts to protect workers against such accidents by mandating compensation from employers would be to dismiss them as interfering with freedom of contract. By extension, laws protecting consumers against accidents caused by products distributed into the stream of commerce by business would also constitute an infringement on the contractual relationship between seller and consumer. Therefore, in the field of tort law classical theory favors lack of compensation for victims of product-related accidents. This is a pro-business position.

The judicial opinions protecting property interests before and after the Civil War adopted the legal-economic theory handed down by Blackstone and adopted by early American legalists at the Republic's inception. It was based on a theory of divine intervention that had much salience in antebellum America. This divine underpinning can be gleaned from the following quotation from Blackstone: "The whole progress of plants, from the seed to the root, and from thence to the seed again; the method of animal nutrition, digestion, secretion, and all other branches of vital economy; are not left to chance, or the will of the creature itself, but are performed in a wondrous involuntary manner, and guided by unerring rules laid down by the great Creator."[79] God had preordained the economic order just as the Creator had determined the natural order. Blackstone's theory of divine intervention paralleled that of the deity in Newtonian physics. Newton believed that divine intervention must have been responsible for the atoms forming the plants and animals that seemed uniquely fitted for earthly inhabitance. Under Newtonianism (which strongly informed classical legal theory) life was not a matter of happenstance but something preordained by divine intervention.[80] In this light, mankind could not undermine the order of things, including the distribution of property.

As mentioned previously, Blackstone's preoccupation with property rights anticipated the laissez-faire worldview of Adam Smith in *The Wealth of Nations*. In turn, Smith's treatise on political economy, the most comprehensive explication of classical economics, had a tremendous influence on classical legal theorists (including David Hoffman). As reflected in Peckham's and Harlan's divergent conclusions, the science of classical legal thought might be indeterminate with regard to political outcomes. Nevertheless, classical ideology tended toward conservative prescriptions.

As providence would have it, *The Wealth of Nations* was published in the same year, 1776, that the Declaration of Independence was signed. While others had espoused piecemeal the ideas put forth in *The Wealth of Nations*, it was Smith who comprehensively articulated free-market tenets. Smith's system was very much deductivist. He began with a fundamental assumption about human behavior: individuals are driven by self-interest. Although the self-interest motive in and of itself did not take into account consequences to others, self-interest served the social good. Competition in the marketplace would act as a self-regulating "invisible hand," assuring that the greatest possible amount of wealth would be created on a societal level and benefit everyone. Contrary to popular belief, Smith was not an apologist for the capitalist class: he harbored suspicion of its penchant for self-aggrandizement, and he expressed concern for the poor. However, he believed that government interference with free market competition would, even if well intentioned, negatively affect the economy.

Smith's worldview is illustrated in his ideas on the returns to labor. In *The Wealth of Nations* he pronounces: "The produce of labor constitutes the *natural* recompense or wages of labor."[81] Anticipating the jurisprudence of the *Lochner* era, Smith notes that "the common wages of labor, depends everywhere upon the contract usually made between two parties." However, he points out that the parties' interests "are by no means the same" and that "workmen desire to get as much, the masters to give as little as possible."[82] While Smith did take the view that supply and demand would be the ultimate arbiter in negotiations between employers and employees, he acknowledged that the owners of production had the advantage. Owners could sustain themselves for long periods without labor. Employees on the other hand led a hand-to-mouth existence and could not survive for long without work. Smith also recognized that business owners were likely to conspire to hold wages down, and do so with more legal protections than were afforded to laborers in their efforts to organize.

The only way for wages to grow was to have the country's wealth rise at an increasing rate. The irony was that since capitalists worked to keep wages at a subsistence level, it was only the capitalists who had the discretionary income to contribute to savings and increase the wealth of the nation. Thus wealth maximization would be attained by free enterprise, not government regulation benefiting labor. Regarding wage regulations, Smith concluded, "law can never regulate them properly; though it has often pretended to do so."[83] In general, he believed in unfettered individualism, and believed that attempts by government to channel individual enterprise (no matter how well intentioned) would inevitably lead to misallocation of resources and a reduction in overall wealth.

At points, Smith expresses a genuine sympathy for the poor, arguing that for the societal good it would be best if they were given a sufficient share of economic goods so that they may be "tolerably fed, clothed and lodged."[84] On the other hand, he notes somewhat dispassionately, if the free market dictates a result such as increased mortality among the poor, society must be reconciled to it.

Smith put forward a powerful case supporting laissez-faire economics. *The Wealth of Nations* appealed to scientific impulses because it provided concrete predictions about events in capitalist economies. The laws of supply and demand served as the postulates for economic science in much the same way as Newton's laws of motion did for physics. They comprehensively describe the way the economic world works. Governor Pownall of Massachusetts, a contemporary of Smith, noted that *The Wealth of Nations* constituted "an institute of the *Principia* of those laws of motion, by which the operations of the community are directed and regulated."[85] This was all set out in an intellectual environment dominated by the ideal of scientific certitude.

In addition, classical economics fit nicely with natural law politics. Under the dictates of natural law, judges justified not using law to interfere with the natural workings of the economy. Natural law was not just an artifice put forward to protect the status quo. While it did serve entrenched economic power interests, it was also a widely held American belief. The popularity of George Combe's *The Constitution of Man* (1828) is evidence that natural law had a strong hold on the Anglo-American psyche. While Combe is known largely for his beliefs in phrenology, the nineteenth-century "science" that linked the size and shape of the brain and its various parts to character traits, he was also a popularizer of natural law theory. Combe argued in *The Constitution of Man* that certain natural laws, if heeded, would lead to individual fulfillment and happiness. In this sense *The Constitution of Man* can be viewed as a "self-help" book. It was wildly popular, selling approximately 350,000 copies between 1828 and 1900, surpassing the sales of Darwin's *The Origin of Species.* While the book mainly sold in Britain, a subsidy from a phrenology benefactor allowed cheap copies to be made available in America as well.

Though Scottish, Combe lectured throughout the United States to spread his message to popular audiences.[86] The tremendous interest in *The Constitution of Man* highlights the popularity of natural law theories and science. Combe's science of the "good life" was grounded in natural laws, analogous to the science of the "good society" espoused by natural law theorists. Natural law theory resonated with the American populace on many levels. It was not until belief in divine intervention and the invisible hand were shattered that the natural law theory edifice would be called into question.

British legal theorists had early on questioned the natural law foundation of Blackstone's legal theory. John Austin, Jeremy Bentham, and John Stuart Mill, all generally considered legal positivists, offered up a competing theory, utilitarianism. (Of course, legal positivism is a school of thought that encompasses many perspectives and theorists, and is not limited to utilitarianism.) In promoting utilitarianism as the guiding light for law, these legal positivists mounted a withering attack on natural law theorists generally and Blackstone in particular. The criticism was based on the view that natural law theory failed to meet the very scientific threshold it had set out for itself. Scientism was turned against natural law theorists.

Austin's critique of Blackstone is particularly harsh and polemical. He criticizes the "method observed by Blackstone in his far too celebrated

Commentaries." The *Commentaries* are derided as not containing "a single particle of original and discriminating thought" and having been directed to the "sinister interests, and to the mischievous prejudices of power."[87] Austin was preoccupied with removing legal theory's metaphorical underbrush (natural law). Since the "natural law" was purely metaphorical, it had no place in a conversation regarding positive law. With regard to Blackstone, this criticism might have been a bit overstated, since although Blackstone is ultimately connected to natural law theory, he arguably articulates some positivist themes.[88]

Austin had no problem with an assertion that because of the "dictates of utility" certain rules were transnational and not limited to any particular time (that is, they would be universal), but he did take offense at the belief that as a general matter natural laws were the "offspring of a moral instinct or sense, or of innate practical principles."[89] Austin pointedly raised the following question: "What . . . is the nature of things?"[90] As a legal positivist, Austin adopted a command theory of law and argued that law was neither "natural" nor subject to intuition (religious or otherwise) but rather was located in the sovereign. He regarded Hobbes's view that "no law can be unjust" as a truism because "positive law is the measure or test of legal justice and injustice."[91]

Jeremy Bentham, in his *A Fragment on Government*,[92] harshly criticized Blackstone. In many ways the work serves a very limited purpose. Bentham's narrow aim is to criticize a subsection of Blackstone's introduction to the *Commentaries* devoted to government formation. However, the narrow criticism has broader implications. Bentham viewed Blackstone as an apologist for the existing social structure. While the *Commentaries* on the surface were limited to stating the law, Bentham believed that they actually functioned to reify political positions underpinning the existing law, and to this he objected. This was all the more dangerous to Bentham because Blackstone had come to have great influence over legal theory and practice. (Bentham knew this from firsthand experience as Blackstone's student.) Bentham viewed Blackstone as an "enemy" and believed that "to wage against [his] works" was essential "for the interests of true science, and of liberal improvement."[93] Bentham did find much to commend Blackstone's narrower project—stating the law. However, by couching the law as deriving from natural law, Blackstone had cut off opportunities for reform. Bentham found this to be nothing short of reprehensible. His central message was the need for reform. To the extent that Blackstone glorified the past, he could be charged with being "obsequious only to the whisper of interest, and to the beck of power."[94]

Bentham's call for reform was based on the perceived need for a scientific approach to social progress. The science—utilitarianism—would come to have a tremendous influence on legal-economic theory. Bentham's utilitarianism was based on the "fundamental axiom, *it is the greatest happiness of the greatest number that is the measure of right and wrong.*"[95] Elie Halevy has directly tied this political vision to the Newtonian revolution: "What is known as Utilitarianism, or Philosophic Radicalism, can be defined as nothing but an attempt to apply the principles of Newton to the affairs of politics and of morals."[96] Bentham believed that "if there be room for making, and if there be use in publishing, *discoveries* in the *natural* world, surely there is not much less room for making, nor much less use in proposing, *reformation* in the moral."[97] He thus directly tied scientific discovery, and by extension the scientific method, to his reform project.

The idea was to have a moral science that mixed experimental and exact science in the same manner as Newtonian physics. This sort of amalgam was in contrast to Blackstone's faulty (according to Bentham) appropriation of science, in which the structure was axiomatic but "is" and "ought" were illegitimately intermingled in an attempt to uphold the political status quo. Blackstone's "ought"—tradition—was not empirically defensible, and his exposition lacked the clarity required under a positivist creed, whereas the utilitarian "ought" (maximizing happiness) was centered on an empirical observation—man's desire to seek out pleasure and avoid pain. What Blackstonian thought and utilitarianism have in common is that they both built on a central axiom through deductivism—similar to Newtonianism.

Utilitarianism is founded on a pleasure-and-pain calculus. It supplants tradition as the first legal principle, therefore putting law on a scientific footing: "From *utility* then we may denominate a *principle*, that may serve to preside over and govern, as it were, such arrangement as shall be made of the several institutions or combinations of institutions that compose the matter of this science."[98] Bentham shared a positivist ethos that a scientific perspective should be adopted wherever possible. Founding moral science on pleasure and pain calculus was inductively sound because, according to Bentham, "*pain* and *pleasure* at least, are words which a man has no need, we may hope, to go to a Lawyer to know the meaning of."[99] Thus the new policy science—utilitarianism—was empirically based and therefore scientifically valid. The natural law scientific view, which idealized tradition, was from a positivist view point metaphysical rubbish. Despite Bentham's vehement criticisms of Blackstone, his utilitarianism may have gone as far toward protecting private property as Blackstone did.[100] However, Bentham did support programs to alleviate suffering by redistributing wealth, at justifiable cost to the better-off, but that sort of assistance stemmed from utilitarian calculus and evaluating the facts, not natural rights.[101] In the end, utility served the same function for Bentham as natural law had done for Blackstone—a mechanism for making political choices.

Bentham, although he did not invent utilitarianism, skillfully used it to sketch out a vision for reform. It was John Stuart Mill who would have an even greater responsibility for spreading utilitarian ideas, particularly in America. Mill's intellectual output and breadth are amazing. In constructing an intellectual genealogy of legal-economic theory, three texts deserve immediate attention: *The Logic of Moral Sciences*, *Utilitarianism*, and *Principles of Political Economy*.

According to Mill the moral sciences help us to understand how human social institutions work. This understanding should be obtained in a scientific manner—as in the physical sciences. Mill did not claim that human science in general could be as "exact" as the physical sciences,[102] because human reactions could not be predicted with the certainty associated with physical phenomena. Nevertheless, credible approximations could be made regarding human behavior. This was sufficient to constitute a "science."[103]

For Mill, the logical starting point for a human science was the mind. He believed that there existed a "Science of the Mind," the basis for which was our observations concerning human behavior. However, we must engage in deductive reasoning to derive testable hypotheses regarding human action. At that point, the scientific method is used to verify the hypotheses. If the hypotheses are verified, then the theory has been held up to scientific scrutiny and is considered valid. This is enough. It is not necessary, and in human sciences it is impossible, to require that the initial empirical observations be immutable or certain. Indeed, observing and hypothesizing these initial beliefs regarding human character are inexact enterprises. By contrast, deploying deductive methodology to derive more specific laws is considered by Mill to be an "exact" science.[104] Methodologically, Mill mimicked Newton's process in deriving the laws of motion.[105]

While Mill is often associated with the proposition that the natural sciences are predominantly inductive, he believed that the moral sciences were essentially deductive. This deductive method was set against what he referred to as experimentalism, particularly in chemistry. Mill associated the chemical method with Sir Francis Bacon, and while realizing that some had misrepresented him, concluded that "Bacon's conception of scientific inquiry has done its work and that science has now advanced into a higher stage."[106] Experience verified laws deductively derived. Specific experience can tell us nothing about general laws in the social context. The deduction would not ape geometry, beginning with one general principle and deducing proofs, but would follow the physical sciences (physics in particular). The reason for preferring physical, as opposed to geometric, science was that the physical laws dealt with complicated issues of causation associated with the moral sciences. The geometric model was too rigid and simplistic: "phenomena of society do not depend, in essentials, on some one agency or law of human nature."[107] However, the proper subjects for social science are those that "though influenced like the rest by all sociological agents are under the *immediate* influence, principally at least, of a few only."[108] Political economy exemplified this theory.

Mill's view regarding complex social science analysis seems to be in tension with his methodological individualism. The multiple causes that influence social life are all exerted through the laws of the mind (psychology) and by extension ethology (the science of human behavior). He believed that although the moral sciences dealt with social phenomena, their basis was individual behavior that could be aggregated in order to draw conclusions. This was not only an objective stance but a subjective one as well.

Mill described ethics as the "logic of practice, or art." In conformance with legal positivist dictates he argued that institutional responsibilities should be based on institutional competence, that the legislature should be entrusted with making broad policy choices and the judge restricted to applying and interpreting (in a narrow sense) rules. Mill's dichotomy of art and science also has much in common with the positivist divide of "is" and "ought." Art proposes ends, and it is left to science to devise the most appropriate means to those ends.[109] Mill was a firm believer in the is/ought dichotomy: "A proposition of which the predicate is expressed by the words *ought* or *should be*, is generally different from one which is expressed by *is* or *will be*."[110] The scientist should never pretend to be doing art— ethics. Art cannot be undertaken in a deductive manner based on universal principles, but is an iterative and ongoing process. In this regard, Mill would share the legal positivist disdain for natural law methods. He believed that those who had taken the deductivist route in ethics had fallen into the geometric trap.

Nevertheless, there is an ethical foundational principle, utilitarianism. In *Logic* Mill described it as the "rule or standard, with which all other rules of conduct were required to be consistent, and from which by ultimate consequence they could all be deduced."[111] While Mill did not believe that *Logic* was the appropriate place to expound on the theory, he would eventually do so in *Utilitarianism*.[112] Mill's utilitarian rule was that "actions are right in proportion as they tend to promote happiness, wrong as they tend to produce the reverse of happiness. By happiness are intended pleasure, and the absence of pain; by unhappiness, pain and the privation of pleasure."[113] In many ways *Utilitarianism* is an extended defense of the doctrine against its critics. Mill revised utilitarianism to guard against the faults he found in previous versions, particularly those of his father (James Mill) and Bentham. He believed that both failed to take into account aesthetic values, and that their narrowness left utilitarianism open to being labeled a sterile doctrine. Mill had been influenced by romantic thinkers and appreciated the need for cultivating "higher" values.[114]

Mill's expanded vision of utilitarianism fit with the expanded role for reform that he advocated. While the elder Mill and Bentham often championed reform programs, their utilitarian theories did not adequately support their political objectives. J. S. Mill believed that a society governed under the utilitarian creed must have as a central goal alleviating poverty and disease: "the grand sources . . . of human suffering are in a great degree . . . conquerable by human care and effort."[115] Education would play a particularly crucial role. It would instill in every individual the qualities (higher virtues) necessary for the greater happiness of all. These basic tenets, which were tied to Mill's utilitarian ethic, would shape his more concrete suggestions regarding the ideal social structure, which he laid out in *Principles of Political Economy*.

While Mill is frequently characterized as a classical economist, his overall view of government intervention is decidedly mixed. Of course Mill argued for individual freedom as a bedrock principle in his *On Liberty*, but this was tempered or (as Mill might say) buttressed by his utilitarian policy commitments. Mill explicitly defined his project as building on Adam Smith's legacy. The idea was to update Smith's classical manifesto, *The Wealth of Nations*, with the knowledge gathered in political economy since its publication. Significantly, Mill acknowledged that there had been many important treatises on political economy written since *The Wealth of Nations*, but argued that none had blended political economy (a scientific enterprise) with social philosophy (a political and pragmatic enterprise). Thence the subtitle to *Principles of Political Economy*: "With Some of Their Applications to Social Philosophy." *The Wealth of Nations* was unique, according to Mill, because Smith never lost track of political economy's practical applications.[116]

The principal point of departure between Mill and other classicals (including Smith, David Ricardo, and Thomas Malthus) was that he replaced the natural law view with a decidedly instrumentalist politics. This break with natural law doctrine reflects Mill's positivist bent. Just as law (a social policy matter) could no longer be predetermined by natural law dictates for the legal positivists, no longer would production and population "laws" (the foundations of economic science) dictate economic policy. In particular, the principal policy concern according to Mill, distribution, was not subject to economic science. While economic production was predetermined—taking on the "character of analytic truths"—distributional considerations were policy choices governed by "human institutions only."[117]

Principles is divided into "books," which are essentially chapter-length treatments. Mill devotes book I to discussing production and book II to distribution. In keeping with its practical focus, the discussion of distribution in *Principles* is broken up into "chapters" devoted to the distribution issue in concrete contexts. There is separate commentary on various forms of land use and economic classes, as well as a general discussion of property distribution.

Mill emphasizes that property ownership is not a natural right, but a state creation dependent upon prevailing sentiment on the issue—"the claim of the landowners to the land is altogether subordinate to the general policy of the State."[118] With regard to what Mill described as "modern Europe," he was quite critical regarding the initial property distribution, which he saw as the result of conquest and not productive efforts. Thence existing rights to property were largely undeserved. Moreover, this maldistribution "purposefully fostered inequalities, and prevented all from start-ing in the race," and the "inequality of chances" led in turn to the "concen-tration of wealth."[119] Mill took a position that subsistence was a necessary condition to political liberty. Unlike his classical predecessors, or even Bentham, Mill would not rule out socialism as an alternative to the laissez-faire system then dominant. But in this as in other matters the issue could not be settled in the abstract. It required detailed policy consideration.

The particular balance between individual liberty and government in-tervention that Mill proposes is spelled out in his book on government. Mill took pains to explain why it was doctrinaire and misguided to suggest that the government should be limited to "night watchman" activities, such as protecting private property. Government intervention did not nec-essarily impinge upon liberty: "When a government provides means of fulfilling a certain end, leaving individuals free to avail themselves of dif-ferent means if in their opinion preferable, there is no infringement of liberty, no irksome or degrading restraint."[120] Thus Mill drew a distinction between government actions that restrained individual choice and govern-ment actions that fostered choice. Legitimate government intervention ranged from assuring assistance to the poor, to providing public goods such as roads and lights, to mandating labor standards. The test of whether a particular activity should be undertaken by the government, as opposed to the private sector, was general expediency (a utilitarian analysis).

It is interesting to explore Mill's thoughts regarding wage regulations. This is an area where both classical economists and legal theorists had argued that freedom of contract should trump prudential arguments for government intervention—recall *Lochner* and, earlier, Smith's views on the subject. Mill believed that the case for child labor laws was easy to make. Generally, those not able to make decisions for themselves should be protected by the state. This logic did not extend to regulating women's labor. While Mill realized that the exploitation of women in the workplace was a serious issue, it was not due to their lacking competence to manage their own affairs ("women are as capable as men of appreciating and managing their own concern") but to the larger "injustices of their present social positions."[121] The solution lay in remedying social and legal in-equalities between men and women so that women would not be subject to male oppression. Labor disparities, in Mill's view, reflected general female subjugation.

With regard to the general labor market, Mill agreed with classical contract freedom views, but with significant qualifications: "There are matters in which the interference of law is required, not to overrule the judgment of individuals respecting their own interests, but to give effect to that judgment: they being unable to give effect to it except by concert, which concert cannot be effectual unless it receives validity and sanction from the law."[122] Mill identified what modern economists would refer to as "large number" and "free rider" problems—which can lead to market failure. For example, it is difficult for large groups of laborers to reach agreement (even in their own interest), and if they do individual laborers will have an incentive to not take part in the agreement. Therefore it is possible that actions in the group interest (such as limiting the numbers of hours worked) are never taken. In such cases, Mill believed in government intervention. Ultimately, Mill would not take a position on whether such a law was required in Britain at the time, but his openness to the possibility is in stark contrast to the categorical rejection by classical economists.

Mill's thought had a tremendous impact on developing American legal-economic theory, which will be discussed in the remaining chapters. The first entry point was Mill's influence on legal realism. Before turning to legal realism it is useful to discuss a form of positivism that made its way onto American soil and against which the realists railed—formalism.

Christopher Langdell is widely recognized as a leading formalist. Langdell, as dean of Harvard Law School in the 1870s, revolutionized the way lawyers were trained. While sometimes painted with the natural law brush, Langdell actually followed the positivist view that rejected natural law edicts. In particular, he broke with the treatise tradition as exemplified by Blackstone by developing the case method. Under this method, lawyers derive legal doctrine by culling through precedent, through cases. This is an inductive process, inferring the general from the particular. Only after the doctrines were gleaned inductively were the rules pertaining to a particular situation reached through deduction. Langdell's stated goal was still (as it was under the treatise regime) to construct an exact legal science: "[it] is indispensable to establish at least two things; first that law is a science; secondly that all the available materials of that science are contained in printed books [(cases in the law library)],"[123] The Langdellian scientific model owed much to Darwinian theory but adhered to a belief in certitude.[124] In addition, his stewardship over the Harvard Law School fit Blackstone's model of the university as a laboratory for legal science. This incarnation did not begin with Langdell but stretched back to 1829, when Joseph Story delivered lectures at the Harvard Law School with the *Commentaries* as a principal text.[125]

With his inductive method of deriving first principles, Langdell marked the beginnings of the radical shift in American legal theory that was soon to come. Natural law and religion were no longer the sources of first principles.[126] Yet Langdell's method effectively set in stone his predecessors' conservative ideology. Given that the common law (dating back to England) had been structured to protect property interests, any first principles derived from the common law would serve a similar function. While these first principles no longer flowed directly from moral intuition, they were only one step removed from it.[127] Importantly, regarding political implications, while Langdell undertook induction similar to Mill, he did not adopt utilitarian reformism.[128]

Langdell embraced inductivism but also extended the deductivist tradition. Arriving at rules to apply to a particular case is still considered a linear science, guided by rationality.[129] The cover of science continues to provide legitimization for law. Thomas Grey has argued that Langdell adhered to the nineteenth-century geometric model (which found its most influential exposition in Mill's *Logic*) by devising a system in which axioms are arrived at inductively and theorems (rules) are derived deductively.[130] It also continues to foster the view that law is an objective, exact, and closed system. Once the doctrine is established (through an inductive investigation) there is no room for policy analysis to inform the legal rules. The rules are prescribed by logical dictates and distributive considerations (as well as sometimes stubborn social facts) are beyond the pale. Langdell's belief that the law constituted an autonomous, consistent, and intelligible body of rules with no room for moral inquiry matches well with classical positivist claims that law and morality are separate inquiries. In this regard, he has been described as the first American positivist.[131]

Langdellian jurisprudence has close affinities with *Lochner* regarding policy implications. Given the inherently conservative basis of the "first" principles, the common law continues to reify existing property relationships. This explains the continued force of conservative jurisprudence even after the Langdellian "revolution" in legal education. It also helps to explain why critics accused Langdell (falsely) of being a natural law adherent.[132]

Nineteenth-century American legal-economic theory blended classical economic and jurisprudential orthodoxy. By century's end, with the rise of positivism, natural law theory could no longer serve as a foundation for legal science. Moreover, classical orthodoxy and its conservative politics would face a serious challenge in early-twentieth-century thought as American intellectuals came to grips with Darwinism (which had already affected Langdell) and ever-pressing social realities.

TWO

THE PRAGMATIC RECONSTRUCTION

OF AMERICAN LEGAL-ECONOMIC THEORY

■ The intellectual moment that set in motion the movement, pragmatism, that would undercut the core principles of classical legal thought was the publication of Charles Darwin's *The Origin of Species* in 1859. Pragmatism is a philosophy that reflects an empirical worldview. Many policy makers in the early twentieth century argued for progressive reforms by framing their arguments in pragmatist terms. As such, they asserted that policies in favor of government intervention were scientifically sounder than the laissez-faire position of classical theorists.[1]

While originally published in England, *The Origin of Species* had a profound impact on American intellectual thought. As a work of science with philosophical implications, *Origin* was as far reaching as Newton's laws of physics. Darwin began with the premise, influenced by Thomas Malthus's *Essay on Population*, that the ability of species to produce was greater than the resources available to sustain unfettered population growth. From this Darwin deduced that there must be a struggle for existence. He concluded that winners in the struggle would necessarily be the strong—the best adapted to local conditions. This aspect of Darwinian theory actually supported classical laissez-faire ideology. If the "have nots" of the world were losing the struggle for existence—dying off—it was due to their own weaknesses. The solution was not to lend them assistance, because that would have the consequence of destabilizing the natural process of selection, the biological equivalent to Adam Smith's invisible hand.

The clearest, and most popular, articulation of the Darwinian view applied to conservative economic policy formulation can be found in Herbert Spencer's *Social Statics*. Although *Social Statics* was written in 1850, before the publication of *Origin*, the popularity of *Origin* helped bolster Spencer's standing as a social theorist.[2]

It is an indication of the richness of Darwin's theory that his influence was not limited to reifying existing nineteenth-century conservatism. Darwin's vision of evolution also fit nicely with emerging notions of progress. The idea that the world was fixed and unchanging was replaced by an ethos of human and social progress.[3] Darwinism also had methodological implications. Scott Gordon has written that Newton's *Principia* and Darwin's *Origin* "stand above all others in the influence they have had on men's minds."[4] Gordon attributes Darwin's influence to his having put the human sciences on the same mechanistic footing as Newton had done for the physical sciences. While Gordon is correct in marking the import of *Origin* in its having provided a scientific underpinning for previously discussed ideas of evolution, he is mistaken in characterizing the footing as mechanistic in the Newtonian sense. The revolutionary aspect of Darwin's theory is that it brought about a tectonic shift in the cultural implications of science. This shift, in combination with more widespread beliefs in progress, would in time—given changing social and political conditions—lead to a progressive appropriation of Darwin.

Formalistic, a priori conceptions of knowledge dominated much of eighteenth-century and early-nineteenth-century American thought. These ideas reflected the Newtonian vision of a determinate universe and the intellectual quest for certainty by way of deductive reasoning. Even those adopting an inductivist approach to science subscribed to the Baconian belief that certainty could be attained through such an endeavor.[5] The intellectual turn spearheaded by Darwin has been described in various ways—anti-formalism, anti-conceptualism, historicism, and contextualism. In any event Darwin's was an indeterminate (probabilistic) world in which the quest for certainty was called into question.

This much was manifest in Darwin's substantive conclusions and methodology. Substantively, according to Darwin God did not script our (human) existence. That existence is the manifestation of an evolutionary process, the results of which are indeterminate. This view directly contradicted creationism's religious certainty regarding the fate of mankind. It also undermined the idea that divine intervention was responsible for the fate of human progress. Newton believed that the divine agent had to have intervened to establish the variety of species.[6] This was the view adopted to the social sphere in the classical era, and it served as the apologia for the existing economic order. Methodologically, Darwin's case for evolution was framed not as a certain but as a probabilistic assertion. Paul Croce has made the case that the "true Darwinian revolution was the sea change away from the assumption that scientific research can provide certainty and toward a brand of science that found plausible, persuasive explanations as patterns in the midst of indeterminate events."[7]

Obviously, Darwin's theory of evolution had no direct implications for the findings of Newtonian physics. However, it was seen as such a revolutionary break from prior beliefs regarding science that its methodological implications did serve as a disciplinary counterpoint to Newtonian method in the intellectual world at large. Nowhere was this more evident than in the philosophical implications of Darwinism. It is significant that despite Darwinism's popular appeal, leading nineteenth-century philosophers of science, including John Stuart Mill, were either critical or did not fully support Darwin on philosophical grounds.[8] Nineteenth-century philosophy was still under the Newtonian spell. Mill did believe that *Origin* followed sound scientific methodology. However, he disagreed with the implication that nature was not the product of intelligent or divine intervention. There was a strong belief in the nineteenth century that any philosophy of science must be made to coexist with a belief in the divine creator (God). Newtonian theory comported with this idea because phenomena not explained by mechanics were ordained to still be subject to predetermined laws dictated by God.[9] Darwin left the unexplained to the chance process of natural selection. Thus in addition to deviance from a divine view, Darwin introduced uncertainty into science, and this was viewed as unacceptable.

The Darwinian turn of thought found its philosophical expression in pragmatism. The origins of pragmatism can be located in the loose configuration of intellectuals commonly referred to as the Metaphysical Club.[10] Members of the club, which was formed in January 1872, included Charles Sanders Peirce, William James, Chauncey Wright, Nicholas St. John Green, and Oliver Wendell Holmes.[11] Of these five figures, two (Peirce and James) could generally be described as philosophers, although Peirce and James had wide-ranging intellectual interests. Green and Holmes were both lawyers by training, while Wright was a mathematician.[12]

The members of the Metaphysical Club did not produce institutional documents or even detailed accounts of their collective ruminations, and the "Club" itself was relatively short-lived.[13] However, the members made significant contributions to American intellectual thought and demonstrate some shared beliefs that are derivative of the Darwinian worldview: temporalism, relativism, probabilism or fallibilism, and pluralistic empiricism.[14]

Temporalism is the pragmatist notion that forms of thought and the nature of things are products of their environment. Thus, they are the product of *evolutionary* processes.[15] There is a direct connection between this temporalism and empiricism. Since all knowledge is contingent on the particularity of the social circumstance, including the history that precedes the present condition, any a priori (universal) theory is to be shunned.

Relativism is the notion that the meaning of expressions and concepts is different in different contexts.[16] It constitutes a rejection of theological and metaphysical claims of the universality of expressions and concepts, external to context. Relativism implies that the worth of rules should be judged by their benefit (under specific but variable conditions) to the greatest number of individuals in the society.[17]

Probabilism and fallibilism reject any mechanistic view of society and instead look at social phenomena as being probable and contingent.[18] They are contingent owing to the limitations of sense-experience and the uncertainty of empirical evidence.[19] Again, as with relativism, this ties in with empiricism because no universal "Truth" can take the place of revisable empirical inquiry. The basis of this view is that the plurality of life experiences and individuals makes it impossible to formulate universal generalities. This view stands in stark contrast to the nineteenth-century British empiricist tradition represented by Mill.[20] However, the positivist distinction between facts (the domain of science) and value did influence the pragmatist point of view. In particular, Chauncey Wright, arguably the intellectual leader of the Metaphysical Club, adopted this view based on his reading of Francis Bacon and J. S. Mill.[21]

Pluralistic empiricism is the piecemeal analysis of complex phenomena.[22] The analysis incorporates disparate areas of knowledge and brings them to bear on the problem at hand. Through this process metaphysical solutions are avoided. A crucial component of this pluralistic empiricism was the need for verifiability as a test for truth.[23]

The general parameters stated above notwithstanding, there was a good deal of diversity in the perspectives taken by the individual members of the Metaphysical Club. Therefore it is best to discuss the members individually, focusing on their unique contributions to American intellectual history generally and more particularly to legal-economic theory. In tracing the genealogy of pragmatism, one is ultimately led to John Dewey, the intellectual heir of the pragmatist tradition that originated in the Metaphysical Club.

Charles Sanders Peirce is widely regarded as the founder of pragmatism. Peirce was born in Cambridge, Massachusetts, in 1839. His father was a distinguished mathematician and professor at Harvard University. Peirce's training and vocation were primarily those of a scientist, which was important in fixing his philosophical views. Peirce, like others in the Metaphysical Club, was deeply influenced by *The Origin of Species* and adopted an evolutionary view of knowledge. The primary intellectual offshoot of this perspective was a disbelief in a priori knowledge and a rejection of Cartesian thought.

Peirce's view of knowledge is set forth in his essay "Questions Concerning Certain Faculties Claimed for Man." In the essay Peirce argues that we do not have the power to constitute knowledge introspectively, independently of previous knowledge.[24] Knowledge or belief is derived from observing external facts and by inference related to the act of observing.[25] Peirce was calling for the type of empiricism that would prove fundamental in shaping the post–Civil War American mind.[26] He framed the method as follows: "[V]alid inference . . . proceeds from its premiss, A, to its conclusion, B, only if, as a matter of fact, such a proposition as B is always or usually true when such proposition as A is true."[27] Peirce stated that this form of argument "might be called statistical argument."[28]

Peirce concluded that it is impossible to make universal propositions and be certain of their validity. However, there could be abstractions derived from "judgments of experience."[29] The general features are derived from the details: "the details are, in fact, the whole picture."[30] In sum, Peirce's view of logical analysis can be described as inductive. In general it would be inductive, as opposed to deductive, analysis that would animate pragmatism.

The consequence of Peirce's view of knowledge was to reject Cartesian philosophy. It is the power of this rejection that makes Peirce such an eminent figure on the American intellectual scene. In his essay entitled "Some Consequences of Four Incapacities," Peirce identified Cartesian philosophy as having four central tenets: (1) universal doubt; (2) belief that individual consciousness is the ultimate arbiter of truth; (3) argumentation based on "single thread inference," which depends on inconspicuous premises (deductive analysis); and (4) an aspiration to "explain all created things."[31]

Peirce attacked these premises one by one. First, there can be no universal doubt (pure objectivity), because we all begin with our individual prejudices. In fooling oneself into believing that universal doubt is possible, the result is inevitably the recovery of the initial beliefs that one thought had been discarded.[32] Second, in Peirce's mind the quest for truth was not an individual endeavor but rather a product of the interaction among a community of philosophers.[33] Third, philosophy could only be as successful as the sciences if it proceeded from "tangible premises" capable of scrutiny (inductive analysis).[34] Finally, there are some areas of inquiry not subject to human inquiry. Therefore, there is no point in venturing to explain certain facts. The Cartesian quest for universal knowledge through introspection and deductive analysis was doomed from its inception.

Peirce's rejection of Cartesian thought was a defining moment in American intellectual history. The formalism that exemplified the classical era would no longer hold sway. In marking this turn against the prevailing ethos, Peirce proposed a form of inquiry that would seem to fit most neatly with Baconian inductivism. Indeed, we can view Peirce's critique of Descartes as an attack favoring the inductive conception of science over deductivism. However, the form of inductivism advocated by Peirce was decidedly different from that proposed by Bacon. Indeed, while admiring portions of Lord Bacon's method, Peirce was highly critical of what he viewed as Bacon's methodological naïveté. The fundamental point of departure was that whereas Bacon held out some hope of attaining ultimate and certain truths through inductivism, Peirce, in keeping with the Darwinian ethos, took a probabilistic view of science.

Peirce's famous essay "The Fixation of Belief" offers up a Darwinian vision of science that would supplant determinism. Peirce proposed that instead of reaching for certainty, belief should be established on the basis of action. Knowledge, in this view of the world, is based on what we "think" to be "true" at the moment, which in turn is measured by that which we are willing to act upon. Unlike in the Cartesian view, the impetus for the fixation of belief was not individual catharsis but community consensus reached through the scientific (inductive) method.

Peirce's provisional view of knowledge powerfully articulated what Paul Croce has identified as the "eclipse of certainty" in American intellectual history.[35] However, his ideas were largely unknown to the broader public. His intellectual peer and good friend William James spoke to a wider audience and explained the more general implications of pragmatism. For this reason James is a more exemplary marker of the broader cultural significance of Darwinism.

While noted as a philosopher, William James was also trained as a scientist, having enrolled in the Lawrence Scientific School at Harvard as a chemistry student in 1861. Significantly, this was only two years after the publication of Darwin's *Origin*. James was located in the vortex of the debate surrounding the meaning of science and its relationship to larger religious and philosophical issues.[36]

The classic expression of James's view of pragmatism, and the statement of the philosophy that would gain the most popular currency, is laid out in *Pragmatism*. The essay was a compilation of lectures that James delivered to lay audiences in 1906 and 1907, attempting to give a nontechnical explanation of the movement earlier titled "pragmatism" by Peirce.[37] James begins by mapping out the philosophical landscape. To his mind philosophers may be broadly categorized as falling under one of two rubrics: "rationalist" or "empiricist." Rationalists are referred to as "tender-minded" and empiricists as "tough-minded." The rationalist begins her analysis from abstract universal principles, while the empiricist starts from facts and builds up the whole as a sum of its parts. James's line of demarcation between the two types of thinking roughly correlates with the distinction between deductivism and inductivism. James is careful to note: "No one can live an hour without both facts and principles, so it is a difference rather of emphasis."[38] However, it is a genuine difference, and one that "has formed in all ages a part of the philosophic atmosphere of the time."[39] James argued that the tenor of his times had, for the better, taken a decidedly empiricist turn: "The optimism of present-day rationalism sounds . . . shallow to the fact-loving mind. The actual universe is a thing wide open, but rationalism makes systems, and systems must be closed."[40] The real-world problem with such a system is that it ignores human suffering, the realities of life, in exchange for a false sense of certainty about the universe. In making this observation James privileged individuals' experiences over philosophical argument.

This privileging of experience is directly related to what James referred to as the pragmatic method, which is based on taking the measure of ideas according to their practical consequences. As between two conflicting ideas, James argued that we would be well served by choosing not the one that might have more appeal in the abstract but the one that leads to the practical results we prefer. James echoed Peirce's anti-Cartesian sentiments in writing that pragmatism "turns away from abstraction and insufficiency, from verbal solutions, and from bad *a priori* reasoning, from fixed principles, closed systems, and pretended absolutes and origins."[41] Pragmatism, and American legal-economic theory in its adoption of pragmatism, turned their back on the sort of formalism championed by Descartes and dominant in classical legal thought.

The pragmatic moment in American history marks a dramatic example of a theoretical rupture. James recognized this when he stated, "the general triumph of [the pragmatic method] would mean an enormous change in what I called in my last lecture the 'temperament' of philosophy. Teachers of the ultra-rationalistic type would be frozen out, much as the courtier type is frozen out in republics."[42] James went so far as to say that the supplanting of empiricism over rationalism was equal in importance to the Protestant reformation. He recognized that the battle between the rationalist and empiricist temperament was a pitched one. The battle would be waged over the claim to science.

James's move to empiricism was not a move away from science but, James would argue, a step closer to science: "Science and metaphysics would come much nearer together, would in fact work absolutely hand in hand."[43] James disagreed with the sharp demarcation of facts (science) and values (metaphysics) drawn by Chauncey Wright.[44] The Jamesean historiography of science linked its development to "inductive logic." True, the early development of science was preoccupied with mathematical argument, but "as the sciences have developed farther, the notion has gained that most, perhaps all, of our laws are only approximations."[45]

The idea of science based on "approximations" reflects the eclipse of certainty brought about by the Darwinian revolution, and it is directly tied to the pragmatic conception of truth: "Darwinism has once and for all displaced design from the mind of the 'scientific.' "[46] Just as in science, there are no absolute philosophical truths, only provisional truths that are measured against experience. James envisioned that we arrive at settled truths through a process of reconciling previously held beliefs with newly proposed ideas. The formalist ideal of absolute Truth is discarded as a relic of rationalism.

Again, one cannot underestimate the importance of Darwin's revolutionary insight in this regard. Darwin made clear that the process of evolution is a chance phenomenon. Variations in organisms occur by chance, and the accident of whether they confer an advantage in survival in the local environment determines whether they are passed on to progeny. There was no preordained plan handed down by God, or any other deistic figure, from on high. James described it thusly: "Darwin opened our minds to the power of chance-happenings to bring forth 'fit' results if only they have time to add themselves together."[47]

Just as the natural world thrives when inhabited by a variety of species, the world of ideas is benefited when a pluralistic approach is adopted. James thoroughly believed in the benefits of a pluralistic approach to the world over an absolutist one. However, true to his anti-absolutist stance, he recognized that there might be an overarching universal purpose. His point was that this position had not been proven and one should no longer take it as a matter of faith. To the extent that experience does allow us to fashion a view in which the world hangs together as a whole, the pragmatist position does not preclude that view. If it did, that would only replicate the absolutist fallacy. For Jamesean pluralism not to dissolve into skepticism, there must be some conception of truth. The pragmatist conception of truth is consequentialist. Granted that an idea is true, what consequence does that have in the world? James frequently summed up this view in the idea of "cash value." What currency does a particular version of the truth have?

The truth is not magically revealed to us through a Cartesian epiphany. It is arrived at through human inquiry and is thus constantly subject to revision as our stock of experience grows. Indeed, the notion of Truth must be replaced with the idea of multiple and malleable truths. This does not mean that we are stuck in a position of being unable to act. James argues that we act on the truth as we perceive it today, though all the while cognizant of its fleeting nature. This makes pragmatism a future-oriented philosophy, always anticipating the bounty of future knowledge harvests.

James viewed the common law as a quintessential example of the pragmatist method at work. Taking a view different from that of the earlier formalists, James argued that common law judges do not derive law from upon high. Law, like any other concept, is not fixed. The laws "have grown up incidentally among the interactions of men's experiences in detail."[48] Judges meld together prior case law with fresh experiences to fashion the law for the case at hand. This theory of law as created by man is the antithesis of the formalist ideal of the judge as mere conduit for the natural law. It is a particular example of James's general view that all truth is socially constructed. In short, "The import of the difference between pragmatism is now in sight. . . . The essential contrast is that for rationalism reality is ready-made and complete from all eternity, while for pragmatism it is still in the making, and awaits its complexion from the future."[49] Of course as applied to law, this position ran the risk of adding an element of subjectivity. It thus might undermine the legitimacy that had previously been claimed based on the view that the law was preordained. However, thinkers influenced by pragmatism believed that they had a more powerful claim to objectivity than revelation, which in any event could hardly be taken seriously post-Darwin—the claim of science. Science had always played a part in previous claims for law's legitimacy. The problem for legal theorists after the Civil War was how to fashion a coherent theory of law based on the then prevailing, Darwinian, vision of science as a probabilistic enterprise. Objectivity would still be the goal. Probabilism is not inconsistent with objectivity. For example, if one makes the statement that there is an 80 percent chance of rain showers based on statistical inference, this is an objective statement. Probabilism merely eviscerates certainty (assuming probabilities of less than 100 percent).

While James's pragmatist musings concerning the quest for certainty might seem removed from the throes of legal-economic theory, they would indeed have profound ramifications. Two figures emerged from the crucible of the Metaphysical Club who would have a direct impact on American legal-economic theory, Nicholas St. John Green and Oliver Wendell Holmes. While Green was not nearly as towering a figure as Holmes, he still warrants attention.

Green's importance lies in an approach which reflected his pragmatist roots and was to be mirrored not only by Holmes but also by later legal realists.[50] Both Green and Holmes resided in the Boston area, where Green was a lecturer of law at Harvard and later a professor at Boston University —to which he had decamped in part to protest the formalism at Harvard under Dean Christopher Langdell's stewardship. Green's affiliation with pragmatism is even more transparent than that of Holmes. Peirce once labeled Green "the grandfather of pragmatism," referring to Green's assertion that belief should be defined as "that upon which a man is prepared to act."[51] Accordingly, belief was not passive but the stuff from which we make our world.[52]

The importance of Green's approach in American legal-economic theory is that it constituted a dramatic departure from the prevailing formalist view. Regarding tort law in particular, it undercut several classical propositions that dominated late-nineteenth-century thinking, including the presumption that all torts could be placed under the umbrella of negligence. In order for the victim to receive compensation, negligence requires a finding of moral fault (wrongful conduct) on the part of alleged wrongdoers who unintentionally cause harm. The other regime for unintentional harms is strict liability, in which no finding of fault is required and therefore the victim is more likely to be compensated.

Green put forth his views on negligence doctrine in 1870 in "Proximate and Remote Cause,"[53] a critique of Shearman's and Redfield's *A Treatise on the Law of Negligence.* At the heart of his attack was a critique of any metaphysical account of negligence, particularly the distinction between proximate cause and remote cause. In his article Green criticizes the adoption and misuse of Francis Bacon's *Maxims of the Law.* "In jure non remota causa, sed proxima spectatur" (In law, look to proximate cause, not remote causes). One requirement for winning a torts case is proof that the injurer's actions were the "proximate cause" of the victim's injury. Essentially this boils down to proving that the injury was foreseeable given the defendant's actions. The implication of Bacon's maxim was that a distinction could be scientifically drawn between proximate and remote (nonforeseeable) cause. Bacon put forth his view on cause not only as a prescription for law but also as a way for philosophers to look at philosophical problems. The separation of proximate and remote cause could be traced to Aristotle through the schoolmen to Bacon, with the maxim finally standing for the proposition of certainty in causal analysis.[54] However, according to Green, Bacon's admonition was one of broad application, and his general prescription with respect to certainty was misconstrued. Bacon's view on certainty in legal causation is an extension of his general belief in philosophic certainty—a decidedly anti-pragmatist view.[55]

Some American courts had indeed adopted the view that the judge could determine causation with certainty, leaving him or her to determine negligence from the facts rather than send the case to the jury.[56] Green felt this to be a mistake, because the methodologies of the schoolmen (assuming causes) and Bacon (enumerating instances and excluding foreign causes) were faulty.[57] Green tells us that "the phrase 'chain of causation,' which is a phrase in frequent use when this maxim is under discussion, embodies a dangerous metaphor."[58] To Green's mind an event does not have a *particular* antecedent, but a *set* of antecedents.[59] Therefore, inquiry centered on causal certainty cannot do the heavy lifting in tort law. That still leaves the question of the appropriate test for determining tort liability: "In actions for negligence, a defendant is held liable for the natural and *probable consequences* of his misconduct. In this class of actions his misconduct is called the proximate cause of those results which prudent foresight might have avoided."[60] Thus the basis for liability is "probable consequences" (probability), not causal certainty. But how is this determined? Green tells us that "[t]here is generally no other way of determining whether events . . . were or might have been anticipated or foreseen, than by an *appeal to experience*."[61] Green's pragmatist legal theory comports with Peirce's and James's thought.

As a doctrinal matter, Green concluded that given the confusion over causation it is "almost impossible to reconcile the cases in this branch of the law [(torts)], even where there is in reality no conflict." The "same cause and effect which would be considered proximate in one class of actions, the attendant circumstances being unchanged, would be considered remote in others."[62] Thus, "use of. . . . [Lord Bacon's] maxim is liable to lead to error by drawing the attention from the true subject of inquiry."[63] The alternative to metaphysical "certainty" was empirical investigation ("appeal to experience") that underlies practical judgment, recognizing the fallibility of any such endeavor.[64]

Green's pragmatist appeal to experience as the guiding concept of tort law, particularly causation in tort, is a precursor to a more general reconstitution of American legal-economic theory. The other lawyer affiliated with the Metaphysical Club, Oliver Wendell Holmes, would build on it. Holmes is probably America's most influential legal theorist. His importance in American legal-economic theory stems from the anti-formalist bent of his masterpiece, *The Common Law*. Published in 1881, *The Common Law* situates the entire corpus of American common law jurisprudence under a pragmatic gaze, wrestling it from its formalist origins. In his campaign against formalism, Holmes became one of Christopher Langdell's harshest critics. If Langdell can be cast as representing classical positivism in America, it naturally follows that Holmes would be critical. Holmes rejected Austin's and Bentham's formalism, which was part and parcel with classical positivism.[65] Similarly, he faulted Langdell for attempting to deduce legal rules from first principles. Of course, while Langdell might be criticized for having a glorified view of logic, his method actually leaned more toward induction (particularly in gleaning broad principles from cases). Moreover, Langdell (as well as the British classical positivists) shared Holmes's disdain for natural law. Holmes described the natural law jurist as naïve.[66] He noted that the motivation for writing *The Common Law* "came from within—from the passionate demand that what sounded so arbitrary in Blackstone, for instance, should be given some reasonable meaning."[67] Holmes's principal objection to natural law was that it purported to ascertain absolute truth, a quest that Holmes thought unachievable. Ironically, Holmes found the same problem in positivism. Thus while Holmes (like his later successors in the legal realist movement) was aligned with positivist theorists in criticizing natural law (for conflating law with morals), the direction that Holmes suggested diverged dramatically from the positivist point of view.

Importantly, the divergence was not over the role of science, but over what constituted the scientific enterprise. Holmes adopted an evolutionary view of law (similar to Langdell's), but unlike Langdell he emphasized that the law was not an autonomous field. For Holmes, law was inextricably connected to other social forces. It is this idea of interconnectedness that Morton White, in his classic *Social Thought in America*, hailed as the hallmark of the "revolt against formalism."[68] It also explains Holmes's skepticism regarding a Benthamite utilitarian science. Holmes believed that utilitarianism extracted away the social context that inevitably (and rightly) influenced legal decision making. There could be no abstract logic to moral science as proposed by the utilitarians.[69] Moral commands were the product of historical evolution and pragmatic resolution. Thus the moral sciences, including law, were practical or pragmatic in nature. This pragmatic approach did not exclude utilitarian-like calculus: "[Lawyers are] called on to consider and weigh the ends of legislation, the means of attaining them and the cost."[70] Holmes, following the much admired Chauncey Wright, was a self-described "bettabilitarian": "we can bet on the universe in its contract with us."[71] However, such utilitarian calculus was not determinative and could not be undertaken in a social vacuum. The common law was an amalgam of logic, social (utilitarian) policy, historical context, and culture.[72]

Holmes connected his vision of science and law in "Law in Science and Science in Law."[73] Holmes begins the essay by marking a decided break: "What do we mean when we talk about explaining a thing? A hundred years ago men explained any part of the universe by showing its fitness for certain ends, and demonstrating what they conceived to be its final cause according to a providential scheme. In *our less theological and scientific day*, we explain an object by tracing the order and process of its growth."[74] Holmes was championing a historical approach to understanding that broke from religious foundations and instead would be based on a Darwinian view. By studying the historical transformation of law the legal theorist would be doing "science in the strictest sense."[75] Holmes continually stressed the science-of-law theme, noting that not only would such a science be facilitated by logic and even history (which he advocated) but that "an even more important part consists in the establishment of its postulates from within upon accurately measured social desires."[76] Holmes was careful to point out that law is not an exact science. Law is the product of competing social norms that change over time. However, we must be as accurate as we can in reflecting and understanding those norms—"inasmuch as the real justification of a rule of law, if there be one, is that it helps to bring about a social end which we desire, it is no less necessary that those who make and develop the law should have those ends articulately in their minds"[77]—and it is "for science to determine, so far as it can, the relative worth of our different social ends."[78]

Regarding tort law, Holmes addressed whether liability for unintentional harm should be based upon fault or strict liability. In answering, Holmes shuns formalistic modes of analysis. He points out the "failure of all theories which consider the law only from its formal side, whether they attempt to deduce the *corpus* from *a priori* postulates [(natural law)], or fall into the humbler error of supposing the science of the law to reside in the *elegatia juris*, or logical cohesion of part with part [(formalism)]. The truth is that the law is always approaching, and never reaching, consistency."[79] To Holmes, "in substance the growth of the law is legislative,"[80] meaning that policy issues underpin law. This is a very telling statement, because the law to which Holmes is referring is the common law and not legislative law. However, Holmes intends the statement not as a novel or radical reconceptualization of the common law but as clarifying what is. Thus, although the public policy rationale behind judicial decision making is "rarely mentioned," it is the "secret root from which the law draws all the juices of life."[81] The common law reflects "what is expedient for the community concerned."[82] The theoretical justification for the common law is reoriented toward policy science, away from claims to objectivity based on universal truths.

Holmes's view of tort law directly contradicted Austin's command theory. Austin argued that since tort law, as well as all other law, was based on sovereign command, then it must also have as its foundation moral culpability. Doctrinally, this boiled down to an argument that negligence was the basis for tort. Holmes attacked this position in a brief but poignant essay, "The Theory of Torts": "liability to a civil action for the amount of the plaintiff's detriment is quite different from a punishment proportioned to the defendant's guilt, so conversely, liability to such an action does not necessarily import culpability, as it has been thought to do by some of Bentham's followers."[83] Holmes pointed to a well-established area of strict liability, "extra-hazardous employments," as proof that moral culpability was not necessary for liability to be assessed. Tort law is designed to influence behavior by taxing it. It is not an inquiry, as Austin would have it, into the actor's state of mind. Even negligence is based not on state of mind but on the actor's conduct. And while the rule of conduct may be set forth under a negligence regime, its application is oftentimes uncertain, given the role that juries frequently play in deciding "hard" cases.[84] In addition, the sources of law are varied: the legislature, public policy, custom, and the community.[85]

Holmes's objection to Austin's conclusion that tort law was solely limited to negligence did not mean that Holmes was an ardent advocate of strict liability. He argued for negligence as the general rule in tort on public policy grounds. Holmes combined some of the dominant political themes from the classical era (individualism and belief in the free market)—he was not a political radical by any stretch of the imagination—with his own version of utilitarianism.[86]

Holmes's argument lacks the empirical support that he himself calls for. He begins by stating the general principle, supporting a negligence regime, that the "loss from accident must lie where it falls,"[87] which, of course begs the question. The principle stems from Holmes's political belief, reminiscent of Adam Smith's "invisible hand," that "the public generally profits by individual activity."[88] As a matter of policy, since "action cannot be avoided, and tends to the public good, there is obviously no policy in throwing the hazard of what is at once desirable and inevitable upon the actor."[89] Holmes is fully aware that other methods of dealing with unintentional harms exist. In particular, Holmes addresses the possibility that the state might bear the costs of accidents by acting as an insurer, spreading the burden of mishaps among its citizens. But to Holmes's mind this insurance function could more efficiently be accomplished by private enterprise. In addition, "redistributing losses simply on the ground that they resulted from the defendant's act" would offend the "sense of justice."[90] Holmes's ideological stance opposing the redistribution of wealth resembles classical dictates. In this regard Holmes implicitly rejects utilitarianism's radical implications as articulated by John Stuart Mill.[91]

The importance of *The Common Law* to the intellectual genealogy of American legal-economic theory is not in its substantive conclusion or political orientation. Its significance lies in the methodological rupture effected by Holmes. Holmes, in the pragmatist tradition, rejects a priori arguments regarding the basis of liability. In this respect, he reflected the emerging anti-formalist strand of American legal thought.[92] Thus his belief in negligence as the basis of liability is not derived from an a priori belief in the superiority of negligence over strict liability. It is shaped by his reading of legal history and made determinate by his ideological beliefs (put forth as policy arguments). Rejecting a priori truths and offering a rhetorical nod to public policy analysis as a basis for choosing a liability rule was a pivotal moment in American legal-economic theory.

The anti-formalist perspective reached fruition in Holmes's later thought, as illustrated in "The Path of the Law." Holmes stressed that theory was his subject, "not practical details," and that theory is "the most important part of the dogma of law, as the architect is the most important man who takes part in the building of a home."[93] "The Path of the Law" includes an oft-quoted phrase: "for the rational study of the law the black-letter man may be the man of the present, but the man of the future is the man of statistics and the master of economics."[94] Holmes particularly recognized that it was necessary to construct a "legal-economic theory," bemoaning the "present divorce between the schools of political economy and law."[95] He noted that a view of the world resembling Newton's mechanics held a strong attraction: "[t]he postulate on which we think about the universe is that there is a fixed quantitative relation between every phenomenon and its antecedents and consequents."[96] According to Holmes, "instead of ingenious research we shall spend our energy on the ends sought to be attained and the reasons for desiring them."[97] This research was not to be "worked out like mathematics from some general axioms of conduct."[98] This last statement further illustrates the criticism of deductivism as a principal mode of human inquiry and strict utilitarianism as a policy guide.

Yet Holmes was very much a consequentialist. He admonished that in the process of "thinking like a lawyer" morals were separated from law because the law was not concerned with subjective thoughts but controlling acts. In this light, the legal system should be designed with an eye toward controlling the behavior of "the bad man" whose concern is with material consequences as opposed to moralistic platitudes. The purpose of law generally is to construct an incentive system that creates desired social consequences. Holmes explicitly faults judges for failing "adequately to recognize their duty of weighing considerations of social advantage."[99]

As to tort law doctrine, in "The Path of Law" Holmes hints at a change in view toward strict liability, particularly in his thoughts on employer liability. In questioning why negligence is an element in employer liability, Holmes, in keeping with his anti-formalism, states, "if any one thinks it can be settled deductively he is theoretically wrong."[100] Holmes juxtaposes the state of society at the time when tort law took shape—one of "isolated, ungeneralized wrongs"—to the state of society at the time of "The Path of Law"—when most torts involved "certain well-known businesses."[101] Holmes posits that if the costs of accidents were borne by "railroads, factories, and the like," they would be factored into the price of products and passed on to consumers at large.[102] This insight by Holmes marks a significant shift in his perspective on torts. It is reflected in his admonition to judges that they should recognize the social, as opposed to the individual, implications of the decisions they render,[103] and it marks a distinct break from a classical view.

Nowhere was this more evident than in Holmes's famous dissent in *Lochner*. It was Holmes, in dissenting from the previously discussed majority opinion, who argued that it was illegitimate for common law judges to decide cases based on "fundamental principles." Specifically, the Constitution "does not enact Mr. Herbert Spencer's social statics" or any "particular economic theory, whether of paternalism and the organic relation of the citizen to the State or of laissez faire."[104] The context of disputes must be fully explored. So, for example, the employer and employee relationship could no longer be examined in a vacuum, ignoring social and power dynamics.

Although much thought and social transformation would remain to be done in developing American legal-economic theory in the wake of the tectonic changes to the post–Civil War intellectual landscape, Holmes's contribution was germinal. First, in *The Common Law* and other related writings Holmes dealt a heavy blow to formalist thought in American law. Second, in "The Path of Law" he demonstrated how the perspective in *The Common Law* could lead to legal policies radically different from those adopted in the classical era. Thus Holmes may be thought of as a precursor, if not the founder, of the legal realist movement that would follow. He recognized his place at the precipice of change: "We are only at the beginning of a philosophical reaction, and of a reconsideration of the worth of doctrines which for the most part are taken for granted without any deliberation, conscious, and systemic questioning of their grounds."[105] And Holmes spoke directly regarding the role of evolutionary theory in this "reconsideration": "In regard to law, it is true, no doubt, that an evolutionist will hesitate to affirm universal validity for his social ideals, or for the principles which he thinks should be embodied in legislation. He is content if he can prove them best for here and now. He may be ready to admit that he knows next to nothing about a permanent best for men. Still it is true that a body of law is more rational and more civilized when every rule it contains is referred articulately and definitely to an end which it subserves and when the grounds for desiring that end are stated or are ready to be stated in words."[106] Holmes desired that legal theory be reoriented toward a pragmatist model. Certainty has indeed been eclipsed:[107] "logical method and form flatter that longing for certainty," yet "certainty generally is an illusion."[108] The legal realists would develop the progressive implications of the pragmatist turn.

John Dewey was in good part responsible for articulating the progressive political implications of pragmatism. Dewey is a towering figure in American thought and one of our most significant public intellectuals, exerting tremendous influence on a whole generation of scholars—including legal theorists. The core of Dewey's method was to first reject formalism in much the same way as Peirce had done.[109] However Dewey, unlike Peirce, expanded his insights to the public sphere and went on to construct a method by which to confront social problems. The crux of this method was to recognize the importance of experience. Dewey's method is laid out in *Experience and Nature*, which has been rightly described as Dewey's most important book of the 1920s and one of the most influential philosophical works of the twentieth century.[110] Dewey's concerns in *Experience and Nature* are particularly relevant to understanding the influence of pragmatism on legal-economic thought because of the direct influence that Dewey had on legal realism. Dewey's impact on legal scholarship is illustrated by Holmes's admiration for *Experience and Nature*,[111] and by the references to Dewey by legal realists.

Dewey describes the approach taken in his book as "empirical naturalism."[112] According to this approach, experience (empirical inquiry) is the only method capable of penetrating the secrets of nature. For Dewey the foundation of knowledge was human experience. Thus he alternatively describes his view as "naturalistic humanism."[113] Dewey contrasted his position with the "supra-empirical" approach set forth by those, such as Descartes, who believed that reason or intuition could transcend nature.[114] Dewey, in the tradition of Peirce, took the sciences as the benchmark for approaching philosophy. He noted that in the natural sciences there was a union of experience and nature.[115] Theory cannot be divorced from empirical reality.

Dewey cited as one example the work of geologists who collect data from a variety of sources and compare them with other results to reach substantive conclusions about past geological events.[116] Again, the point is that traits (be they physical, philosophical, or social) are discovered inductively and not constructed a priori from universal truths. Like Peirce, Dewey attributed the philosophical evasion of experience to the Cartesian school of thought, which "relegated experience to a secondary and almost accidental place."[117] Not only did the evasion of experience in philosophy have metaphysical implications, but more importantly for our discussion, Dewey connected this evasion to what he considered a "striking dissimilarity of results yielded by an empirical method and professed non-empirical methods."[118]

According to Dewey, the failure of a non-empirical method is threefold. First, there is no verification of what it leads to in ordinary experience.[119] Second, the constitutive elements of experience are not enlarged and enriched in their meaning.[120] Third, the subject matter becomes "abstract" in the negative sense and is divorced from its contact with "ordinary experience."[121] Dewey stresses that any philosophical inquiry must refer us "back to ordinary life-experiences and their predicaments, render them more significant, more luminous to us, and make our dealings with them more fruitful."[122] Thus, applying Deweyan thought to legal theory, the law must render its effects on the lives of everyday people more comprehensible and place those effects at the center of analysis, as contrasted with a priori ideals making up what Dewey referred to as the "original material" of analysis.[123]

Dewey bemoans how some fail to examine the connection between "instrumentalities" and the "conditions of life and action."[124] The result of their misguided analysis is "a picture of a world of things indifferent to human interest because it is wholly apart from experience."[125] In other words, "we are about something and it is well to know what we are about.... [and] [t]o be intelligent in action and in suffering even when conditions cannot be controlled."[126] The "something" cannot be examined outside its "special context" and "particular need in order to effect specifiable consequences."[127] "Social reform" was the "something" that Dewey was "about."

For Dewey philosophy, like all intelligent inquiry, is to serve the purpose of criticism.[128] Dewey implores philosophers and others engaged in intellectual work to focus their criticism in an effort to further "social reform."[129] Specifically, criticism "includes a heightened consciousness of deficiencies and corruptions in the scheme and distribution of values that obtains at any period."[130] Dewey's criticism is driven by his own progressive political vision of social reform. Thus in Dewey we hear the philosophical call to arms that would inform many reform movements of the early twentieth century, including the progressive impulses in American legal-economic theory.[131]

Science was to play the role of appraising values by evaluating their "causes and consequences."[132] This of course is a very empirical conception of the sciences, highlighting the need for statistical analysis and calling for "a degree of distance and detachment":[133] scientism still holds sway. Dewey championed the inductive method of analysis as opposed to deductivism, going so far as to assert that the "*act* of knowing . . . is always inductive."[134] In arguing that scientific criticism had been woefully missing in philosophy, Dewey specifically referred to "economics" as one of the "prerequisite tools" to undertake critical analysis.[135] However, he dismissed classical economics.

Dewey's views are illustrated in two essays written after the First World War, *The New Social Science* and *Elements of Social Reorganization*, in which he urged America to construct a new vision of the economic and social order in light of the lessons of the war. Dewey was critical of the assumption put forth by classical economists, including Adam Smith, that the "dynamic order . . . [is] the result of the cumulative intelligence of an indefinitely large number of beings, each devoting his own intelligence to the things to which it is peculiarly adapted."[136] He considered this view to "constitute an essential mythology."[137] In reality, he argued, "the present order rest[ed] upon habit, intrigue, private deflections . . . secret business"[138] and other "non-intelligent" forces. In the face of the new reality, coming out of the war, the proper methodology for social science was to establish "large working hypotheses concerning the uses to which these forces are to be put."[139] Doing so would necessitate empirical description not "framed up" by the old mythology. In rejecting the old mythology (unfettered capitalism), however, Dewey eschewed lapsing into what he considered to be the alternative mythology of Marxism. There should be no dictatorship of the proletariat.[140] There would be a more intelligent and humane capitalism,[141] an intelligent capitalism that emphasized the social and public as opposed to the private.[142] This new perspective would shore up the "weak points in our social fabric."[143] An accommodationist perspective regarding capitalism would be a common theme in the Progressive era. Irrespective of his willingness to accept capitalism as the general economic framework, Dewey's views toward government intervention were radically different from those of classical theorists.

Dewey's principal concern was employment opportunity. However, in listing the afflictions that contributed to an "inhuman" standard of living Dewey touched upon a host of progressive causes, including "socially unnecessary deaths, illnesses, accidents and incapacitations that come from the bad economic conditions under which so much of modern industry is carried on."[144] The scope of Dewey's concerns was therefore broad enough to implicate many of the policy issues that would preoccupy legal theorists, particularly tort law scholars.

Dewey's methodological and political break reflected a more general one in American intellectual thought. Institutional economists worked along similar lines. Just as classical economics is closely associated with formalism, so is institutional economics with pragmatism. Institutional economics and pragmatism derive from the same intellectual and political milieu.[145] The connection and significance of pragmatism to institutional economics was aptly summed up by John R. Commons, one of the leading institutional economists: "We [institutionalists] . . . follow most closely the social pragmatism of Dewey; while in our method of investigation we follow the pragmatism of Peirce. One [(Peirce's philosophy)] is scientific pragmatism—a method of investigation—the other [(Dewey's philosophy)] is pragmatism of human beings—the subject matter of the science of economics."[146] Just as classical economics would have a tremendous influence on classical legal thought, institutional economics would exert its pull on legal realism. The basic tenets of institutional economics are a focus on society as opposed to the individual, emphasis on the larger forces (institutions) that underlie a market economy, descriptive (inductive) analysis, and humanistic concern (coupled with generally progressive political beliefs) for those at the economic margins of society. Overarching these tenets were pragmatist notions that economic theory should stress context rather than abstraction.[147]

Institutionalism was in its ascendancy in the 1920s, so much so that in the words of the noted economist Paul Horman in 1928, "[institutional economics] represents the most marked trend at the present time in the United States."[148] Four economists clearly in the institutionalist camp—Thorstein Veblen, John R. Commons, Henry Seager, and Richard Ely—are essential in drawing connections to American legal-economic theory.[149]

Responding to the increasing omnipotence of corporations, Thorstein Veblen is best known for placing his intellectual imprint on the phenomenon. As to Veblen's general intellectual bent, Morton White appropriately describes him as being part of the revolt against formalism along with Dewey[150] and Holmes.[151] Veblen rejected the abstract, individualistic methodology of classical economics. In his classic work on corporate power, *Absentee Ownership*, Veblen charged the corporation with being principally concerned with finance and credit, as opposed to producing goods.[152] Contrary to the "folklore" of classical economics that the corporation acted as a "creative force in productive industry,"[153] the corporation was a tool for finance capitalists in their quest for increased wealth.[154] A similar tone was struck in *The Theory of Business Enterprise*, in which Veblen states that the result of businessmen's focus on "pecuniary gain" is their lack of interest in the "bearing [of business operations] upon the welfare of the community."[155] In fact the modern corporation had destructive effects on the community, "making the disturbances of the system large and frequent."[156]

A theme that runs throughout *The Theory of Business Enterprise* is the conflict between business and consumer interest. This conflict resulted from changing historical conditions: "In the older days, when handicraft was the rule of the industrial system, the personal contact between the producer and customer was close and lasting. Under these circumstances the factor of personal esteem and disesteem had a considerable play in controlling the purveyors of goods and services."[157] This revision of perspectives on the corporation given different historical circumstances reflects a contextual view of society, stemming from the pragmatic turn in American thought. According to Veblen, one implication of the changed relationship between consumer and producer was that in earlier times "producers were careful of their reputation for workmanship, even apart from the gains which such a reputation might bring," whereas "[u]nder modern circumstance, where industry is carried on a large scale, the discretionary head of an industrial enterprise is commonly removed from all personal contact with the body of consumers."[158] Veblen's view of the relationship between producer and consumer can be taken as a brief for government intervention to protect consumers.

Of course, the classical rebuttal to calls for consumer protection would be that consumers knowingly assume the risk associated with particular products. Veblen, however, did not believe that informed choice existed in the industrial state. To his mind, the specter of mass advertising undercut arguments regarding consumer choice. The purpose of advertising was not to inform the public but to create a "monopoly of custom and prestige."[159] Thus according to Veblen, advertising conditions consumers to purchase products not by investigating their worth or risk but on the strength of name recognition. This was the basis for his paternalistic attitude toward consumers.

Veblen argued that the upshot of the corporate finance system was a "magnificent scale of unemployment, privation, and underfeeding."[160] Accordingly, the social ills produced by unfettered industrial forces necessitated that industry should be regulated for the greater social good.[161] Again, as with Dewey, Veblen's view of the corporation is in direct opposition to the view expressed in classical theory. Adam Smith, who also had an appreciation for the workings of business interest, concluded that its furtherance was for the good of society. However, classical legal theory, as represented in the *Lochner* opinion, abstracted away any analysis of corporate power. Contextual issues of power are front and center in Veblen, owing to the inductivist nature of his enterprise and his generally progressive political leanings.

John R. Commons was a contemporary of Veblen and was influenced by his view of the corporation.[162] Commons took Veblen's more acerbic observations on the workings of business and translated them into an approach to thinking about institutions generally. These insights were transformed into politically mainstream programs, most notably workers' compensation. In his *Legal Foundations of Capitalism* Commons concentrated on "going concerns." Going concerns were associations throughout society joined by individuals to consummate transactions. The two going concerns that most interested Commons were labor and corporations. Commons took the position that there needed to be a structure through which labor and corporations could more efficiently transact their negotiations. The method of choice was collective bargaining, since a more socialistic approach would have been disfavored by an American public "so stubbornly individualistic that social responsibility, in so far as it exists *effectively*, has come about only piecemeal."[163]

Commons's perspective on the economic order had profound implications for legal-economic theory. For Commons the common law, statute law, business rules, and the like constituted the "working rules" of going concerns. Laws structured institutional arrangements. Commons, like other progressive intellectuals of the time, took the principal policy concern in shaping institutions to be social insurance. The early-twentieth-century social insurance movement in America was centered to a great extent on the American Association for Labor Legislation (AALL),[164] founded in 1906 as an outgrowth of the American Economics Association.[165] The AALL was devoted to promoting a broad range of social insurance, including workers' compensation, unemployment insurance, and old age insurance. The social insurance movement was central to the historical development of American legal-economic theory because the policy arguments and methodology that played a large role in the movement, particularly with regard to workers' compensation, would later be used to call for reshaping tort law.[166] The AALL stressed the scientific investigation of issues related to social insurance and reliance on empirical (statistical) evidence.[167] In doing so, according to Commons, it took an interdisciplinary approach and used the "best results of the work done in medicine, hygiene, economics, sociology, and jurisprudence" to argue for its cause.[168]

A key figure in examining how the shift in economic perspective marked by institutionalism affected legal-economic theory is Henry Seager. One of the preeminent economists of his time, Seager in 1922 was elected president of the American Economics Association. He was a major figure in the social insurance movement, as evidenced not only by his participation in the founding of the AALL but by his position as president of the association (1911–12, 1914–15) and member of the Committee on Social Insurance.[169] The ideas put forth by Seager in Social Insurance (1910)[170] are striking precursors of later justifications for using a strict liability regime rather than a negligence regime to resolve disputes related to accidents resulting from manufactured products. While Seager's contribution to the intellectual foundations of tort law theory have not been generally noted, his work in Social Insurance was specifically cited by Harold Laski, who was affiliated with the legal realist movement.[171]

Social Insurance was a manifesto concerning the need for social insurance to guard against the economic consequences of accidents, illness, premature death, unemployment, and old age. Of greatest concern in constructing an intellectual genealogy of tort law are Seager's thoughts regarding accidents. Before moving to that specific discussion, however, it is useful to sketch Seager's ideas concerning social insurance in general.

The social conceptualization that lay at the core of Seager's view was that the "creed of individualism is no longer adequate" in an industrial society where "clear appreciation of the conditions that make for the common welfare . . . and an aggressive program of governmental control and regulations to maintain [them]" are the order of the day.[172] Seager was particularly concerned with the ideology of individualism, such as the views of Adam Smith, and believed that the ability to adopt social insurance schemes hinged upon changing the "state of the public mind"[173] regarding individualism. Seager argued that this transformation, and a consequent social insurance program, would be vital in guarding against the dislocation caused by social ills. Social dislocation came in the form of economic hardship for families suffering a loss of income and insufficient savings. Workers had very little money to save, and the "failure of wage earners to provide . . . against [emergencies was] . . . proof that collective remedies must be found and applied."[174] The gravity of the problem was illustrated by Seager in emphasizing that "more than courage is needed to enable a widow left without resources to bring up her children as they would have been brought up had the father lived."[175]

In addition, and Seager stressed this point, the evils were not limited to the individual families. Seager believed that one consequence of a family's economic desperation would be to add to the pool of unskilled and low-paid workers,[176] as children and women were forced into the workplace and injured workers (presumably male) were forced out of their trades and into lower-skill employment.[177] This pressure would result in lower wages for all and a general decline in living standards: poverty. According to Seager, poverty was an "insurmountable obstacle to the realization of the individualist's millennium" and made the "program of individualism little better than a program of despair."[178] The problem of poverty was neither natural nor the result of individual fecklessness. The distribution of wealth is a societal, not an individual, phenomenon.

Law, particularly as it defines the ownership of property, plays a key role in determining the distribution of wealth. Its distributional consequences, like those of other institutions, are not necessarily at the forefront of consciousness, but frequently manifest themselves in any event. Seager believed that it is the job of economic science to shed light on these consequences. Seager was not as critical of corporations as Veblen was, but he believed that industrialization had had a profound impact on America: "[F]or other great sections of the country—the sections in which manufacturing and trade have become the dominant interests of the people, in which towns and cities have grown up, and in which the wage earner is the typical American citizen—the simple creed of individualism is no longer adequate. . . . [Owing to the] industrial revolution . . . with the introduction and spread of capitalistic methods of production, the individual wage earner has become more and more helpless in his efforts to control the conditions of his employment."[179]

In sum, Seager's view of the world is collectivist in nature and his principal public policy concern is poverty. With the breakdown of the small-scale agrarian economy, it made no sense to think of labor in individual terms, and it would be a mistake to describe industrial activity as anything but collective. The focus on the social, as opposed to individualistic, aspect of economic relationships marked a distinct break from the classical era.

Seager's concern with the consequences of economic dislocation was tied to the general institutionalist view regarding the distribution of wealth. Richard T. Ely is the institutionalist who most forcefully argued that distributional issues are central. In *Property and Contract in their Relations to the Distribution of Wealth* (1914) Ely wrote: "[D]istribution gives a standpoint from which to discuss public questions. . . . Our study leads us, therefore, to consider nearly all the topics in economics from the standpoint of distribution."[180] In examining the question of distribution, Ely emphasized that "[w]e have to consider in real life the present distribution."[181] Ely's focus on distributional considerations marked a decided break from the dictates of classical economics. Ely argued that distribution analysis should focus not on the individual but on "units"—such as rich people, poor people, and labor. In doing so, Ely hinted at his own progressive redistributionist tendencies, noting that "certain . . . economic units do not have sufficient incomes for the satisfaction of real needs."[182] He specifically referred to sweatshops and the need to increase wages for workers. The focus on "units" and distributional concerns had important implications for tort law, particularly the choice between a negligence and a strict liability regime.

Seager attacked negligence doctrine because of the barriers that it posed to compensation. Seager had a very sophisticated understanding of negligence law and submitted it to much of the same critique that legal scholars and judges would later level in arguing for strict liability. The motivation for his critique was his belief that a negligence regime bars recovery to many who are injured: "the whole burden of loss and expense which it entails, as well as the pain and suffering which it causes, must be borne by the injured workman and those dependent upon him."[183] This contradicted the individualistic principle that "everyone should be responsible for his own acts and omissions, and only for his own acts and omissions."[184] Seager admonished that only if society "turn[s] from abstract principles to a consideration of the social consequences of the policy"[185] will there be a move away from individualism and towards a more adequate compensation program. In his attempt to move away from "abstract principles," Seager used statistical data to make his case.[186]

To substantiate his claim that compensation was inadequate, Seager relied upon reports that insurance companies compensated victims in fewer than one-eighth of reported accidents.[187] It was significant to Seager that more than half the accidents were the result of risks inherent to industry and could not be attributed to the fault of the employer or employee.[188] In addition, a good many of the remaining accidents were noncompensable because of affirmative defenses.[189] What was the solution for Seager? To take industrial accidents out of tort law: "[n]egligence is clearly too narrow a basis on which to rest society's policy with reference to accidents."[190] Because a certain number of accidents were inevitable, even once prevention measures were taken, a system of compensation not based on fault (workers' compensation) would be needed to assure what Seager considered justice.

Seager argued that corporations had the capacity to insure themselves against this contingent liability and to "pass on the cost of insurance to consumers as one of the normal items in the expense of production."[191] The theme of justifying corporate strict liability because of the corporation's ability to act as a conduit in passing on the cost of accidents (loss spreading) would later prove significant in American legal-economic theory. However, it was in tension with the more hostile approach toward corporations adopted by Veblen. It could be argued that Seager was simply a more astute economist than Veblen—recognizing that whether the corporation actually absorbs the costs of accidents depends largely on the sensitivity of consumer demand. Or the cost-spreading approach to mitigating losses by consumers may simply have been more politically palatable (assuming a moderate political consensus) than the "soak the corporation" approach adopted by Veblen. Ultimately, Seager's view would prevail.

Commons and Seager clarified the policy basis behind the coming revolution in tort law theory, which reflected more general shifts in American intellectual thought. While Veblen's initial anti-corporate admonitions were important in focusing the American intellectual psyche on the role of corporate power, his radical critique would be supplanted by the more instrumentalist view of the corporation as a conduit for spreading losses. It was outside legal academe that the transformation of tort law theory received both its philosophical underpinning (rejection of formalism and focus on humanistic concerns) and its policy basis (social insurance and concern over the distribution of wealth). Now it would be up to legal scholars to complete the transformation.

The peak years of legal realism in American legal theory are generally dated between 1910 and 1945, with the 1920s through 1930s marking its height.[192] The essential tenets of legal realism that reflect institutionalist and pragmatist influences are concerns for connecting law with social and economic reality, and the use of social science as an analytical tool. There was also a highly visible strand of legal realism, of which Jerome Frank was a staunch champion, which was more critical than instrumentalist. In his classic *Law and the Modern Mind* (1930) Frank took a psychoanalytic view of legal theory, borrowing from Freud. While Frank colorfully (and with great rhetorical flourish) reflected the legal realist challenge to objectivism and certainty, his critique did not include the programmatic bent characteristic of the brand of legal realism influential in legal-economic thought.

The contextualist impulse in legal realism owes much to the general rejection of formalism in American thought. In this regard, the intellectual connection between legal realism and Holmes is important. However the legal realists, like most others in the pragmatist movement and unlike Holmes, were politically progressive and motivated by a desire to ameliorate human suffering associated with an industrialized society. In addition, while Holmes rhetorically exhorted that in legal studies the "man of the future is the man of statistics and the master of economics,"[193] the legal realists actually took up this methodological charge in arguing for social reform.[194] The legal realists' approach to legal-economic reform was very much pragmatist in nature. Science of the inductive sort would be a pillar of legal realism. The deductive formalism of the classical era had to be beaten back.[195]

Nowhere was this intellectual shift in American legal-economic theory more prevalent than in tort law. The work of Harold Laski—a British socialist intellectual and leading legal realist, and one of Holmes's most intimate intellectual soul-mates—is exemplary. He carried forward Holmes's insights on strict liability, as presented in "The Path of Law." Laski's centrality to the intellectual history of American legal-economic theory stems not only from his connection with Holmes but also from his affiliation with leading thinkers of the Progressive era, particularly institutionalists and legal realists. The breadth of Laski's intellectual contacts is demonstrated in his founding in 1919 of the New School for Social Research with Dewey, Veblen,[196] and others,[197] and his commitment to a progressive social agenda by his influential role in Britain's Labour Party.[198]

Laski presented his view on tort law theory in "The Basis of Vicarious Liability."[199] For him the central question was how to justify the doctrine of vicarious liability: liability of employers for actions taken by their employees. Laski aptly pointed out that there was nothing in American or English legal tradition that on its face rationally justified the doctrine. However, this was exactly the point. The ascension of vicarious liability marked a turning point in legal-economic theory.

Like Henry Seager, Laski argued that it was time to move away from the individualistic conceptions that had served as the philosophical basis for negligence, and turn toward a more public and collectivist vision:[200] "[I]t becomes increasingly evident that society cannot be governed on the principles of commercial nihilism. To assume that freedom and equality consist in competition is simply to travesty the facts. We come once more to an age of collective endeavor."[201] The philosophical basis of Laski's position can justly be labeled pragmatism. Laski tells us that "[w]e cannot run a human world on the principle of formal logic . . . [or] fit the life we live in *a priori* rules."[202] We must "attempt to see the individual in his social context."[203] Laski was attuned to the pragmatism of his day and had an ongoing debate with Holmes regarding the merits of pragmatism in general and, particularly, which of the emerging versions of pragmatism was most worthy of attention.[204] Regarding liability, Laski had firm ideas about the principles that should guide one's thinking. Laski identified one of the most important theoretical underpinnings of vicarious liability as minimizing social dislocation.[205] He viewed the corporation as a social unit against which the public must be protected.[206] Institutionalism influenced Laski, particularly through Henry Seager's works. Laski's views on economics in general and his antipathy toward classical economics in particular are set forth in a letter to Holmes. Laski describes an economist who "defines economics as the alternative between scarce means to achieve maximum satisfaction" as demonstrating the "mental limitations of the expert" and justifying why the "public does not take the economists very seriously."[207]

Laski's position on vicarious liability illustrates how the Holmesian legal view affected reform-oriented legal intellectuals, That view was also adopted by Leon Green, one of the leading figures in the legal realist movement and a giant in the field of tort law.[208] Green's assault on causation in negligence was a significant contribution to tort theory. This critique of causation was strikingly similar to that of Nicholas St. John Green (to whom he was not related), providing a distinct connection to pragmatist thought. However, where Nicholas Green discussed causation on a philosophical level, Leon Green engaged in doctrinal analyses.

Leon Green's view is set forth in "Are Negligence and Proximate Cause Determinable by the Same Test?"[209] In it Green criticizes any mention of proximate cause in a long line of cases in Texas. To his mind, discussions of proximate cause only confused and masked the true issue: negligent behavior, as measured by the probability (foreseeability) of injury stemming from a particular activity. In making his argument, Leon Green drew the same conclusion as Nicholas Green: it is impossible to reconcile the cases in tort law through proximate causation analysis. Whenever courts used the term "proximate cause," it stood as a proxy for probability of injury (negligence) and not causal relation. Like Nicholas Green, Leon Green believed that negligence should be determined by "probable consequence"[210] and that in place of vacuous proximate causation analyses courts should look to "experience"[211] as their guide to determining liability. According to Leon Green, only by analyzing cases in a probabilistic manner and appealing to experience could courts avoid the "niceties of metaphysics which have so long beclouded the point [(negligence doctrine)]."[212] Like his forebear, Green criticized attempts to provide a metaphysical underpinning for liability and urged that the determination should be based on a "probability test solely."[213] Green's analysis was an important contribution to tort law theory. The critique of causation in negligence paved the way for a conception of torts based on probable consequences and the acceptance of statistical inference as a policy justification in tort law analysis.

A figure even more closely associated with the legal realist movement is

Karl Llewellyn. Although Llewellyn's contribution was in the area of contracts, his ideas had important connections to tort law.[214] As a legal realist, Llewellyn trumpeted themes very similar to those in the pragmatic thought of Holmes and Nicholas Green. He believed in the shifting nature of law, the need for law to change in response to a changing society, and the use of law as a public policy tool.[215] In his text on the law of sales, Llewellyn summed up his ideas on the evolutionary nature of law: "[D]octrine changes to somewhat adjust to new insight. But the justification must be in terms of purely static law—and the older authorities pay the price—twisted out of recognizability. The other approach, taking account of the time dimension and the fact of development, finds classic expression in *MacPherson v. Buick*."[216] Llewellyn readily recognized the direct, and potentially problematic, relationship, between legal realism and pragmatism: "Legal realism is a name for pragmatic and empirical thinking about the law; its confusions are due to an uncritical acceptance of dogmas of raw empiricism and pragmatism without any consideration of the philosophical issues these dogmas raise, but certainly do not resolve."[217]

Llewellyn's contribution to American legal-economic theory is principally due to his ideas on warranty, and to the theoretical arguments underlying them. The ideas were set forth in a two-part article entitled "On Warranty of Quality, and Society,"[218] which is an explicit appeal to history and a call to contextualize legal doctrine: "It is a sad commentary on our dogmatics that sales cases over a hundred and fifty years and more than fifty jurisdictions have been treated as if they floated free of time, place and person. Whereas it is time, place, person and circumstance which give them meaning."[219] Within this general framework, Llewellyn would go on to lay out the history of warranty law dating back to early English common law.

One of the themes that figured prominently in Llewellyn's analysis was the disparity in bargaining power among contracting parties.[220] In examining the bargaining issue, Llewellyn adopted a pragmatic assessment rule: "(1) Bargain to the parties' taste has been, and is, praise-worthy in our law *wherever experience has not shown the contrary*. (2) A bargain, however, shows itself not to be a bargain when lop-sidedness begins to scream. . . . (3) The problem is this: that the contract is not a natural right but a legal construct."[221] The idea that contractual bargaining was not in any sense "natural" but a process undertaken within a socially constructed legal regime marks a sharp contrast to the natural law thinking of the classical era as evidenced by Justice Peckham's decision in *Lochner*. To Llewellyn the core issue was the "helpless consumer . . . who takes what he gets, because he does not know enough, technically, to test even what is before his eyes."[222] According to this paternalistic view, Llewellyn saw the development of law related to corporate liability for the products they produce, whether in tort or warranty, tending toward strict or "absolute liability."[223]

As part of his historical and policy analysis, Llewellyn admonishes legal scholars to weigh different legal and policy doctrines "against the flux of conditions, needs and theories."[224] Since coming out of the Civil War, America had been transformed from an agricultural yeoman economy to one that included a "combination of power-factory, technical advance, natural resources uncovering, expansion of railroad mileage and unity, the Republican Party, the tariff, and the general incorporation laws, [which] set the stage nationally for widening a seller's mercantile obligation."[225] Llewellyn emphasized the need for social insurance, which justified shifting the costs of accidents from consumers to manufacturers of products. In *On Warranty II*, Llewellyn discussed the need to "spread risk" and emphasized the importance of being concerned with the "distribution of risk."[226]

Llewellyn used an institutionalist framework for his policy arguments. References by Llewellyn in "On Warranty" to Walton Hamilton,[227] the institutionalist economist and Yale Law School professor who had been influenced by Veblen,[228] confirm this observation. Moreover, his affection for the institutionalist school of thought is evident in another article, which appeared in the leading economics journal of the day, laying out his public policy ideas: "The Effects of Legal Institutions upon Economics."[229] In it Llewellyn is frank about the need for lawyers to turn to economics to formulate legal theory. He makes a crucial connection between the legal realists' anti-formalism project and the policy prescriptions of the institutionalist school: "The jurist is protesting against the dogma of his fathers that law is unchanging, eternal, discoverable always by deduction. Only recently has he come to see it as a thing, in flux, and made discovery of non-legal factors which condition its growth and action. Whereas the economist takes that for granted.[230] Llewellyn goes on to say that "[w]hen one approaches the law not with the idea of formulating its rules into a system, but with an eye to discovering how much it does or can effect, and to the principles both of its effect and of its change, economic theory offers in many respects amazing light."[231] The importance of economics was that it provided the scientific tools with which to consider how best to harness the power of institutions for the good of society.[232]

The institution that was foremost in Llewellyn's mind was the corporation, and his views on the corporation and its role vis-à-vis the consumer was similar to Veblen's. Consumers were seen as the helpless prey of vulture capitalists. Llewellyn concluded that wealth should be redistributed from "wealthy" corporations to "poor" consumers. He tied his general position on the redistribution of wealth to tort law, particularly workers' compensation, products liability, and strict liability for hazardous activities. He saw movements in all these realms as dealing with the relationship between capital, labor, and the consuming public, and he believed that the law should be used to regulate the distributive function of the marketplace. Llewellyn recognized that this distributive function, as opposed to the market's productive function, was too easily ignored, but only at our peril. This view of course contrasted starkly to the laissez-faire ideology of the classical era.

The jurisprudential implications of the break with the classical ideal of scientific jurisprudence as deductivist is found in Benjamin Cardozo's *The Nature of the Judicial Process*,[233] a landmark in American legal-economic theory. Cardozo makes little reference to pragmatist philosophers,[234] but pragmatist sentiments abound and there are several references to Holmes, as well as a general admonition that "the juristic philosophy of the common law is at bottom the philosophy of pragmatism."[235] In subscribing to this philosophy Cardozo stresses that "truth is relative, not absolute,"[236] a vision of truth linked to the explicit anti-formalist position that Cardozo takes throughout his book.[237]

However, Cardozo rejects any sort of radical anti-formalism. In Cardozo's view, judging consists of four types of analysis: (1) logical progression of rules; (2) historical development; (3) custom; and (4) justice, morals and social welfare.[238] The inclusion of logical progression as a part of judicial development bespeaks Cardozo's unwillingness to make a clean break with judicial formalism. Nevertheless, in the context of a changed society Cardozo makes it clear that "in our day and generation . . . the greatest of [the forces shaping judicial change is] the power of social justice which finds its outlet and expression in the method of sociology."[239]

Cardozo's focus on judicial decision making in context is evolutionary in perspective;[240] Cardozo takes an interdisciplinary approach in thinking about how judges are to construe the law at various points in society's evolution: "Courts know today that statutes are to be viewed, not in isolation or *in vacuo*, as pronouncements of abstract principles for the guidance of an ideal community, but in the setting and the framework of present-day conditions, as revealed by the labors of economists and students of the social sciences in our country and abroad."[241] This broad jurisprudential manifesto would inform legal-economic thought regarding tort law.

Fleming James led the intellectual charge for expanding strict products liability in torts during his career as a law professor at Yale University beginning in the 1940s.[242] James based the promotion of strict products liability on three pillars: the futility of constructing a unifying theory of torts; a zeal for loss spreading as a guiding concept; and a belief in social science as a method for approaching the myriad of tort law issues.[243] These three themes were deeply rooted in the pragmatist tradition.[244] Holmes's role as a precursor to the legal realist movement is evident in James's "Tort Law in Midstream."[245] James makes references to Holmes's *The Common Law* and *Collected Legal Papers*, but more important in situating James's work as essentially pragmatic is how his critique of tort law coincides with Holmes's and the legal realists' conception of tort law as a disparate set of rules and doctrines (with no a priori unifying concept).

James stressed that torts "covers a heterogeneous mass of stuff." This view of torts, which reflects James's view of society at large, is a direct offshoot of the anti-formalist turn in American thought, particularly as presented by the legal realists who preceded James. James puts forth three categories of torts: intentional torts, negligent torts, and torts based on strict liability. Just as Oliver Wendell Holmes, Nicholas Green, Leon Green, and Harold Laski took it as part of their project to criticize the move toward providing an overarching theory of torts, James criticized the notion that any one of the concepts associated with his three categories of torts, particularly fault in negligence, could be used to coherently conceptualize all of tort.[246] James's purpose was to open up doctrinal space, a project initially undertaken by Holmes, so that strict liability would take on a larger role in the torts corpus.

James attacked the individualistic creed. Again, this is a common theme linking James to the pragmatists, particularly the position taken by Henry Seager. Rejecting individualism led James to argue against negligence, which he criticized as being founded on the notion of individual fault or blameworthiness. In fact, in attempting to address his critics, James criticized those who "prefer the individualism which they believe underlies the present law of negligence."[247] "[N]otions of individualism," he admonished, "that underlay the development of negligence law during the last century do not in fact underlie accident law today, and no philosophy and no amount of wishing will make it so."[248]

The parallels in perspective between James and Seager are not surprising, given that in the landmark treatise *The Law of Torts*, which James wrote with Fowler Harper,[249] an entire chapter is devoted to "social insurance."[250] At the beginning of the chapter a direct reference connects the torts project that James wished to pursue with "workmen's compensation in 1910" and "1930's social insurance legislation."[251] The importance of social insurance is discussed, along with the litany of ills that concerned the social insurance theorists discussed previously: "pecuniary loss through such vicissitudes of life as accident, old age, sickness, and unemployment."[252] This linkage of James with the workers' compensation movement is a linchpin in the genealogy of strict products liability.[253]

James and Harper stressed the contrast between the themes of social insurance in the workers' compensation movement and the fault principle, recognizing that dissolution of the fault concept was as essential to constructing their vision of strict products liability in torts as it was to the workers' compensation movement. Fault encompassed the individualistic, laissez-faire ideals in American society that James rejected. Its origins lay in an "earlier, mechanistic imputation of blame,"[254] a view inspired by Newtonianism which legal realists criticized. James believed that it should be rejected because: "Human failures in a *machine age* cause a large and fairly *regular*—though probably reducible—toll of life, limb, and property. The most important aspect of these failures is not their moral quality; frequently they involve little or nothing in the way of personal moral shortcoming."[255] Relying on the same argument—the irrelevance of fault in a modern industrial economy—as Seager did in proposing workers' compensation, James and Harper emphasized that individuals are engaged in activity that causes "certain" and "calculable" loss.[256] To this point, James was enamored with accident studies and their economic implications.[257]

As for the economic theory consistent with James's and Harper's vision, it was decidedly of the institutionalist sort. This is important to emphasize, because by the time strict products liability was implemented, the neoclassical school of economics had clearly beaten back institutionalism.[258] In a later edition of *The Law of Torts* it was recognized that the thoughts of Guido Calabresi, a leading torts theorist, were somewhat allied with the positions taken in the treatise. Calabresi's neoclassical economics arguments for strict liability, which will be discussed in chapter 3, are described as having helped to "illuminate the approach taken in this text, although they employ different emphases and suggest different conclusions."[259] Calabresi's use of neoclassical economics is contrasted favorably to that of Richard Posner, another pioneer of law and neoclassical economics who will also be discussed later.[260] However, the point cannot be overemphasized that regardless of the "brand" of neoclassical economics, the "economics" James had in mind was incongruous with the tenets underlying neoclassical economics. His vision of legal-economic theory was deeply rooted in institutionalist ideas and praxis, as is evidenced by his belief in the inductive (statistical) method.

Regarding statistical studies, James declared that the greatest was the Columbia Study, compiled in 1928–30 by a group of scholars at Columbia and Yale,[261] partly at the instigation of William O. Douglas and Leon Green, both members of the Yale faculty at the time. The study had four parts: case studies on the effect of accidents on individuals, records on court congestion, studies of the constitutionality of compensation laws, and insurance studies. The report was very much in the pragmatist tradition, as evidenced by this statement: "The value of [a] principle [(negligence)] is to be tested by its results, rather than by a priori moral considerations."[262]

Emma Corstvet conducted the Columbia Study under the supervision of the dean of the Yale Law School, Charles Clark.[263] Corstvet was influenced by institutionalism. As an undergraduate she had studied with Commons at the University of Wisconsin, and she later studied at the London School of Economics.[264] Corstvet's method was contextual, as is best illustrated in an article that she wrote based on data from the Columbia Study. The article, "The Uncompensated Accident and Its Consequences,"[265] begins with a short exercise in storytelling. Corstvet tells of families, each with a member disabled or killed in an accident, and the emotional and financial consequences they faced:

[I]n Connecticut, Steve Carlson, a laborer, was injured in an accident, his hip smashed. While he was in the hospital and for sometime afterwards, his wife and children managed. They borrowed from relatives, used up small savings, exhausted their credit with the grocer. The rent fell behind. Finally, a year later, the family gave up and was taken in by his parents until such time as 'maybe his sickness gets better.' There was no compensation. There was no newspaper report of this unimportant series of events; it is recorded only in statistics which state that about a million people were injured that year by automobiles.[266]

A little later in the year, Pasquale Miniotti was killed while crossing a street. A brief notice in the local paper stated that the driver had been found by the coroner to have been drinking and was arrested for homicide but later released. The widow got $500 life insurance, more than half of which she foolishly spent on the funeral. Seven months later she was living on occasional gifts from her former husband's employer and on gifts of food from neighbors. The landlady had not yet had the heart to put her out. There had been no compensation.[267]

The stories, and additional illustrations woven throughout the article, place the empirical data in human context. It is significant that Corstvet makes the point: "The concern of this article is not with reduction of accidents, itself an important problem. . . . It is with . . . the blunt consequences of lack of money."[268] At this point in the intellectual evolution of strict products liability, compensation, not deterrence, was at center stage. The concern was for the social dislocation associated with uncompensated accidents, a concern that had been prominent in the workers' compensation movement. The case studies and statistical analyses contained in the Columbia Study intrigued James because they lent support to his belief that the then-existing tort system undercompensated victims and led to social dislocation. According to the Columbia Study, only about 60 percent of accident victims received any compensation at all.[269] In addition, those suffering permanent disability did not obtain sufficient compensation to cover continued medical expenses and wage loss.[270]

Loss spreading was the chief economic means that James attempted to employ. His emphasis on loss spreading was a product of his concern regarding the distribution of wealth and its human consequences—values associated with institutionalism. James's view was that "[w]e should not only select but also adjust our tools to the particular job in hand, and that is to be measured in terms of *human* needs and values and not of legal concepts."[271] To this end, as evidenced by his emphasis on the Columbia Study, James saw the tort system as a tool for compensation rather than deterrence. In *The Law of Torts*, we are told that reducing accidents could be achieved through "pressure of safety regulations with penal and licensing sanctions, and of the self-interest in avoiding the host of non-legal disadvantages that flow from accidents."[272] However, "[W]hen this is all done *human* losses remain. It is the principal job of tort law today to deal with those losses. They fall initially on people who as a class can ill afford them, and this fact brings great hardship upon the victims themselves and causes unfortunate repercussions to society as a whole. The best and most efficient way to deal with accident loss, therefore, is to assure accident victims of substantial compensation, and to *distribute* the losses involved over society as a whole or some very large segment of it. Such a basis for administering losses is what we have called *social insurance*."[273] This statement echoes the humanistic concerns that animated James's views. It also illustrates how the concept of the corporation as a conduit for spreading losses and achieving distributional goals was at the core of James's conception of strict products liability.

While James was the most theoretically sophisticated of the tort scholars who helped to implement strict products liability, William Prosser was the most instrumental in its ultimate adoption into law. Prosser's influence was due in large part to his doctrinal contributions.[274] James emphasized the policy aspects of strict products liability; Prosser, while acknowledging the relevance of social engineering and policy aspects (remnants of the institutionalist influence), focused on setting forth a doctrinal approach to strict products liability. James fulfilled his function through his duties as a principal author of the *Restatement (Second) of Torts*. Restatements of the law, written by leading lawyers, judges, and academics and published by the American Law Institute, are summaries of the state of the law in various fields that serve two often contradictory functions. As their title implies, they "restate" existing law, but they are highly influential and also frequently lay out which direction the law ought to take.[275]

This focus on doctrinal reconfiguration can be seen in Prosser's contribution to the debate over warranties in "Implied Warranty."[276] Prosser sets out to examine the development of warranty law in much the same way as

Llewellyn had done in his "On Warranty" articles, beginning with the history of warranty. At the outset, Prosser recognizes that initially breach of warranty was a claim in tort (because it was treated as a form of misrepresentation) and that this entanglement has present-day consequences.[277] In particular, the tort strands in warranty analysis provided grounds for the argument to extend implied warranty to the ultimate consumer.[278]

As to the reasons why an implied warranty of quality could be so easily read into the law of contracts, Prosser offered three. First, the seller is assumed to have represented certain facts to the buyer and the failure of the product to meet the buyer's supposed expectations constitutes deceit.[279] Deceit was read into the transaction because of the "seller's supposed superior judgment or information about the goods."[280] Prosser characterized this as a tort theory and correctly stated that as applied it represented a "strict liability" rule.[281] Second, the basis of warranty was the actual agreement by the parties, irrespective of whether the agreement remained unexpressed in the contract.[282] A holding of liability in this instance is based on the court's creative reading of the contract. Nevertheless, at bottom it is a contract analysis. Third, "law," irrespective of what the parties initially desired, imposes warranty.[283] The basis for imposing liability was policy: "the loss due to defective goods is placed upon the seller because he is best able to bear it and distribute it to the public."[284]

Although he listed all three rationales, Prosser was careful to note that as far as liability was concerned, which of the three was actually deployed made little difference, because as a general matter courts were "tending to an increasing extent to favor the buyer and find the warranty" regardless of the rationale put forth.[285] Thus Prosser recognized that doctrinal machinations were mere placards for intellectual and policy shifts. Those shifts had been effected under the influence of pragmatism. However, under Prosser's steady hand the ultimate triumph of strict products liability would occur in the form of Section 402A of the *Restatement (Second) of Torts*, which Prosser was instrumental in having adopted.[286]

Section 402A of the *Restatement* is the principal doctrinal statement for liability stemming from the use of manufactured products.[287] The language in Section 402A that gives it much of its doctrinal meaning is the imposition of liability even if "the seller has exercised all possible care in the preparation of his product." The decision not to allow a defense of "all possible care" in products liability cases effectively placed such cases in the category of strict liability as opposed to negligence. This is an important policy choice: as noted earlier, a strict liability rule means that the victim is more likely to be compensated than under a negligence rule, which requires the plaintiff to prove some sort of fault (or wrongful conduct) by the defendant. Section 402A was very influential. The vast bulk of American courts adopted some form of strict products liability in its wake.

Strict liability doctrine had been championed since the early twentieth century by legal realist academics and like-minded judges. The basis for the legal realist position was a pragmatist philosophical orientation and a view of economic relationships influenced by institutional economists. The development of strict products liability was an acknowledgment that by the middle of the twentieth century American legal-economic theory looked a lot different from the way it did at its inception in the classical era. Methodologically, there was a shift toward empiricism and inductive inquiry generally and away from deductive formalism. Politically, the worship of laissez-faire ideology was supplanted by more progressive politics and redistributionist leanings. However, there was a similarity between the classical and pragmatist eras: the reliance on science as the foundation for legal-economic theory. The lessons of Darwin had a profound impact in spurring the shift from formalism to pragmatism. The pragmatist point of view lent credence to the legal realist argument that the prior claim to science in the classical era no longer withstood critical scrutiny, nor satisfied the prevailing standard of objectivity as probabilistic and contextual. While the critique of absolutist notions of Truth (certainty) implicitly called into question the possibility of objectivity, into the twentieth century science would remain a constant in legal-economic theory. However, its contours would change yet again—philosophically, methodologically, and politically.

THREE

NEOCLASSICISM AND THE REPRISE OF FORMALISM

■ The philosophical roots of the scientific position that would serve as the foundation for the neoclassical era in legal-economic theory are to be found in the "analytic turn"—the historical moment, beginning in the early twentieth century (as pragmatism was ascendant), that marked the emergence of ideas later to develop into what is today referred to as analytic philosophy (logical positivism, logical empiricism, and linguistic philosophy).[1] The contrast between the analytic vision of science that came to dominate America after the Second World War and the pragmatist vision that it displaced has been summed up by Cornel West: the major effect of the dominance of logical positivism was to "turn attention away from historical consciousness and social reflection and toward logic and physics."[2]

The philosophical discussion will center on A. J. Ayer's *Language, Truth and Logic* as a historically significant exemplar of the analytic turn, particularly in developing logical positivism and importing it to America.[3] Ayer's contribution is important because his was the first comprehensive English-language exposition of analytic dictates. The analytic movement was formed in the crucible of European thought. The principal influence can be traced to the Vienna Circle, founded by Moritz Schlick in 1925, a configuration of Viennese intellectuals that included not only philosophers but also physicists, mathematicians, psychologists, sociologists, and lawyers.[4] Given their emphasis on scientific thought as the touchstone for philosophical inquiry, it is not surprising that members of the Vienna Circle should have been heavily influenced by what certainly counts as one of the two greatest scientific discoveries in the twentieth century—Einstein's theories of relativity (the other being quantum theory, which will be discussed in chapter 4).[5]

While Darwinian theories of evolution had a profound effect on the conception of science as inductive in nature, providing a respite from mathematical formulations (at least in America), theoretical physicists were soon to reassert their preeminence. As discussed previously, Newton had augmented his physics with metaphysical speculations that space and time were absolute phenomena. In addition, he had proposed the existence of a ubiquitous ether. While Newtonian mechanics worked perfectly well, and still does today, for making a large range of physical predictions, in the nineteenth century physicists began discovering phenomena that were either incompatible or inconsistent with his system. Einstein would be largely responsible for answering some of the most fundamental unresolved questions in physics. In doing so he revolutionized how we view the physical world and, more importantly for us, reestablished the supremacy of the view that science is in large part deductive and determinate.

An experiment by Albert Michelson and Edward Morey in 1887 had failed to detect the ever-elusive ether. Until that time physicists did not have instruments sensitive enough to ascertain its existence. Ether was just assumed to exist, because in order for Newton's ideas of absolute time and space to be consistent with other laws of physics, in particular James Maxwell's electromagnetic theory (which revealed the connection between electrical and magnetic forces), there must be an ether. In addition, Newtonian physics required that the speed of light be variable. However, mathematical representations constructed on the basis of electromagnetic theory indicated that the speed of light remained constant. The Newtonian worldview, which had previously seemed unassailable, had been called into question. Against this backdrop, in 1905 Einstein came up with a revolutionary hypothesis: time and space are relative to one's reference frame—the speed of light is constant. As a result, there was no need to hypothesize the existence of an ether.

Einstein (in his popular rendering of relativity theory) began by discussing the physical meaning of geometrical propositions.[6] While geometry was an axiomatic enterprise yielding exact answers, it had nothing to do with measurement in the real world. Therefore, a geometric statement could not be defined as "true." To have a real measurement, there must be an object to be measured. Einstein's musings on the subjects of truth and geometry have obvious philosophical implications, and philosophers had long debated the possibilities and limitations of the geometric method.[7] To define an object's position in space, we must be able to measure it. Einstein believed that the "purpose of mechanics [(physics)] is to describe how bodies change their position in space over 'time.' "[8] However, he quickly noted that this definition begs the question of what we mean by "position" and "space." He posed the issue as a thought experiment. Suppose that someone stands at the window of a rail car moving at uniform speed (constant and straight) and drops a stone on to an embankment. The person dropping the stone will see it as falling straight, while someone watching at a distance from the track will view it as falling on a parabolic curve. The "position" of the stone could be described as straight or parabolic depending on the reference point (on the train or removed from it). Space, according to Einstein, was not a very helpful expression and should be replaced by "motion relative to a practically rigid body of reference."[9] The stone's path (or position) is relative to the position of the observer (reference point). There is no independent point of reference.

Einstein noted that measurement is a matter not only of space but of time: "[i]n order to have a *complete* description of the motion, we must specify how the body alters its position *with time*; i.e., for every point on the trajectory it must be stated at what time the body is situated there."[10] But time is also relative. Perhaps the most famous example of this principle is the clock experiment (two identical clocks will keep different time depending on one's frame of reference). Here is another illustration, provided by Einstein. Assume that two bolts of lightning strike locations A and B along a rail line, simultaneously from the point of view of the person standing on the embankment at the midpoint between A and B. How is the same event measured by a passenger on a train who is also at the midpoint between A and B? If the train is headed toward B the passenger will see the lightning at point B before point A, and the lightning strikes will not appear to be simultaneous. Time is not absolute.[11] If fact, seconds are ticked off more slowly when a clock is in motion than at rest.[12] "Time" depends on the relative position (motion) of the observer. Time relativity is only one of the strange phenomena revealed by relativity. Einstein also demonstrated how a rod would appear to be shorter when in motion than when at rest, and the greater the velocity the shorter the rod would appear.[13]

For scientists Einstein's theory is appealing, because he offers up a method that reconciles the measurement differences—a series of "transformation equations" (originally formulated by the Dutch physicist Hendrik Antoon Lorentz). While time and space were not absolute, they were comprehensible and measurable by an "objective" observer, the physicist, because the laws of physics were applicable in all reference frames.

These popular examples of special relativity theory are misinterpreted by some outside the scientific community as indicating the relative nature of physical phenomena. David Cassidy has argued that Einstein's relativity theory has had a great impact on the nonscientific community and resonated with European culture in the years following the First World War despite an inability to truly understand it or outright misinterpretations.[14] It is often the misperceptions that resonate with the public: "[i]nfluential theories such as relativity seem to strike a special chord across a range of ideas, or metaphors embodying those ideas, that are in currency at a given time."[15] The devastation and carnage of war made broad segments of Europe and the United States receptive to the idea of a world separated from its moorings. For some Einstein's special relativity confirmed their suspicion that there are no overarching norms to guide the polity (since there were none on the physical level). As Cassidy describes it, "the familiar features of the mechanical worldview seemed suddenly undercut by relativity theory, while the old view's 'deterministic' elements seemed at fault for current uncontrollable difficulties."[16] That Einstein's theory was labeled relativity theory did not give much comfort to those seeking a secure foundation. Although the popular understanding of relativity was based on a false perception of it and a failure to heed to Einstein's own admonitions regarding its limitations, the very name raised the specter of a world without social, political, or moral moorings. Some responded to the cultural angst of the time by redoubling their efforts to push a scientistic agenda as a cure-all. Ironically, they found solace in Einstein as well.

While Einstein's theory of special relativity was a remarkable achievement, his general theory, published in complete form in 1916, went even further to secure his fame and broaden the cultural prestige of physics. One implication of the special theory of relativity (in conjunction with electromagnetism) was that nothing could travel faster than the speed of light. However, this rule was contradicted by Newton's theory of gravity, according to which gravity seemed to work "instantaneously." Newton's theory was based on a geometric model of space as flat, and thus there was a need for an "invisible force" to explain gravitational attraction. Einstein viewed this explanation as empty conjecture and found the implication of instantaneous force troubling. He instead developed the revolutionary hypothesis that space is curved, shaped by bodies of mass, such as our sun, that occupy the universe, as well as other forms of energy and the global properties of the universe. Thus gravitational pull is caused by bodies of mass succumbing to the curvatures in space, much as a ball rolls around a roulette wheel.[17]

Sir Arthur Eddington empirically confirmed Einstein's theory of curved space in 1918 and Einstein, the iconic genius who had changed our conception of space, was the subject of a film entitled "The Einstein Theory of Relativity" (1919) that was shown in movie theatres. After the social chaos of the First World War, there was need for a renewed sense of human progress, much as had been needed in Europe in the seventeenth century. The spectacular achievements of Einstein were the answer. Just as Newtonian physics was seen to point the way to the future of Europe, Einstein's discoveries inspired confidence in the progress of the species under the comforting umbrella of science.

It is little surprise that Einstein's impact should have been profound in the philosophical community, particularly on the Vienna Circle.[18] There was a natural affinity between logical positivism and Einstein's theories, and an earlier critique of Newton's notion of absolute time and space by one of the founders of logical positivism, Ernst Mach, who argued that time and space were relative, had been an inspiration for Einstein.[19] Schlick viewed Einstein's triumph over the Newtonian worldview as particularly important because it also marked in his mind the positivist triumph over Kantian metaphysics. In an effort to prove the point, Schlick wrote a series of papers highlighting the relationship between logical positivism and Einstein's scientific worldview.

According to Schlick, Kantian critical philosophy was a "product of the Newtonian doctrine of nature."[20] In particular, Kant had based his philosophical system on the idea of absolute space and time, in a manner consistent with his conception of a priori knowledge. Since the notion of absolute time and space was scientifically disconfirmed, it was necessary to reconsider the entire Kantian edifice. The logical positivists rejected any form of a priori reasoning as metaphysical rubbish. While Kantian critical philosophy had aspired to be an "exact science," as did logical positivism, it did not meet logical positivists' criteria for attaining this exalted status.

Relativity theory fulfilled the promise of exact science. It embodied the quest for certainty that had preoccupied western intellectual thought. Indeed, according to Schlick relativity theory had paved the "way to attain to the most universal laws and to discover the ultimate invariants."[21] Schlick, who had been trained as a physicist, believed that Einstein's scientific breakthrough validated the positivist philosophical view. Einstein was able to form his vision of relativity only after rejecting the inclusion of nonobservable phenomena, such as the ether and "the Deity," adopting the philosophical position that "*only something observable should be introduced as a ground of explanation* in science."[22] Since logical positivists took the position that there was no distinction between science and philosophy (regarding "philosophy, not as something distinct from the sciences, but as something in them"), nonobservables could not serve as a basis for knowledge acquisition generally.[23] There was a consistency between Einstein's and the logical positivists' views. To the extent that Einstein came to influence the scientific view of the world, the logical positivist position would also take hold.

While they established an intellectual foothold in Europe, the ideas associated with Schlick and the Vienna Circle did not enjoy widespread dissemination in the English-speaking world until *Language, Truth and Logic* was first published in 1936, and members of the Vienna Circle immigrated to the United States.[24] *Language, Truth and Logic*[25] has been referred to as the Vienna Circle's manifesto.[26] In it all genuine propositions are divided into two classes: "those which concern 'relations of ideas' and those which concern 'matters of fact.' "[27] The former represent the tautologous "propositions of logic and pure mathematics" which are "necessary and certain only because they are analytic . . . [and] cannot be confuted in experience . . . [because] they do not make any assertion about the empirical world, but simply record our determination to use symbols in a certain fashion."[28] For example, the statement "$2 + 2 = 4$" is necessarily true but says absolutely nothing about the world as opposed to the empirical statement that "there are four eggs in the jar."[29] Aside from examining the self-consistency of logical propositions, the role of the scientific philosopher includes establishing criteria for determining the truth or falsehood of the other class of propositions—empirical propositions. This emphasis on observational confirmation tracks the scientific method.

There is the danger that "propositions and questions which are really linguistic are often expressed in such a way that they appear to be factual."[30] Analytic propositions lack factual content; they are not susceptible to proof or invalidation through factual inquiry.[31] But if not to illuminate factual properties, what is the use of analyses? According to Ayer: "They call attention to linguistic usages, of which we might otherwise not be conscious, and they reveal unsuspected implications in our assertions and beliefs."[32] More pointedly, as the complexity of argument increases, the risk of faulty logic also increases. Thus there is a need to introduce symbolic devices to simplify expressions and guard against faulty reasoning.

After establishing which classes of statements fell within the domain of philosophical analysis—that is, analytic and empirical statements—Ayer set forth his view on a class of utterances that did not qualify as statements at all, namely ethical utterances. Ayer's ideas on ethics would become influential in determining what met the cultural perception of constituting an objective argument in postwar America.[33] *Language, Truth and Logic* regards ethical enunciations as "unanalysable" and "mere pseudo concepts." Therefore, the "presence of an ethical symbol in a proposition adds nothing to its factual content." Ayer illustrates his point by examining how the word "wrong" is used in grammar. If one were to say, " 'you acted wrongly in stealing that money,' " the statement could be reduced to " 'you stole that money,' " because adding the ethical concept "wrong" to the sentence does not add factual content to it. Ethical statements can "arouse feelings," but they fall outside the domain of science. They do not constitute logical (analytic) propositions or empirical propositions (given that their truth-validity is not capable of empirical investigation).[34]

In addition to the influence of *Language, Truth and Logic*, the migration of Vienna Circle members to America was crucial in bringing the ideas of the analytic movement to bear on American conceptions of science. With the onset of the Second World War, members of the Vienna Circle were almost wholly dispersed.[35] The flight from Nazi terrorism brought to American soil crucial figures in the logical positivist movement, such as Rudolf Carnap, Hans Reichenbach, Alfred Tarski, Herbert Feigel, and Carl Hempel.[36] The influence of logical positivism grew after the war as students under the tutelage of logical positivists spread their ideas to others. Its ascendancy was no doubt aided by the tremendous popular appeal of Einstein and his cultural influence. Science, particularly physics, had reached a position of tremendous prestige.

The neoclassical period is strikingly similar to its classical predecessor. In the classical era, Bacon and Descartes had established the philosophical basis for science and set the stage for the rise of scientism. The triumph of scientism, which appealed to the thirst for certainty, was manifested in Newton. Its greatest philosophical synthesis is found in Kant's formulation of "exact science." Logical positivism, marking the analytic turn, set forth the domain of what would "truly" constitute an "exact science" once the errors of Kant had been put to rest. Einstein is held up as exemplifying the power of exact science. Rationalism again reigns supreme.

Giovanna Borradori has noted that "[f]rom the thirties to the sixties, from the eve of the Second World War to the Vietnam War, American philosophy ceased to be a socially engaged interdisciplinary enterprise, becoming instead a highly specialized occupation . . . , [f]eaturing precise formal problems and hostile to any form of historical-literary erudition."[37] Carl Schorske, in his *Fin-de-Siècle Vienna*, has stated that analytic philosophy "[i]n the interest of a restricted and purer functioning in the areas of language and logic, . . . broke the ties both to history in general and to the discipline's own past."[38] Schorske also notes the general receptivity to Austrian ideas in America after the Second World War. For Schorske, the decade after the war's end marked a time of crisis for America,[39] similar to the political and cultural crisis in fin-de-siècle Vienna,[40] in which "the historical and social optimism that had been associated with the New Deal and the struggle with the Nazis finally broke down."[41] In particular, "Its shared Enlightenment premises were gravely weakened by a combination of political factors in the early postwar years: the deepening of the Cold War, the first Soviet coup in Czechoslovakia, new revelations of Stalinist iniquities, and the effects, so powerful and so astonishingly ramified throughout all social classes, of McCarthyism. It was not so much that these political developments caused the intellectuals to shift political positions or abandon politics entirely, though many did so. More fundamentally, the crisis seemed to force a shift in the general philosophic outlook in which liberal or radical political positions had been embedded. In short, the liberals and radicals, almost unconsciously, adapted their world-views to a revolution of falling political expectations."[42] In such a social environment, America would be fertile terrain not only for the method of analysis, but also for an attack on progressive ideals.

Legal realism was particularly vulnerable to attack. Its pragmatist method and progressive political orientation did not comport with the new formalism. Stephen Feldman has noted that after the Second World War legal realism had reached the point of "epistemological crisis," particularly in the "area of substantive and ethical values."[43] In an era in which the specters of Soviet and Nazi tyranny loomed large, even the whiff of relativism associated with legal realism made it an untenable theoretical position. Institutional economics, which had served as the policy core of legal realism, suffered a similar fate and was displaced by neoclassical economics. This displacement would have a direct influence on the eventual rise of law and neoclassical economics as the dominant legal-economic theory in America, supplanting legal realism. Before discussing the law and neoclassical economics movement, it is important to set the rise of neoclassical economics in historical relief

Neoclassical economic thought ascends in an intellectual environment shaped by the philosophical implications of Einstein's theories. The claim is not that neoclassical economists necessarily understood the intricacies of Einstein's theory or even their philosophical implications. The ideas dictate scientific parameters and to the degree that the mantel of science confers legitimacy, the ideas are appropriated (even if at times disingenuously). F. A. Hayek is an important figure in the historical evolution of neoclassical economics and its links to larger philosophical movements. While Hayek never joined the Vienna Circle, he was exposed to its ideas. Hayek appreciated that the intellectual engine of Austria in the 1920s and 1930s was "almost entirely the influence of Ernst Mach," and acknowledged that his "introduction to . . . philosophy—scientific method . . . was through Machian philosophy."[44] Stephen Kresge and Leif Wenar identify Hayek with the general "intellectual and cultural eruptions from Vienna and Central Europe to which the rest of the world has been forced to respond."[45] While Hayek would ultimately "emancipate" himself from positivism and declare it "misleading in the social sciences," its influence on his intellectual evolution is undeniable.[46]

Hayek's migration to England would play an important role in shaping the debates that are crucial to understanding the evolution of law and neoclassical economics. Hayek directly influenced the law and neoclassical economics project at the University of Chicago.[47] Ronald Coase, in his brief intellectual history of law and neoclassical economics, credits Hayek with helping to launch the law and neoclassical economics program at University of Chicago Law School. The institutional symbiosis between Hayek and the law and neoclassical economics movement is also typified by the appearance in the United States of Hayek's *The Road to Serfdom*, publication of which by the University of Chicago Press was encouraged by two economists at Chicago who were leading figures in the law and neoclassical economics field: Aaron Director, the first editor of the *Journal of Law and Economics*, and Frank Knight, an influential scholar in the economic and political realms.[48]

The Road to Serfdom was the vehicle for Hayek's statement of his beliefs.[49] Hayek called it "a political book" and acknowledged that all that he had to say was "derived from certain ultimate values."[50] Written while Hayek held a professorship at the London School of Economics, *The Road to Serfdom* was conceived as a direct response to a socialist ethos that permeated the European continent and endangered the liberal underpinnings of English politics. The goal of the book was to sound a "warning to the socialist intelligentsia of England"[51] that their program would lead to the very totalitarianism so many had fought against. Despite its focus on the British intellectual scene, the book had an enormous impact in the United States.[52] Over 600,000 copies of a Reader's Digest condensed version of the book were sold in 1945. Since its publication, over a quarter of a million copies of *The Road to Serfdom* have been sold.

Hayek's book produced a more extreme reaction, both positive and negative, in the United States than in England. Part of the consternation on the left in the United States no doubt was due to its boldness and scope.[53] While the argument that "hot socialism" would poison a society might not have unsettled some on the American left, Hayek made similar claims regarding the welfare state.[54] The contention of *The Road to Serfdom* was that the core beliefs of socialism had become so deeply embedded in the conceptual framework of intellectual thought that they threatened to undermine liberal society under the guise of the welfare state or egalitarian rhetoric. There would, for example, be knee-jerk calls for state intervention in the economy when "judicious use of financial inducements might evoke spontaneous efforts."[55] What lent *The Road to Serfdom* its polemical force was Hayek's linking of governmental measures aimed at curing social ills to the dangers of totalitarianism, particularly the sort seen in Nazi Germany. Hayek boldly and flatly asserted, "[i]t is necessary now to state the unpalatable truth that it is Germany whose fate we are in some danger of repeating."[56]

The core of the anti-statist stance of *The Road to Serfdom* was a belief in the uniqueness of individual activity and thought ("ethical individualism"). According to this view it was unacceptable, in fact impossible, for anyone other than the individual to make decisions for him or her without imposing an alien set of values. Thus seemingly benign policy prescriptions dissolved into naked, unjustifiable coercion. To avoid it, "individuals should be allowed, within defined limits, to follow their own values and preferences rather than somebody else's."[57] In the anti-government sentiments and emphasis on incentives of *The Road to Serfdom*, we see the ideological seeds of the American law and neoclassical economics movement. The ways in which the anti-statist ideal set forth in *Serfdom* would be reflected in social institutions are clear in Hayek's discussion of the legal system and are fundamental in linking his intellectual project to the law and neoclassical economics movement. Hayek's views on the legal system were shaped by his core belief that "competition" is the "central means of co-ordinating human effort" and the "*conviction* that, where effective competition can be created, it is a better way of guiding individual efforts than any other."[58] In the quest to protect the individual, it is free-market competition, not government intervention, that is presumed to be for the good.

So, what of the law? "[I]n order that competition should work beneficially, a carefully thought-out legal framework is required." In sum, the law facilitates competition, the system most conducive to individual freedom, by setting the boundaries of competition. The law should "recognize the principle of private property and freedom of contract." It is a neutral arbiter facilitating individual preferences and defining the "right to property as applied to different things." For example, some legal structure may be needed to ensure accurate communication of the price of goods and services, which is vital information for buyers.[59] The rights associated with property, notwithstanding anti-statist ideals, were not absolute. Efficiency was the ultimate criterion: the "systematic study of the forms of legal institutions which will make the competitive system work efficiently." Regarding legal rules specifically, *The Road to Serfdom* advocated a system in which "[t]he only question . . . is whether in the *particular instance* the advantages gained are greater than the *social costs* which they impose."[60] Hayek's emphasis on legal rules, particularly as they affected the costs of engaging in an activity that are not borne by those who undertake it (social costs),[61] is the touchstone connecting him with the law and neoclassical economics movement.

Hayek gave a detailed analysis of social costs and the limits of government intervention as a tool for minimizing these costs. However, to the extent that legal rules limiting property rights represent an activist role for government, Hayek stated that though the scope of this permissible intervention on individual autonomy was not defined, "the tasks provide, indeed, a wide and unquestioned field for state activity."[62]

Hayek's laissez-faire ideology is similar to that of Adam Smith in the eighteenth century. His views would have a profound, if not always transparent, impact on economic policies across the globe. Daniel Yergin in his *Commanding Heights* has chronicled the influence of Hayek's ideas on broad policy issues.[63] In the 1940s Hayek's free-market stance was pushing against the tide of history. Keynesian economics, about which more will be said in chapter 4, had redistributionist implications and had taken hold in economic policy circles by the time Hayek wrote *The Road to Serfdom*. As Yergin astutely chronicles, Hayek had set forth an anti-statist argument that would not find its way onto the larger public policy (macroeconomic) stage until the rise in the 1980s of Margaret Thatcher and Ronald Reagan, who mounted a political and intellectual overthrow of the pro-government intervention ("commanding heights") consensus. While this broader movement was taking shape, a quiet revolution was taking place at the microeconomic level. One of the products of that revolution was the law and neoclassical economics movement.

Just as with classical economics, understanding the connection between ideology and the substantive workings of neoclassical economics is crucial to appreciating the historical context for its prestige as a social science. Law and neoclassical economics, a subdiscipline of neoclassical economics, also carries the garb of science under the analytic turn. This claim on science is particularly strong in the analytic era when law and neoclassical economics is compared to its predecessor in legal-economic theory, legal realism.

Lionel Robbins, in *An Essay on the Nature and Significance of Economic Science*, provided neoclassical economics with its mature definition as "economic science."[64] Robbins acknowledged that although economic theory had been well established, there was no common definition of what the discipline was about or, more importantly, not about: "[w]e all talk about the same things, but we have not yet agreed what it is we are talking about." He declared that what neoclassical economists talked about was a defined set of problems: "the unity of a science only shows itself in the unity of the problems it is *able* to solve." Robbins then set forth the neoclassical definition of economic science: "Economics is the science which studies human behaviour as a relationship between ends and scarce means which have alternative uses."[65]

Before fleshing out his definition of economics, Robbins wanted to address what economics was specifically not about so as to eliminate confusion. According to Robbins, many economists had mistakenly believed that economics was about the causes of material welfare (monetary gain).[66] However, the subject of economic analysis extends beyond activity affording monetary rewards and costs, to the choice between monetary and nonmonetary activity:[67] "The conception we have adopted may be described as *analytical*. It does not attempt to pick out certain *kinds* of behaviour, but focuses attention on a particular *aspect* of behaviour, the form imposed by the influence of *scarcity*. . . . There are no limitations on the subject-matter of Economic Science save this."[68] This definition fits with the application of neoclassical economic analysis to legal rules, particularly social cost analysis. As long as one views an activity as a matter of choices involving scarce resources—for example, whether to allow an accident to occur or expend the resources to prevent the accident—it can then be the subject of economic analysis.

The theory of human behavior under which these choices were to be examined was not drawn from empirical investigation. Robbins asserted that the "*belief* in these propositions is as complete as *belief* based upon any number of controlled experiments"—the central neoclassical proposition was the "assumption that the different things that the individual wants to do have a different importance to him, and can be arranged therefore in a certain order." This ordering constitutes an "elementary fact of experience" from which one "can derive. . . . equilibrium of exchange and of the formation of prices," or, more generally, neoclassical consumer demand theory. Indeed, all "propositions of economic theory, like all scientific theory, are obviously *deductions* from a series of postulates."[69]

The reliance on a deductivist methodology is a crucial component of neoclassical economic science that can be traced to its classical roots. Logical positivists would place this methodology under the rubric of tautologous logical propositions. The logical positivists were influential in defining what types of statements were not within the domain of science (recall Schlick's nonobservables). In economics the quintessential "nonobservable" is utility, the pleasure that one derives from something. Since individual utility is nonobservable, it is impossible (as a scientific matter) to make interpersonal comparisons between individuals' utility level. The technical distinction is between cardinalism (a belief that utility can be measured) and ordinalism (a belief that it cannot be measured). While this distinction might seem esoteric, it has tremendous political consequences—a very rough form of cardinalism underlay many arguments for redistribution. Neoclassical economists dismissed cardinalism as unscientific. They regarded the sort of pro-redistributionist utilitarian analysis associated with Jeremy Bentham and J. S. Mill as an exercise in moral philosophy, not scientific investigation.

Ernest Screpanti and Stefano Zanagni ponder why " the passage from cardinalism to ordinalism occur[red] only during the 1930's if . . . all the necessary presuppositions were already available at the beginning of the century," and in noting the importance of Robbins's *An Essay on the Nature and Significance of Economic Science*, they point to the logical positivist movement as a key explanation:

> There was a widespread opinion, among the economists gathered together by Robbins at the LSE [(London School of Economics)], that the notion of 'individual preferences' was epistemologically safer than that of 'levels of welfare.' Logical positivism had had a dramatic impact on Anglo-American social science, and the entry point in England had been the LSE. At the beginning of the century, positive epistemology had not yet begun to disturb the sleep of the economists. It was not until the philosophical settling achieved by the Vienna Circle that economists, too, began to speak of "observability" as a demarcation criterion between science and fiction, and of neutrality with respect to value judgments as a separation criterion between science and ethics. The notion of 'individual preferences' seemed able to dispose of the concept of inobservability of utilities and, at the same time, to give a new foundation to the normative character of the interpersonal comparisons which motivate social policies.[70]

Robbins's work defined distributional issues as not falling within the category of the analyzable: we "assume, too, a given initial distribution of property."[71] Concerned that the law of diminishing marginal utility[72] might be mistakenly used to argue for redistributing wealth in an effort to maximize total social utility, Robbins declared that the diminishing marginal utility justification for redistribution "rests upon an extension of the conception of diminishing marginal utility into a field in which it is entirely *illegitimate*"[73]—because interpersonal comparisons of utility are not scientifically valid. Robbins argued that although individuals could order their preferences (ordinalism), the magnitude of the preferences could not be measured (cardinalism).[74] We cannot measure whether $10,000 taken from Person B will benefit Person A more than its confiscation displeases Person B.[75] Therefore, there is no basis from which to measure overall social welfare post redistribution. Any attempt to make such a measurement "falls outside the scope of any positive science" and "is essentially normative." Such analysis is deemed "ethical" and "does not at all follow from the positive assumptions of *pure* theory." This argument placed redistribution outside the bounds of the analyzable in neoclassical economics. It put a scientific imprimatur on the status quo as much as classical theory had done.[76] Any argument for the redistribution of wealth was deemed political.

The neoclassical synthesis, accepting the status quo distribution of wealth and equating deductivism with economic science, had the effect of displacing institutional economics as the dominant paradigm in American economic thought. Yuval Yonay aptly chronicles this struggle for the soul of economics.[77] He reduces the methodological dispute to whether emphasis should be placed on inductive (institutionalist) analysis or deductive (neoclassical) analysis.[78] The neoclassical claim was that the inductivism, stressed by institutionalists, amounted to little more than the unsystematic collection of facts, a decidedly unscientific enterprise. Yonay concludes that both institutionalists and neoclassical economists used a mix of deductivism and inductivism to varying degrees, and that the real dispute was over the meaning of theory. Neoclassical economists argued that the theoretical orientation of institutionalism—its emphasis on historical analysis and focus on institutions—was not adequately abstract to derive the sorts of predictions required under the mantel of science.

The issue of whether "values" (including concern over the distribution of wealth) should be a part of economic analysis also split most neoclassicists from institutionalists. Appropriating the distinction between facts and ethics drawn under logical positivism, neoclassical economists argued that economic analysis must, to be a science, exclude any discussion of values. Institutionalists countered that any economic analysis worth doing had to be geared toward the betterment of society and thence must explicitly consider its values. Moreover, the neoclassical criterion of efficiency (or maximization of wealth) was itself a value choice. By contrast, institutionalists were concerned with the maldistribution of wealth and the continuation of poverty and economic insecurity. The neoclassicists enlisted the prestige of science in waging their battle.[79]

The new scientific approach to economic analysis had tremendous political consequences, most notably providing a scientific argument for maintaining the existing distribution of wealth and a rebuttal to those who believed that there was a scientific argument in favor of changing it. It had a logical and political force in a postwar culture that took the analytical definition of science as gospel and harbored suspicions, Keynes notwithstanding, toward the political consequences of an activist government. In the 1960s this force would begin to affect American legal-economic theory.[80] The first point of entry was Ronald Coase's "The Problem of Social Cost." Its intellectual forerunner was the work of the English economist A. C. Pigou, in particular his book *The Economics of Welfare*.[81] Before discussing Pigou's substantive treatment of social costs, it is useful to review his methodological and ideological stances, and how they figure in his social cost analysis.[82]

Pigou began *The Economics of Welfare* by declaring the "hope that a scientific study of men's social actions may lead . . . to practical results in social improvement." To this end, Pigou, quoting Whitehead's *Introduction to Mathematics*, stated, "in our most *theoretical* moods we may be nearest to our most practical implication."[83] The emphasis on "practical implication" dictated the form that theory would take. *The Economics of Welfare* proposed two possible avenues for "positive science": "On the one side are the sciences of formal logic and pure mathematics, whose function it is to discover *implications*. On the other side are the realistic sciences, such as physics, chemistry and biology, which are concerned with actualities."[84]

Pigou took this distinction, which reflected the divide between an analytic and pragmatist approach to the philosophy of science, from Bertrand Russell's *Principles of Mathematics*, an important text of the analytic turn.

It is clear that in the foreground of the methodological formulation in *The Economics of Welfare* was the distinction between the analytic and the empirical emphasized in the analytic movement. As is made clear by Pigou's concern with scientific method and logic, neoclassical economics always had a structure that heeded, if it did not submit to, analytic dictates, even before those dictates dominated the postwar intellectual milieu. Regarding economics, Pigou said: "It is open to use to construct an economics science either of the *pure type* represented by pure mathematics or the *realistic type* represented by experimental physics. . . . For pure economics . . . it would not be relevant to inquire what the value of *x* is among the actual men who are living in the world now. Contrasted with this pure science stands realistic economics, the interest of which is concentrated upon the world of *experience*."[85]

For Pigou "it must be the realistic, and not the pure, type of science that constitutes the object of our search . . . and endeavor to elucidate, not any generalized system of possible worlds, but the actual world of men and women as they are found in *experience* to be."[86] In laying out the argument for an economics based on "experience" and focused on "practical interest," *The Economics of Welfare* set forth a middle ground between the thoroughgoing inductivism of institutional economics and the deductivism of the neoclassical school: "But, if it is plain that a science of the pure type will not serve our purpose, it is equally plain that *realism*, in the sense of a mere descriptive catalog of observed facts, will not serve it either."[87] As for *The Economics of Welfare*, the goal was to "study certain important groups of causes that affect economic welfare in actual modern societies."[88] Pigou's work, while having a core neoclassical analytic structure, incorporated institutionalist insights. His methodological "blending" is understandable given the requirements of science of the "pure" (analytic) type and his impulse to engage in realism owing to his progressive political leanings.

Pigou's ideological commitments were revealed in his *Socialism versus Capitalism*.[89] While the study largely concerned the relative merits of capitalism and socialism, its ultimate resolution of the problem was to propose a capitalist economy augmented by strategic government intervention. Pigou was concerned with poverty, or more precisely with inequality in society. Pigou highlighted the problem of inequality with statistics concerning the distribution of property and income. The statistics illustrated huge inequalities in both property and income. For Pigou, the result of these inequalities was a system catering to the "whims of the rich." Pigou revealed his ethical objection to this state of affairs by labeling it a "*maldistribution* of productive resources."[90] Pigou's reliance on empirical investigation revealed the realist vein that augmented his analytic arguments, including those concerning social costs.

In examining Pigou's contribution to the issue of social costs, it is important to note that he saw a direct link between property rights and income.[91] Specifically, redefining property rights to deal with the problems of social costs was a method for achieving the redistribution of income that Pigou saw as an ethical imperative. As discussed earlier, Robbins would later articulate the turn in neoclassical economics that removed distributional issues from the concerns of the economic scientist. While the issue of social cost became central to law and neoclassical economics, in keeping with the developed construction of neoclassical economics, there would be little discussion of distributional issues.

Pigou's focus on property rights was not limited to a concern with the ethical dimensions of inequality under capitalism. He also addressed the inefficiency of laissez-faire capitalist policies. Of specific concern to the development of law and neoclassical economics was Pigou's focus on economic contexts where marginal private cost did not equal marginal social cost. The inequality could lead to the inefficient allocation of productive resources. Neoclassical economists refer to such instances as "market failure." In *The Economics of Welfare* Pigou drew a distinction between marginal "social" and marginal "private" net product. Marginal social net product is defined as the "total net product of physical things or objective services due to the marginal increment of resources in any given use or place, no matter to whom any part of this product may accrue." Marginal private net product is "that part of the total net product of physical things or objective services due to the marginal increment of resources in any given use or place which accrues in the first instance . . . to the person responsible for investing resources there."[92] In some conditions marginal private net product "is equal to, in some it is greater than, in others it is less than the marginal social net product."[93] Problems arose in cases of divergence in social and private product, because "industrialists are interested, not in the social, but only in the private, net product of their operations."[94] The emphasis on "industrialists" meshed with Pigou's conception of there being a "maldistribution" of resources, implied a need to redefine property rights to curb industrial power, and echoed institutionalist sentiments.

The Economics of Welfare argued that "self-interest . . . will not tend to bring about equality in the values of the marginal social net products except when marginal private net product and marginal social net product are identical."[95] The remedy for this divergence, given the failure of "simple competition," lay in "specific acts of interference with normal economic processes . . . [that] increase the dividend." One illustration of the problem is especially relevant to law and neoclassical economics: "Person A, in the course of rendering some service, for which payment is made to a second person B, incidentally also renders services or disservices to other persons (not producers of like services), of such a sort that payment cannot be exacted from the benefited parties or compensation enforced on behalf of the injured parties."[96] This divergence could not be handled through bargaining because it "arises out of a service or disservice to persons other than the contracting parties." The "state" would be required to intervene and grant "bounties" or assess "taxes" on behavior.[97] The Economics of Welfare did not espouse a socialist alternative to the neoclassical enterprise. Pigou envisioned a program of "gradualness—to mould and transform, not violently to uproot" society in an attempt to mitigate the "glaring inequalities of fortune."[98]

In the postwar intellectual and ideological climate as reflected in the enthusiastic reception of Hayek's The Road to Serfdom in the United States and the analytic turn, the political and intellectual logic of Pigou's position would serve as a point of departure for policy makers arguing for government intervention. However, in adopting the neoclassical paradigm, Pigou and his postwar successors opened themselves up to criticism by others using the paradigm who favored a laissez-faire approach to government. Pigou's appropriation of neoclassical economics to argue for government intervention to solve the problem of social costs brought about an almost immediate response by free-market neoclassical economists. The response, initiated by Frank Knight, would later culminate in Ronald Coase's classic critique of Pigou, "The Problem of Social Cost."[99]

Frank Knight has been hailed as the "founder of the libertarian Chicago school of economics"[100] and as one of the foremost exponents of economics as the "grand exercise in rarified abstractions."[101] Knight's Risk, Uncertainty and Profit, published in 1921, is a profoundly influential text in neoclassical economics, one fundamental to understanding the method-ological approach to economic analysis that would later underlie Knight's refutation of Pigou's position on social costs.[102] While the book predated the reign of logical positivism, it was a methodological manifesto that echoed certain analytic themes that would resonate with the postwar scientific ethos. The first chapter opens with the bold statement that "[e]conomics, or more properly theoretical economics, is the only one of the social sciences which has aspired to the distinction of an exact science." When we take up the mantel of "exact science," the contours of science must be mapped out. To begin with, it must be "somewhat abstract and unreal." Abstraction and analytic treatment give economic theory the capacity to make sense of complex economic relationships.[103]

Methodologically, according to *Risk, Uncertainty and Profit* the economics profession encompassed the spectrum ranging from mathematical economists and pure theoreticians, who adopted a "closed system of deductions from a very small number of premises as assumed by universal laws [(analytic statements)]," to those, particularly institutionalists, who proposed a purely descriptive science and repudiated any form of abstraction and deduction.[104]

Like Pigou in *The Economics of Welfare*, Knight rhetorically eschewed both extremes and proposed a middle way. "Pure theory" (the deductive method) was the first and most crucial step in economic investigation. The conclusions drawn from the deductive arguments would be tested against "observed fact."[105] Knight's dichotomy between "pure theory" and "observed fact" followed the logical positivist definition of science as constituting analytic and empirical statements. In light of empirical observations, the economist would revise her or his premises if necessary.[106] The corollary to this view of economics is that the "empirical laws" formed by inductive observation must follow from the "general principles of the science" if they are to be credited with significance. In sum: "There is, then little if any use for induction in the Baconian sense of exhaustive data collection and collation of facts, though in some cases this may be necessary and fruitful. On the other hand, there is equally little use for deduction taken as doing more than suggesting hypotheses, subject to verification."[107] Knight's methodological position would put him in direct conflict with the institutionalists. Indeed, Knight has been described as the "dean of the opposition to institutionalism" in America after the First World War.[108]

Knight's "middle way" in *Risk, Uncertainty and Profit* decidedly favored deduction by way of intuitive insights, not empirical inquiry: "[C]ommon-sense generalizations have a very high degree of *certainty* in some fields, giving us, in regard to the external world, for instance, the "axioms" of mathematics. . . . Our knowledge of ourselves is based on introspective investigation, but is so direct that it may be called intuitive. . . . Many of the fundamental laws of economics are therefore properly "intuitive" to begin with."[109] In this regard, Knight's framework departed from positivist conceptions of science. Intuition, obviously nonobservable, provided Knight with a framework for choosing a priori starting points for deduction that positivists never claim. For Knight, there was a need for intuition because economic behavior was based on "human conduct."[110]

While intuitionism may seem antithetical to logical positivism, it has always played a role in science. The theoretical work of Einstein provides an illuminating illustration. The logical positivists, Mach in particular, focused on Einstein's rigor in not assuming the existence of any phenomenon that could not be observed. However, the motivation behind much of his insight was his intuition that there should be a simplicity and elegance in any true explanation of the universe. Indeed, one of the attractions of Einstein's views for Schlick was that they provided explanations without all the caveats and complications of Newtonian theory. A similar desire to impose order out of complexity underlay the neoclassical rejection of institutionalist method. The "intuitive" premises on which economic science would be based were necessarily limited in number to ease the task of simplifying the complex economic order. *Risk, Uncertainty and Profit* laid out the fundamental premise: free competition prevails in the marketplace.

Knight believed that the free-market competitive premise was buttressed by certain *intuitive* assumptions regarding economic actors, which were key to analysis: "All discussion of economics assumes (and it is certainly "*true*") that every rational and competent mind knows (a) that some behavior involves the apportionment or allocation of means limited in supply among alternative modes of use in realizing ends; (b) that given modes of apportionment achieve in different 'degrees' for any subject some general end which is a common denominator of comparison; and (c) that there is some one 'ideal' apportionment which would achieve the general end in a 'maximum' degree, conditioned by the quantity of means available to the subject and the terms of allocation presented by the facts of his situation."[111] These assumptions, which Lionel Robbins in *An Essay on the Nature and Significance of Economic Science* later enshrined in the science of neoclassical economics, were labeled "intuitive" because for Knight it was obvious that "[w]e '*know*' these propositions better, more confidently, than we know the *truth* of any statement about any concrete physical fact or event, whether reported by someone else or made by ourselves on the basis of our own experience, and fully as certainly as we know the *truth* of any axiom of mathematics or of logic."[112] Belief in the neoclassical paradigm is not solely commitment to principles of science, but a form of human inquiry based on fundamental and indisputable *truths*. "Science" (logic and empiricism) can only expose a "fraction of human knowledge" and "no knowledge of human or of social data, or specifically of economics."[113]

Risk, Uncertainty and Profit did not discredit theoretical economics, but bolstered it by clarifying its theoretical limitations, maintaining a subjectivist foundation, and arguing for economic premises based on intuitionist insights. Knight's intuitionist augmentation of the neoclassical system can be contrasted with Pigou's realist infusion, which Knight rejected. On the surface, it would seem that Knight's methodological approach was nonideological. However, Knight recognized that science and politics were inextricable. In so doing, Knight highlighted the political contrast with Pigou.

In taking a methodological stance, Knight made his commitments clear: "[i]n the demarcation of economics, the interests of the individual . . . are regularly and properly taken as factual data." Knight recognized that his assertion was open to contestation: "*Individualism*, as a subject of approval or disapproval, is a social policy and an *ethical category*." Knight's belief in individualism, as an "ethical" norm, influenced his choice of an economic approach based on methodological individualism.[114]

The basis for Knight's ethical leanings as they relate to neoclassical economics was stated in his presidential address delivered at the Sixty-Third Annual Meeting of the American Economics Association in 1950.[115] Knight began with the statement that the core of what he would talk about was the "conflict of values." As if to make clear the depth of his commitment to his own value system, he characterized his own values as "Truth" and those outside his value system as "other values." The purpose of his presentation was to "give considerable preference to the truth over other standards."[116]

Knight's ethical commitment, which rings forth throughout "Role of Principles," was to individualism: "[M]en have a right to want and strive to get whatever they do want, and to have the tastes and 'higher' values they do have, as long as their conduct does not infringe the equal rights of others."[117] For Knight, this ethical commitment was inseparable from economic theory: "Economic principles are simply the more general implications of the single principle of freedom, individual and social, *i.e.*, free association in a certain sphere of activity."[118] In a later passage Knight went on to state: "All this about the abstract and interpretive character of economic theory or principles has little to do with their significance. That is because their main value is connected with policy determination, under the *fundamental ethical* principle of *freedom*."[119]

Knight believed it important to preserve his "fundamental ethical" principle from the "increasing resort to legislative and bureaucratic interference and control."[120] Striking an anti-statist chord that seems to foreshadow *The Road to Serfdom*, Knight warned of the dangers of authoritarian control by big government. Government intervention in response to demands for justice and "a radical shift from business to democratic politics" is "screwy thinking" that would lead to a "moralistic approach" equating "social evil to sin."[121] Knight recognized that in the "distribution of economic resources atomistic motivation tends powerfully toward cumulatively increasing *inequality*," and "those who already have more capacity are always in a better position to acquire still more, with the same effort and sacrifice."[122] Elsewhere Knight argued that while social justice was a laudable goal, "[i]t is hopelessly undefinable [and] meaningless."[123] Since social justice and the redistribution of wealth were unattainable and ill-defined goals, they should not serve as bases for economic policy.

One specific policy issue addressed by Knight in response to Pigou, was the divergence between social and private costs. Ronald Coase in "The Problem of Social Cost"[124] later addressed the issue in much the same manner and quite properly acknowledged his intellectual debt to Knight. Knight took up the issue in "Some Fallacies in the Interpretation of Social Cost."[125] The fallacies to which Knight referred were those of F. D. Graham and in "Pigou's monumental work on *The Economics of Welfare*."[126] The fundamental issue was "whether 'society can increase the production of exchange value by interfering with free bargaining relations." Knight credited Pigou with the thesis that free-market transactions could actually "reduce the production of wealth." However, "[t]he fallacy to be exposed is a misinterpretation of the relation between social cost and *entrepreneur's* cost."[127]

Knight began by analyzing an example involving two roads: one broad enough to accommodate all anticipated traffic, but poorly surfaced; the other well surfaced, but narrow and with limited capacity. Pigou had argued that in a free market there would be too much use of the narrow road, because individual truckers would be unwilling to use the broader road if their private gain was not increased. However, if these truckers were to use the broader road without increasing the costs of those already on it, this would increase the value of the narrow road to all those remaining.

Pigou considered this a case clearly necessitating government intervention in the form of taxation. Moreover, Knight noted that Pigou extended this solution "over the whole field of investment." Knight argued that government intervention was not necessarily required if there was a system of property rights: "It is in fact the social function of ownership to prevent this excessive investment in superior situations."[128] In making this assertion, *Knight* pointed out flaws not only in *The Economics of Welfare* but in economic theory in general: "Professor Pigou's *logic* in regard to the roads is, as *logic*, quite unexceptionable. Its weakness is one frequently met with in economic theorizing, namely that the assumptions diverge in essential respects from the facts of real economic situations."[129] If the two roads in Pigou's hypothetical were "subject to private appropriation and exploitation, precisely the ideal situation which would be established by the imaginary tax will be brought about through the operation of ordinary economic motives." The tax in the free market context could take the form of a "toll" charged by the owner of the narrow road that would "exactly equal the ideal tax above considered."[130] Thus, according to Knight, although *The Economics of Welfare* captured the analytic logic of the problem, it failed to incorporate the intuitive fact of economic man as an agent in search of profit. Instead, Pigou incorporated a view of the world more in line with an institutionalist approach. Knight did recognize that the analytic science ("logic") used to describe the problem of social cost was the same for both men. Their differences were driven by divergent political views.

Imbedded in Knight's discussion of social costs and private property was his underlying belief regarding private property as expounded in *Risk, Uncertainty and Profit*: the social theory of private property thus rests not so much on the premise that productive resources will be more effectively used in the creation of goods for consumption as on the *belief* one can achieve a greater stimulus to progress by inducing men to take the risks of increasing the supplies of productive resources themselves, including both material things and technical knowledge and skill.[131] Where Pigou saw private property as an evil perpetuating inequality, Knight saw it as an essential component of social progress. In his view, infringements of private property to remedy the problem of social costs should be circumscribed.

The political lines of demarcation between Knight and Pigou exemplify divisions in neoclassical economics and would carry over onto law and neoclassical economics. But both also subscribed to what can be described as a moderate consensus. Conservatives, following Knight, as well as liberals, following Pigou, agree that a capitalist economy should be the foundation of our economic system. The disagreement is over the desired level of government intervention. Liberals lean toward moderate intervention in the free market to remedy what they perceive to be the maldistribution of wealth in favor of the rich. Conservatives believe that such government interference is often misguided and, according to Hayek and his followers, can have catastrophic political consequences. The problem for liberal practitioners of neoclassical economics is that the discipline, at least as defined by Robbins, leaves little room for explicit consideration of distributional concerns. This dilemma, and its inevitable consequence, a centrist politics, would also be evident in law and neoclassical economics when the idea of social cost was adopted as the principal theoretical tool for analyzing tort law issues.

Ronald Coase introduced Knight's argument regarding social costs to the legal academy in a highly influential article, "The Problem of Social Cost."[132] The article set forth the methodological structure of law and neoclassical economics,[133] and was an exemplar of the anti-statist tendency of the discipline.[134] Coase wrote the article to contest the progressive appropriation of neoclassical economic theory represented by *The Economics of Welfare*,[135] thus continuing, into the 1960s and at the inception of law and neoclassical economics, the battle within neoclassical economics between anti-statist and progressive economists that had begun with Frank Knight's critique of Pigou forty years earlier. Coase acknowledged his intellectual debt—"Knight happens to be one of the most important influences in developing my views"[136]—singling out *Risk, Uncertainty and Profit* as a key text in his intellectual development. Coase had this to say about the influence of Knight's "Some Fallacies in the Interpretation of Social Cost": "[T]he title of my paper came from Knight. . . . [I]f there are traces of what Knight says in my work, it wouldn't surprise me."[137]

"The Problem of Social Cost" is a clear example of deductive methodology, combined with subjectivist insights and an anti-statist overlay, all as proposed by Knight. It abstracted away the complex relationships at the heart of Pigou's analysis of social cost in an industrial state, reducing them to a simple dispute between a farmer and a rancher. This allowed the issue of social cost to be subsumed under the paradigm of methodological individualism. The hypothetical is as follows: (1) a rancher and a farmer are on neighboring properties; and (2) as the size of the cattle herd is increased, so is the damage to the farmer's crops. The central axiom driving the analysis is that the "price system operates smoothly."[138] There is also the initial premise that transactions (bargaining) costs are zero. As with any deductive system, conclusions flowed ineluctably from the premise, in this case the conclusions that costs would be internalized and production maximized.[139] Coase used a mathematical illustration to demonstrate the commonsense nature of the bargaining process at the core of his thesis that through mutual agreement joint production could be maximized without government taxation. He did not attempt to empirically verify his thesis by investigating instances of bargaining in the context of externalities. He simply took the structure of his argument and presumed that because it was logical, real-world results would conform accordingly.

Coase argued that his analytic statement of the social cost problem (the hypothetical involving the rancher and the farmer) corresponded "exactly" with how economic actors responded. His posing the issue in analytic terms corresponded with the logical positivist view that this sort of analysis could reveal relationships not previously recognized. However, his assertion that his analytical statement of the problem corresponded to reality, without empirical investigation, deviated from logical positivist dictates that statements about the real world should be studied empirically.

There was no empiricism in "The Problem of Social Cost." However, Coase stated his "*belief* that economists, and policy-makers generally, have tended to over-estimate the advantages which come from governmental regulation."[140] Thus Coase, like Knight, referred to the need to bolster analysis with empirical study, but failed to follow through.[141] Also like

Knight, Coase ultimately based his analytic technique on an anti-statist underpinning, influenced by Hayek.[142] The analytic argument, as Knight noted, supplied a superstructure to promote anti-government beliefs. This was made clear when Coase returned in the last two sections of his article to discussing the Pigouvian tradition.

Coase began his critique by reexamining Pigou's example of damage done by sparks flying from a railroad car. Coase used a numerical illustration, following the same axiomatic methodology with which he began the article, to argue that efficiency may be unaffected whether liability is attached to the railroad activity or not. However, he added, "[o]f course, by altering the figures, it could be shown that there are other cases in which it would be desirable that the railway should be liable for the damage it causes." Thus, as was stressed by Hayek, the issue again boiled down to an empirical question: "[w]hether it is desirable or not depends on the particular circumstances."[143]

Although Coase acknowledged that whether Pigou is correct is an empirical proposition, in surveying the influence of Pigou's thought he regretted that a "doctrine as faulty as that developed by Pigou should have been so influential."[144] Later, in reflecting on his article, Coase would continue to bemoan Pigou's influence: "[e]ven those sympathetic to my point of view [in "The Problem of Social Cost"] have often misunderstood my argument, a result which I attribute to the extraordinary hold which Pigou's approach has had on the minds of modern economists."[145] It was on this basis that "most economists" would prescribe a system of government taxation to remedy the problem of social cost.[146] For Coase, "such tax proposals are the stuff that *dreams* are made of. In my youth it was said that what was too silly to be said may be sung. In modern economics it may be put into mathematics."[147]

"The Problem of Social Cost" set forth the methodological parameters of neoclassical economics as it began to assert itself in the 1960s as a tool for reconceptualizing legal-economic theory under the guise of science. Yet Coase recognized that the article was a political statement, and he forthrightly acknowledged a point that he attributed to Frank Knight: "problems of welfare economics must ultimately dissolve into a study of aesthetics and morals."[148] Coase surveyed the political landscape of neoclassical economics and found the scales to be much too heavily weighted toward liberal appropriation. His response was to resuscitate Knight's criticism of Pigou. As such, Coase's article can be viewed as part of the long march toward the conservative appropriation of the classical dictates of Adam Smith, with its attendant politics. However, Coase's argument established an institutional footing in a setting where the soil was fertile: legal academia. Ironically, part of the groundwork was laid by legal realism (which law and neoclassical economics would displace as the dominant legal-economic theory). The legal realists were responsible for establishing the ethos in legal academe that legal theory should focus on policy analysis. Law and neoclassical economics can be seen as a direct response to that. The entry point for law and neoclassical economics was the University of Chicago School of Law, where a group of largely conservative economists and lawyer-economists (following Knight and Coase) laid the foundation for the spread of its ideas.

Because of the continued need for the veneer of objectivity in law, a forthright admission regarding the political nature of neoclassical economics would not serve the legitimating function of legal-economic theory. Instead, the principal popularizer of law and neoclassical economics, Richard Posner (then a professor at the University of Chicago School of Law), emphasized its scientific trappings. His efforts marked a bold attempt to harness the prestige of science in the service of legal-economic theory at a time when the realist vision had collapsed and mainstream legal theorists (while holding onto the idea of objectivity in law) had for the most part rejected the idea that legal theory constituted a science in any true sense. The significance of *Economic Analysis of Law*,[149] Posner's major contributions to the popular spread of law and neoclassical economics, lay not in the sophistication of its analysis but in the sheer breadth of its coverage and its accessibility to those not familiar with neoclassical economics. It thus marked the migration of law and neoclassical economics to the realm of "normal science."[150] In setting forth the ground rules for this normal science, *Economic Analysis* functioned as a methodological treatise on law and neoclassical economics. Posner's methodological commitment was plainly stated: "This book is written in the *conviction* that economics is a powerful tool for analyzing a broad range of questions of legal interpretation and policy but that most lawyers . . . have difficulty connecting economic precepts to concrete legal problems."[151]

Posner began with a statement of economic reasoning mirroring that of Lionel Robbins: "Economics is the *science* of human choice in a world in which resources are limited in relation to human wants."[152] At a time when scientism still carried significant cultural and ideological weight, this statement set the stage for the total displacement of legal realist residue in legal-economic thought. Posner in reviewing Guido Calabresi's seminal work *The Costs of Accidents*, which applies law and neoclassical economics to accident law, was one of the first to recognize this displacement. Referring to the realist paradigm, Posner remarked: "[F]rom at least Brandeis' time there was also a branch of legal scholarship [(legal realism)] that emphasized facts rather than logic, generally facts that demonstrated that the premises of a body of law were out of touch with contemporary social reality. They can more accurately be described, however, with no invidious intent, as anecdotes. The 'facts' marshaled by Brandeis and other fact-oriented legal reformers were for the most part stories (not necessarily untrue) told to legislative committees, rather than a product of rigorous *empiricism*."[153] It is implicit that the "branch of legal scholarship" to which Posner refers is legal realism. Posner viewed the displacement of legal realism as the progressive triumph of a scientific paradigm: "One *displaces* a scholarly approach not by showing that it has limitations but only by producing a *better* approach." Posner viewed this displacement as already under way, given that there were a "growing number" of legal scholars "who believe that over a broad range of subjects they will make greater progress utilizing the theories and empirical procedures of the social sciences than continuing to depend exclusively on the methods of traditional legal scholarship." Of course, the social sciences referred to by Posner would include neoclassical economics, not institutional economics. In this regard *The Costs of Accidents* was "an ambitious effort to employ a social science perspective (again that of economics) in a field of law in which . . . there was no supportive tradition, no pioneering work by economists or other social scientists, on which to rely." In so doing, it was a "*bold break* with conventional legal analysis of tort questions . . . [and] may be a portent of the future direction of legal scholarship in fields that . . . remain bastions of the traditional approach."[154]

As the work that would do much to secure the displacement referred to by Posner, *Economic Analysis of Law* "explores and tests the implications of the *assumption* that man is a rational maximizer of his ends in life."[155] All of Posner's analysis flowed deductively from this premise. A related premise was that "people respond to *incentives*—that if you change a person's surroundings so that he could increase his satisfactions by altering behavior, most of the time he would do so."[156]

With these individualistic and subjectivist premises in place, three fundamental concepts logically followed. First was the "inverse relationship between price charged and quantity demanded." This relationship represented the standard neoclassical law of the downward-sloping demand curve. Second, the cost of producing a good was equal to alternative price. This notion was tied to the concept of opportunity cost in economics. Posner stressed that by emphasizing opportunity cost he dispelled the "fallacies about economics—that it is about money." "On the contrary, it is about resource use."[157] One recalls Robbins's statement that economic science was about choice in the face of scarcity, as well as his insistence that the scope of economic analysis extends beyond "monetary issues." Economic analysis was about structuring society so as to maximize the value of resources available to quench human wants. This insight led to the third and final economic principle flowing from Posner's initial premise: "the tendency of resources to gravitate toward their highest valued uses if exchange is permitted."[158] These principles culminated, deductively, with the conclusion that "[b]y a process of voluntary exchange, resources are shifted to those uses in which the value to the consumer, as measured by the consumer's willingness to pay, is highest. When resources are being used where their value is greatest we may say that they are being employed efficiently."[159] It is clear from these excerpts that *Economic Analysis of Law* adheres to the subjectivist tradition and, like Coase's work, sees unfettered competition as maximizing societal wealth, a goal for economic science initially championed by Adam Smith.

Of course, "[w]illingness to pay is in turn a function of the existing distribution of income and wealth in society." However, "[t]he economist cannot tell us whether the existing distribution of wealth is just."[160] The inability of law and neoclassical economics to deal with issues of distribution, taking them off the legal-economic public policy stage (the "analyzable"), was enshrined in its principal text, *Economic Analysis of Law*. When issues of distribution were raised, the neoclassical economist had to remain silent: "The economist's competence in a discussion of the legal system is limited to predicting the effect of legal rules and arrangements on value and *efficiency*, in the *strict technical senses*, and on the *existing distribution* of income and wealth."[161] This refusal to discuss distributional issues demarcates science and ethics and also corresponds to Robbins's definition of economic science. However, it ignores the inherent symbiosis and consequent contestation between politics and analysis ("technical senses") that was at the core of neoclassical economics' historical formation.

This political contestation was immediately evident in the formation of law and neoclassical economics, with Guido Calabresi's liberal application of economic analysis to torts. Calabresi must be credited not only with carving out a liberal position within law and neoclassical economics but also with expanding the implications of social-cost analysis. Of particular interest is the field of manufacturer liability, in which the legal realists had crafted a doctrine of strict liability based on institutionalist insights. The general concept of social cost may be extended to the context of manufacturer liability for products placed into the stream of commerce. If tort law theory generally can be seen as being concerned with the social cost of private actions, products liability may be viewed as a particular case for social-cost analysis. For example, an automobile manufacturer who places a car into the stream of commerce incurs certain private costs of production. These costs are internalized by the manufacturer and factored into the price of the automobile. To the extent that the automobile causes accidents once on the road, the costs of those accidents represent social costs. The Coase theorem suggests that if there are negotiations between the manufacturer and victims, the problem of these social costs, given certain assumptions regarding transactions costs, may be solved without government intervention into the market. Obviously, this suggestion had very severe implications for the viability of institutionalist and legal realist assumptions about the need to intervene in the market on behalf of consumers. The policy question in constructing products liability law was the extent to which Coase's solution applied in the consumer products market. Coase's article, while having addressed the general issue of social cost, left open a wide terrain of policy questions with regard to products liability law doctrine and torts. Guido Calabresi would soon fill the void.

With the rise of law and neoclassical economics, the legal realist foundation for Section 402A strict products liability posed a problem for progressive legal-economic theorists: How to justify a doctrinal legacy whose theoretical foundation has been called into question? For more conservative legal theorists the immediate question was whether the doctrine should survive at all: Does the refutation of legal realism require that products liability law be shifted to the category of negligence? This doctrinal question is of the utmost political importance because, as noted earlier, strict products liability arguably disfavors injurers (in this case business interests) and most definitely leans toward compensating victims (in this case consumers).

Calabresi's *The Costs of Accidents*[162] was a direct attempt to rescue the doctrinal legacy of strict products liability constructed by Fleming James and other legal realists from the fate that the burgeoning law and neoclassical economics movement foreshadowed.[163] Tellingly, it stated: "[T]here has been a realization on the part of theoretically inclined writers that the analyses that had seemed to support the trend toward nonfault liability are woefully unsophisticated."[164] Specifically, such phrases associated with the loss spreading concept as "distribute the risk" and "let the party who benefits from the cost bear it" "can no longer be accepted as sufficing to determine who ought to bear accident costs."[165] Social insurance, compensation, and the suffering of victims, major focal points in the legal realist construction of strict products liability, were described in *The Costs of Accidents* as "rather misleading, though occasionally useful" concepts.[166] We must move beyond these concepts if we are to construct a theoretically defensible framework. While recognizing that economic analysis was not the only approach to tort law, Calabresi asserted that "it remains the fundamental tool for analyzing problems,"[167] and that the dictates of neoclassical economics cannot be avoided.

The Costs of Accidents pointed to the potential inconsistency of various possible goals of loss spreading. The goals included the broadest possible spreading, shifting losses to the wealthiest (deep pockets), and shifting losses to those causing harm.[168] To deduce how to choose among these concepts, *The Costs of Accidents* set forth the following standard: "[I]t is *axiomatic* that the principal function of accident law is to reduce the sum of the cost of accidents and the costs of avoiding accidents."[169] The choice to regard as "axiomatic" the goal of tort law as minimizing the costs of accidents reveals Calabresi's fidelity to neoclassical dictates. It constituted a political choice regarding ends and mirrored Robbins's vision of economic science in *An Essay on the Nature and Significance of Economic Science.* It had political content because it curtailed the possibility of more generally redistributive accident compensation policies.

The problem, as stated in *The Costs of Accidents*, was "allocation of resources." Calabresi recognized that the approach assumed as an essential basic postulate that "no one knows what is best for individuals better than they themselves do."[170] In *The Costs of Accidents* this postulate was carefully labeled "ethical"[171] because Calabresi would disavow it as inconsistent with his avowedly paternalistic point of view. The postulate is the subjectivist core of neoclassical economic theory. Implicit in it is that "as long as individuals are adequately informed about the alternative and so long as the cost to society of giving them what they want is reflected in the cost to the individual, the individual can decide better than anyone else what he wants. Thus, the function of the prices of various goods must be to reflect the relative costs to society of producing them, and if prices perform this function properly, the buyer will cast an informed vote, in making his purchases; thus the best combination of choices available will be achieved."[172]

The fundamental differences between Calabresi and more conservative adherents of law and neoclassical economics are Calabresi's paternalist instinct and his focus on market failure, both of which are captured in the following statement: "Ultimately, my skepticism here reflects in part my *belief*, explained later, that people individually do not or cannot voluntarily insure against accident risks to the degree they collectively deem desirable."[173] It is revealing that Calabresi recognized this fundamental political assumption as his "belief," just as Coase did for his own assumptions.[174] Calabresi later did explicate the extent of his paternalist beliefs, and that explanation goes a long way toward situating him very much as a political progressive.[175] Calabresi eschewed what may be referred to as the "pure paternalist" position (he refers to it as the "old paternalistic" position, or paternalism in "its most extreme form"): that generally "people do not know what is best for themselves." Calabresi rejected this position, which he said "calls into question the very notion of a free market," not for any explicit policy reason but because it "does not command much [political] assent in our society."[176]

The old paternalist position was contrasted with a "semipaternalist" position that politically was a "more measured, more acceptable version of the paternalistic notion." The notion was not that people generally did not know what was best for them, only "that in the area of accidents they often do not."[177] Thus the general idea of a free market is not called into question, but consistent with the neoclassical tradition there is a basis for intervention in the market (in the guise of strict liability) to remedy market failure in the context of accidents. Calabresi advanced the standard neoclassical arguments for finding market failure in the context of accidents. First, individuals do not have the data necessary to make the choice between undertaking risks and taking out insurance, whereas manufacturers "can view the risk as a statistic" and "evaluate it clearly." Second, even if the information were available, it is doubtful that consumers would have the capacity to process it. This is so because individuals have a tendency to deny or discount the possibility of being in an accident. Finally, there is the general failure, beyond the context of susceptibility to accidents, to believe that one will be subject to misfortune. This final argument is more consistent with the "general paternalistic view," or pure paternalism.[178]

Despite his paternalist leanings, Calabresi did not articulate the institutionalist or realist response to the problem of economic dislocation, or focus on conditions of social misery. This had been the position that Pigou took in appropriating neoclassical economics and refuting the assumption that distributional concerns fell outside the parameters of economic science. It was also the position taken by the legal realists who had argued for strict products liability. Instead, Calabresi expressed his redistributive arguments in more abstract terms. Calabresi's straddling of legal realism and neoclassicism is evident in the way he defines goals and subgoals in accident law: "First, it must be just or fair; second, it must reduce the costs of accidents."[179] At first glance it would seem to be this evocation of justice and fairness that sets *The Costs of Accidents* apart from other works in law and neoclassical economics, just as Pigou's concern with the distribution of wealth set him apart from Knight. However Calabresi, unlike Pigou, did not draw upon realist insights to put forth an argument for the redistribution of wealth. In this regard *The Costs of Accidents* conformed to the methodological restriction found in *An Essay on the Nature and Significance of Economic Science*: the redistribution of wealth falls outside the rubric of the analyzable.

The Costs of Accidents attempted to avoid the contradiction of seeking justice within the neoclassical economics paradigm by setting up justice as a larger normative goal separate and apart from neoclassical economic analysis. At the same time, the possible role of justice was downplayed: "Justice, though often talked about, is by far the harder of the two goals to analyze." Specifically, statements about justice, while often appealed to, were "rarely backed up by any clear definition of what such support means, let alone by any empirical research into what is considered fair."[180] This view is reminiscent of Knight's that social justice is "hopelessly undefinable."[181] Calabresi acknowledged that one may "readily document specific injuries that occur in existing systems, such as the fault system or workmen's compensation"[182]—a not-so-obvious reference to the empirical studies done by institutionalists and legal realists. Calabresi also admitted the rhetorical purpose of these studies in stating that the "requirements of fairness those systems may meet are difficult to define and therefore are usually stated as generalities, in hope of striking a responsive chord."[183] The characterization of the purpose of earlier empirical studies of accidents was correct, but Calabresi was concerned that this mode of analysis (arguing for legal changes with particular distributive consequences) was insufficient because it "may be an inadequate guide to what our reaction would be if the system were changed." In the end *The Costs of Accidents* accepted justice as a "constraint that can impose a veto on systems," but conceded that its "elusiveness . . . justifies delaying discussion of it."[184]

In *The Costs of Accidents* Calabresi simultaneously recognizes justice and fails to incorporate it in policy analysis. The failure can be attributed to the impulse in neoclassical economics to omit distributional issues, as evidenced in Lionel Robbins's *An Essay on the Nature and Significance of Economic Science*, and also to Calabresi's stated goal of setting forth a theoretically sophisticated analysis of tort law. Subject to the definition of analysis coming out of the analytic turn, a definition ensconced in American academe after the Second World War, there was no place in "scientific" discourse for justice. In A. J. Ayer's words, utterances regarding justice were emotive gestures adding *nothing* to the scientific quest for knowledge. This view of science was combined with postwar suspicions regarding government intervention. In addition, the hesitancy in *The Costs of Accidents* about pursuing justice may have sprung from the failure of explicitly pro-egalitarian social insurance arguments by legal realists who supported strict products liability. Calabresi hinted at this when stating that others have "sought to use accident law as a means of reducing inequalities in income distribution." However, Calabresi tells us that "we usually would do far better to attack the particular problem directly than through accident law."[185] This argument is based on the standard neoclassical view that distributional concerns should be addressed through macroeconomic policies, about which more will be said later.

Despite explicitly disavowing the legal realist redistributionist project, Calabresi did not make a clean break. Instead, as discussed earlier, he relied upon paternalist sentiments and attempted to resuscitate the loss-spreading argument under a more theoretically sophisticated guise. In this regard, Calabresi's appropriation of neoclassical economics differed from its appropriation by adherents of the Chicago School of law and neoclassical economics as represented by Coase and Posner, who rejected both arguments. Calabresi inserted the societal "costs" of economic dislocation into his policy calculus as "secondary costs," while acknowledging that "[e]conomists, unlike lawyers, tend to treat secondary costs under the rubric of justice."[186] In fact, secondary cost was merely another term for loss spreading.

Calabresi framed his argument for loss spreading in two ways. First, "taking a large sum of money from one person is more likely to result in economic dislocation . . . than taking a series of small sums from many people." Second, "even if the total economic dislocation were the same, many small losses would be preferable to one large one simply because people feel less pain."[187] These arguments were of dubious merit within the neoclassical tradition. As noted in *The Costs of Accidents*, the first proposition was a straightforward "empirical generalization" about which there might be little argument. However, the policy import of the proposition could be questioned under neoclassical analysis. The second proposition, that it was preferable to take a small amount from many rather than a lot from a few, became highly controversial given the neoclassical economics disavowal of the theory of the diminishing marginal utility of money, particularly Robbins's declaration in *An Essay on the Nature and Significance of Economic Science* that the theory was illegitimate under the definition of economic science. Calabresi recognized that diminishing marginal utility theory "has been in substantial disfavor among *modern* economists," meaning neoclassical economists, and he agreed that the premises underlying the theory were open to question. However, Calabresi argued that the "basic justification for loss spreading remains strong" because "social dislocation[s], like economic ones, will occur more frequently if one person bears a heavy loss than if many people bear light ones."[188] Of course, this begs the initial question posed by an exponent of the neoclassical school: How does economic dislocation figure into economic science as defined under the dominant neoclassical economics paradigm? The answer is that it does not fit, because it constitutes an argument based on the normative goal of alleviating human suffering.

Calabresi adhered to the methodological contours of neoclassical theory, and his redistributionist arguments were susceptible to critique from those who did not share his political agenda. This much was evident given the rest of Calabresi's analysis of the topic and the subsequent attack by Posner. As an adherent of neoclassical economics, Calabresi had to consider how the possible benefits of loss spreading and deep pockets were mitigated by the need to reduce the "primary" costs of accidents (both the costs of the accidents themselves and the costs of their reduction). Here Calabresi made a point clearly at odds with the legal realist tradition: "If the secondary cost of avoidance were our sole aim, there would be no justification for limiting compensation to accidents and not giving equal compensation for illness, old age, and all the other troubles of this planet."[189] In fact, as discussed earlier, the overarching policy recommendation of progressives during the pragmatist era (as informed by their general paternalist position) had been social insurance as a means of alleviating crippling poverty regardless of its cause, and their focus in tort law was on pain and suffering, not "primary" cost reduction.

The extent to which primary cost reduction (accident avoidance)—as opposed to secondary costs (loss spreading)—dominated the analysis in *The Costs of Accidents* is illustrated by the discussion on the various systems of loss spreading: social insurance, private insurance, and enterprise (strict) liability. The doctrinal implication of the social insurance and enterprise liability systems was that both might be used to support a strict products liability regime. However, the social insurance approach had even broader implications and could be used to argue that accident costs should be borne by the government and not be part of the private law tort system. A private insurance approach tended to argue for a negligence regime.

Of the three systems, social insurance would provide the maximum loss spreading. A system could tie loss spreading to a tax structure with particular distributive consequences. This option, of course, had potentially radical political implications. Calabresi rejected it on the grounds that it would not facilitate an optimal level of deterrence (primary cost reduction). This conclusion was based in part on his skepticism regarding the efficacy of government regulation. As for private market deterrence, Calabresi argued that it allowed individuals the "freedom to choose" whether to engage in risky activity.[190] However, it could have the shortcoming of failing to spread losses very widely. The market would operate so that like risks would be clustered and the insurance base limited. For law and neoclassical economists of the Chicago School, including Posner, this posed no problem, since a major premise was that individuals knew what was best for them. Calabresi broke from this subjectivist assumption by expressing, as earlier stated, his "*belief* . . . that people *individually* do not or cannot voluntarily insure against accident risks to the degree they *collectively* deem desirable."[191] Calabresi's skepticism regarding a private insurance regime is consistent with the paternalist impulse in *The Costs of Accidents* and necessarily undercuts the case against restricting the "freedom to choose." Of course, for those with anti-statist leanings and a belief in methodological individualism, the collectivist analysis in *The Costs of Accidents* marked the creeping socialism they so abhorred.

Enterprise liability, a basis for strict products liability, marked a moderate ground between social insurance and private insurance. As between enterprise liability and social insurance, *The Costs of Accidents* argued that the enterprise method provided more market deterrence than the social insurance method.[192] It also had some desired distributive consequences, although they were not as broad as those associated with social insurance.

Calabresi's attempt to place a neoclassical economics gloss on products liability marked the death of the legal realist vision of strict products liability. Not that the doctrine disappeared altogether, but as law and neoclassical economics tenets displaced the justifications of the legal realists, they dictated the debate over how we conceptualize products liability. Nowhere was this more evident than in the policy discussion and doctrinal drift toward negligence in *Restatement, Third, of Products Liability*.[193]

Neoclassical economics rejects social insurance, leaving only private insurance and enterprise liability as plausible among the three possibilities originally advanced by Calabresi. Of the two, *The Costs of Accidents* favored a system of enterprise liability and a doctrine of strict products liability. However, given the analytic and nonempirical nature of Calabresi's arguments, and the inevitable contestation of his position by more conservative adherents of neoclassical economics, Calabresi's intellectual foundation for strict products liability was unsteady. Calabresi's loss-spreading rationale did not carry much weight in mainstream neoclassical economics and would meet with immediate suspicion among law and neoclassical economics theorists. While he and others would also make efficiency-based arguments for strict liability, efficiency analysis is so malleable that it is often impossible to arrive at a definitive conclusion regarding the correct policy choice. As stated by Posner: "1. Economic theory provides no basis, in general, for preferring strict liability to negligence, or negligence to strict liability, provided that some version of a contributory negligence defense is recognized. Empirical data might enable us to move beyond agnosticism but we do not have any. 2. A strict liability standard without a contributory negligence defense is, in principle, less efficient than the negligence-contributory negligence standard. Empirical data could of course rebut the presumption derived from theory." The final arbiter would be values (including political judgment).

The political nature of law and neoclassical economics is evidenced in Posner's review of *The Costs of Accidents*. He notes, "Calabresi easily sweeps rival approaches, employing more conventional legal analytical methods, from the board."[194] However, "his reasoning is *analytic* rather than empirical and the analysis is not compelling."[195] Posner rejected Calabresi's application of law and neoclassical economics because it was in the Pigouvian tradition of expressing concern over distributional issues. In thinking about his differences with Calabresi over the policy implications of law and neoclassical economics, Posner is troubled by Calabresi's unwillingness to jettison the progressive policy prescriptions of the legal realist era. Posner comments on Calabresi's "unwillingness to reject proposals for reform that—as he shows so convincingly—themselves rest on shaky conceptual foundations." Posner concluded that "the explanation must be sought outside the text."[196]

Posner is right. The solution must be found outside the text. The history of American legal-economic theory from its inception and into the twenty-first century has been one of an obsession with scientific reasoning in the service of political beliefs—be they conservative or liberal. Law and neoclassical economics is merely the latest act on the stage of this intellectual drama. Kevin Phillips has associated the emergence of the Chicago School of law and neoclassical economics with the laissez-faire reconfiguration of the political landscape during the Reagan years.[197] As such, neoclassism is very much akin to the classism of Adam Smith. However, the political topography of law and neoclassical economics is more complex than this. Calabresi's contribution may be seen as a moderate intervention, distinguishing the neoclassical era from its classical predecessor. In this regard law and neoclassical economics, like all legal-economic theory, is a reflection of its political times. If the Posnerian wing of the movement were viewed as reflecting the politics of Reaganism, Calabresi would seem to reflect the moderate politics of "Clintonism" (and its predecessor, Carterism).

Irrespective of its politics, the one characteristic shared by law and neoclassical economics and classical legal thought was their formalist structure. While neoclassical formalism (which we may summarize as the "Calabresi-Posner research program") could hold sway given a particular vision and deference to science, it was in fact on shaky ground from the start.

FOUR

THE DISSOLUTION OF AMERICAN LEGAL-ECONOMIC THEORY

■ What makes our particular historical moment unique is that unlike in earlier ones, the very idea of science is being interrogated, and by implication, notions of objectivity are coming under heavy assault in a variety of intellectual fields. As a result, the scientistic dream of constructing legal theory based on a scientific conception of universal truth, which has been the centerpiece of American legal-economic thought, has been heavily criticized. Not since the classical era has a legal-economic movement clothed itself so fully in scientific garb as has law and neoclassical economics. The belief in its universal application and its superior claim to scientific status is summed up pithily in the title of a roundtable remembrance of Chicago school law and economics, "The Fire of Truth."[1] The title harkens back to Frank Knight, whom participants of the roundtable recognized as an intellectual forebear, and the description in his presidential address to the American Economics Association in 1950 of the values latent in neoclassical economics as "Truth."

Strangely enough, the seeds of our postmodern turn were sown by the scientific theory that marked the apex of the modernist quest: Einstein's theories of relativity. As discussed earlier, the theory of relativity did not throw physics into a relativistic quagmire. Indeed, it expanded our understanding of the physical world to vistas previously unimagined. However, outside physics, in the broader social milieu, Einstein's theory was viewed as having radical implications for a relativistic worldview.[2] Einstein rightly declared these inferences from his work misguided. Yet even mistaken perceptions can have profound effects on the larger culture. Einstein had unwittingly set in motion the tides of twentieth-century skepticism.

Perhaps the most unsettling aspect of both Einstein's special and general theories of relativity was his insight that an understanding of the physical universe is not necessarily accessible to common experience. Our common perceptions can be deceiving, time is not fixed, and space is not flat. These new realities, which divorced science from lay perception, called into question the modern notion that science should be a mediating force in civil society: as disputes arose, they could be resolved by means of common-sense analogies to the scientific method.

Yavon Ezrahi traces this marriage of science and the larger culture, particularly in liberal democratic societies, to Newton, whose vision of science was viewed as having shed the light of reason on a tattered culture.[3] If the complexities of the physical universe could be picked apart and analyzed like the parts of a machine, the same could be done with the social world. Relativity did not have the same salutary cultural effect as the clean certitude of Newtonian physics. The shift in perception was so profound that it led the famous French philosopher Maurice Merleau-Ponty to declare that Einstein had brought about a "crisis of reason."[4] Subsequent developments in physics would only deepen the crisis. Although nonscientists were incorrect in their view of relativity theory, the next major discovery in physics, quantum mechanics, would in fact reveal a physical world with philosophical implications that tended toward indeterminism.

During the period in which Einstein was formulating his theories of relativity, physicists began peering deeper into the structure of matter, focusing on quanta. Early in his career, Einstein described light as consisting of individual light quanta (units of energy) traveling through space at high velocity—dispelling the previous theory that light energy was only a continuous, wave phenomenon. Einstein's work in this area built on Max Planck's, who had earlier been doing research on the properties of quanta—arguing that the quantum is the fundamental measurement of radiated energy. His work led to the development of quantum mechanics, the mathematical representation of atoms. Niels Bohr put forward the complementarity idea: an atom could be described as a particle (discrete nucleus and electrons—this is the "pinball" model of atoms that we see in high school texts), or as a nucleus and matter waves (representing event probabilities). Bohr argued that the two descriptions were complementary ways of describing the same phenomenon depending on context. In 1926 this insight culminated in the famous Copenhagen interpretation of quantum events. In contrast to the certainty that characterized the Newtonian mathematical representation of the physical universe and Einstein's theories of relativity, there was a probabilistic element to quantum mechanics.

The location of electrons, the elementary particles that are the fundamental constituents of matter spinning around the nucleus of the atom, could not be predicted with certitude and the results of measurements could not be reproduced. Specifically, one could not predict with certainty both the location and momentum of an electron, although one could predict one or the other. The location and momentum of a particle are determined by a probability distribution and characterized by a wave function. Therefore, all measurements have some degree of uncertainty. These error possibilities are accounted for in a probability function. Classical physics would account for errors in experimentation, but not the inherent uncertainty in the system itself. The prediction problem gave rise to the famous "uncertainty principle" of Werner Heisenberg, who argued that at the subatomic level it was impossible to have precise predictions. Heisenberg noted that while it was "possible in principle" to observe an electron in orbit, "in the act of observation at least one light quantum of the y-ray must have passed the microscope and must first have been deflected by the electron."[5] This change in momentum guarantees an uncertain measurement. The uncertainty made for a contrast with Newtonian mechanics and Einstein's theory, according to which the state of a system could be precisely determined.

The notion of strict determinism had been thrown into doubt. Heisenberg discussed the philosophical implication of quantum mechanics in his *Physics and Philosophy: The Revolution in Modern Science.* The revolution came in two forms. First, quantum mechanics brought about a radical view of the relationship between observer (physicist) and world. The Newtonian perspective took as a given that the observer could view and catalogue the world without affecting it. Heisenberg argued that this was not the case at the subatomic level. Second, Heisenberg fundamentally questioned the classical view of the physical world. According to Heisenberg, the subatomic world (as opposed to the large phenomena described by Newton and Einstein) is probabilistic. In both Newton's and Einstein's view, the physical world was deterministic. Heisenberg's goal was to discuss the "ideas of modern [quantum theory] physics in a not too technical language, to study their philosophical consequences," which he characterized as "not simply a continuation of the past; it seems to be a real break in the structure of modern science."[6]

In many ways quantum theory marks an eclipse of certainty similar to that effected by the Darwinian revolution. David Lindley has summed up the implications for objectivity of quantum subatomic reality as follows: "It makes no good sense to talk of an objective world of real facts if those facts cannot be apprehended without altering them in the process. There is no longer any meaning to be attached to the idea of a real, objective world; what is measured, and therefore known, depends on the nature of the measurement."[7]

Heisenberg was aware of the larger philosophical implications. He argued that classical physics had operated under the "illusion" that we could describe the world objectively without taking into account our presence. This is possible when thinking about large-scale events but not at the subatomic level. However, quantum physics does not introduce subjectivism into the system. It merely acknowledges our limitations and agency.[8] Heisenberg traced the classical attempt to divorce the observer and the observed to Descartes's *Discourse on Method*, commenting that the "influence of the Cartesian division on human thought . . . can hardly be overestimated." He describes Descartes as the "first great philosopher of [the] new ([modern]) period of science." However, "it is just this [Cartesian] division which we have to criticize . . . from the development of physics in our time": "Natural science does not simply describe and explain nature; it is a part of the interplay between nature and ourselves. . . . [The Cartesian] separation between the world and the I [is] impossible."[9] Quantum physics also called into question positivist demands. Under positivist requirements for clarity, terms such as "position" and "velocity" must be clearly defined. However, in quantum science this requirement cannot be met because of the uncertainty associated with quantum mechanics.[10] In the end, Heisenberg concludes that "it will never be possible by pure reason to arrive at some absolute truth."[11]

The lessons of quantum mechanics were not lost on the larger public. An article in the *New York Times* in 1928 entitled "A Mystic Universe" discussed how the "new physics" of relativity and quantum mechanics forced us to "rid ourselves completely of established notions and forms of thought," and suggested that it was only a matter of time before it would "reshape our lives for us as the Newtonian science did."[12] John Dewey drew the same lesson from quantum theory in *The Quest for Certainty*. Dewey noted that "Heisenberg's principle compels a recognition of the fact that interaction [of the observer] prevents an accurate measurement of velocity and position for any body."[13] For Dewey, "[t]he change for the underlying philosophy and logic of science is . . . very great, [and] [i]n relation to the metaphysics of the Newtonian system it is hardly less than revolutionary."[14] Indeed, it marked the end of "the quest for certainty" in physics.

The implications of the theory were so profound that Einstein, clinging to a classical vision of determinism, refused to accept it, declaring in the now-famous quote that God "does not play dice with the world."[15] Einstein's view reflected his fundamental intuition that there is an underlying order to the world. In response, Max Planck is reported to have asked who Einstein was to presume how God would or would not structure the universe. Einstein ended his career in science searching for a "unified field theory" that would be a totalizing theory of the physical world—a theory of everything. His was a failed effort.

Thomas Kuhn has demystified the idea of scientific progress from a historical perspective. His *Structure of Scientific Revolutions* called into question the status of science, severely damaging its cultural prestige. Ironically, Kuhn's *Structure of Scientific Revolutions* first appeared in the *International Encyclopedia of Unified Sciences*, the manifesto for logical positivism. In light of the connection between the logical positivist project and the stated goal of a unified science, Kuhn's basic thesis seems conspicuously out of place. Citing such tectonic shifts in scientific conceptions as Einstein's theories versus Newtonian physics and the Copernican model of the stars versus Ptolemy's, Kuhn argued that these radically divergent paradigms could not be melded in a continuous tale of scientific progress.[16] They in fact signaled revolutions or ruptures in intellectual thought. The conflicting paradigms were incommensurable.

Kuhn's potentially radical historiography implies that there is no end to the scientific quest. What was deemed 'normal' science was only so because the next "better" theory had not yet arrived, but if history was any indicator, it would. It was therefore nonsensical to declare a fixed scientific

Truth. Kuhn did not have a sense of the maelstrom he had unleashed on the larger cultural understanding of knowledge, and would later disavow what he felt to be radical relativist misinterpretations of his theory.[17] However, his historical accounting had already affected the cultural psyche.

In addition to Kuhn's historical assault on the grand claims of science, there would be developments in the philosophical community also calling into question the notion of Truth. Because of the symbiotic relationship between science and philosophy, it is not surprising that as science lost its determinist footing, philosophy began to experience cracks in its own edifice. Nowhere was this more evident than in the unraveling of logical empiricism. Logical empiricism's demise was foreshadowed by one of its principal founders—Rudolph Carnap. Echoing Moritz Schlick, Carnap had announced the mission of logical empiricism (to place philosophy on a scientific footing) in *The Logical Structure of the World* (1967).[18] No sooner had this manifesto of logical empiricism been published than it met with immediate criticism within the movement, forcing Carnap to reconceptualize his views. Carnap eventually accepted that there was no viable theory of truth and that the notion of truth had more to do with language than reality.[19]

While the logical empiricist program of "technical" philosophy, under the rubric of logical positivism, progressed unabated in the United States after the Second World War (in large part because of the popularity of Ayer's *Language, Truth and Logic*), grand claims to the project of unifying science under the umbrella of philosophy fell into disfavor. This turn was spurred on by the recognition that meta-claims to objectivity could no longer be sustained.

Two of the most influential figures in American philosophy, W. V. Quine and Alfred Sellars, are in good part responsible for demonstrating the point. In perhaps the most important argument in postwar American philosophy, which Kuhn directly acknowledged as having shaped his historical views,[20] Quine argued in "Two Dogmas of Empiricism" that two of the pillars of logical empiricism could not be sustained: (1) the demarcation between logical and synthetic truths; and (2) the premise that scientific statements could be reduced to immediate experience.[21] Without these false dogmas in place, philosophers could no longer lay claim to embarking on an endeavor that would lead to objective representation. While the technical work of the logical empiricists (such as looking at the structure of language and the logic of statements) would go on unabated, much like the work of science in general, the hope of a grand theory of knowledge, the philosophical equivalent to a unified theory, had to be abandoned.

Hilary Putnam, analytic philosopher turned neopragmatist, has offered up a fascinating account of the connection between the current states of physics and philosophy.[22] He tracks what he takes to be two parallel intellectual phenomena: quantum mechanics and the philosophical development of a logical paradox ("the puzzle of the Liar"). Putnam's discussion builds on a quote from Friedrich Nietzsche's *The Birth of Tragedy*, "as the circle of science grows larger it touches paradox at more places." For Putnam, the increasingly paradoxical nature of science mirrors the same in philosophy. Putnam takes as his point of departure quantum theory. Specifically, he considers the fact that (unlike in Newtonian physics) measurement results in quantum theory are unpredictable. Uncertainty reigns supreme.[23]

Putnam juxtaposes quantum uncertainty with the Newtonian " 'God's-Eye View' of the whole universe."[24] His insight into the philosophical implications of this view is telling: "The dream of a picture of the universe which is so complete that it actually includes the theorist-observer in the act of picturing the universe is the dream of a physics which is also a metaphysics. . . . The dream has haunted Western culture since the seventeenth century."[25] Niels Bohr's Copenhagen interpretation of quantum theory marks the end of the dream.

Putnam draws similar conclusions to those drawn from quantum mechanics regarding the possibility of objectivity when looking at the domain of logic. A philosophical exploration of the "Liar's paradox" has revealed that the logical positivist dream of a totalizing language based on logical propositions was doomed from the start.[26] Putnam concludes: "[I]n giving up the idea that we can generalize about all languages; in giving up the idea that we have a single unitary notion of truth applicable to any language whatsoever, we have arrived at a strange position—a position, I want to suggest, somehow reminiscent of the position we find ourselves in quantum mechanics."[27] Just as physicists have been forced to give up on the notion of a "God's-eye view" of objectivity, philosophers have resolved that there is a split between the "reality" of language and its observation. No longer is philosophy burdened with the ideology of scientism. This would have significant implications for not only philosophy but the larger intellectual world as well, including legal theory.

With the demise of scientism, American legal-economic theory is for the first time left unfettered. The political contestation that has been cloaked in science is revealed. Nowhere is this more evident than in the dissolution of law and neoclassical economics. Here, what can be referred to as the Calabresi-Posner research program can be taken as a case study. In this regard, it is important to recognize, as discussed in chapter 3, that law and neoclassical economics is itself an offshoot of general neoclassical economic theory. The field, including the Calabresi-Posner research program, is therefore subject to the disciplinary restraints of economic analysis.

Guido Calabresi is the central figure in the research program because he was the first, with *The Costs of Accidents*, to undertake a comprehensive neoclassical analysis of torts. It is useful to reiterate the core policy goal of the research program as proposed by Calabresi: "[I]t is axiomatic that the principal function of accident law is to reduce the sum of the cost of accidents and the costs of avoiding accidents."[28] This axiom would guide development of the program. However, it is *not* an axiom of neoclassical economics analysis but rather a policy prescription.

In making his prescription for the economic analysis of tort law, Calabresi warned that issues traditionally considered outside the parameters of neoclassical economic analysis should be taken into account—most notably distributional concerns. However, Richard Posner objected to Calabresi's endeavor by reminding those who would participate in the scientific enterprise of law and neoclassical economics that "[t]he economist's competence in a discussion of the legal system is limited to predicting the effect of legal rules and arrangements on value and efficiency, in the strict technical senses, and on the existing distribution of income and wealth."[29] This claim to distributional agnosticism was based on the lack of a "theoretical [economic?] basis for [the] conclusion" that a "transfer of money from a wealthy man to a poor one is likely to increase the sum of the two men's total utilities."[30] This argument against the interpersonal comparisons of utility was a linchpin in the science and politics of neoclassical economics championed by Lionel Robbins (and discussed in chapter 3).

On the heels of *The Costs of Accidents*, Calabresi and Jon Hirschoff published "Toward a Test for Strict Liability in Torts."[31] In it Calabresi began fleshing out themes that were buried in *The Costs of Accidents* but later developed into a position opposed to that of Posner on the distribution and maximization of wealth, marking the beginning of Calabresi's break with the research program. This break was politically significant. As discussed earlier, while it is possible to combine standard neoclassical analysis with progressive policy recommendations (a possibility exemplified by Pigou and Calabresi), nothing in the neoclassical framework inherently favors progressive outcomes. There are so many imponderable variables in efficiency analysis that often plausible arguments can be made for either conservative or progressive policies. Classic examples of this are the arguments for and against strict liability in tort. If a vital part of the liberal (Calabresi's) agenda is to promote policies that redistribute wealth from rich to poor, law and neoclassical economics is at best a clumsy instrument. Calabresi's appeal to focus on distributional concerns may be viewed as an effort to tip the policy scales toward a progressive agenda.

Calabresi and Hirschoff first argued that even within the efficiency paradigm the relevant point of analysis is "categories" of plaintiffs and victims rather than individuals.[32] What is even more significant is that Calabresi and Hirschoff use their categories not only to do efficiency analysis but also to begin a conversation on distribution. They emphasize that when different liability rules "have different distributional effects . . . distributional differences may well *determine* the approach taken."[33] How much consideration should be given to distribution? The answer depends partly on how they define distribution: "For the purposes of this article, we are lumping together as distributional all those effects of liability rules which do not relate to minimizing (a) the sum of accident costs and avoidance costs, and (b) the administrative costs entailed by the minimization."[34] The distributional category includes preferences to "fractionize losses" (spreading), move "toward a given distribution of wealth," promote "dynamic efficiency" (entrepreneurship), and uphold notions of "just desserts." All of these come under the ideal of "justice."[35] The acknowledgement of distributional goals is significant because in *The Costs of Accidents* justice is no more than a veto constraint on efficiency. Calabresi and Hirschoff turn neoclassical analysis on its head. As opposed to lying in the background, distribution is in the foreground.

While Calabresi and Hirschoff had gone a step toward questioning distributional agnosticism in legal-economic theory, there was obviously much work to be done.[36] This work would take place on several planes: moral philosophy, historical accounting, and political theory. I want to focus on utilitarianism as a particularly relevant strand. The revival of utilitarianism in American legal-economic theory marks its resurrection from the ashes of British legal-economic thought as represented by Jeremy Bentham and John Stuart Mill. Utilitarianism received some attention in *The Costs of Accidents* and would later be more fully developed by Calabresi and others who argued for the centrality of distributional considerations in economic analysis. Utilitarianism is also unique as a conception of justice because of its close (even if at time hostile) affinity to neoclassical economics.

The utilitarian position, while alluded to in *The Costs of Accidents*, took center stage in legal academe with Ed Baker's "Utility and Rights: Two Justifications for State Action Increasing Equality."[37] Baker's project was not initially directed specifically toward law and neoclassical economics, but rather toward promoting the "numerous proposals . . . that would move American society toward greater economic equality." The goal was to "develop and compare theoretical justifications for state interventions in the market which would guarantee to every member of society either minimum income or minimum satisfaction of 'just wants.' "[38] The contemporary legal-economic theory backdrop for Baker's analysis was critical legal studies (CLS), about which more will be said later. While it is a tricky proposition to label someone a "crit," given the movement's rather loose affiliations, Baker's ties with CLS can be traced through his invitation to the initial organizing conference in 1977 and his having no fewer than twelve works (including "Utility and Rights") listed in a bibliography of CLS.[39]

Baker's utilitarianism, borrowing from Bentham, had as its core the maximization of social welfare, based on the central thesis that "societal utility is systematically maximized by a distribution of wealth where equality is greater than it would be if the total wealth of the society, not utility, were maximized."[40] This thesis is borne out on the basis of three assumptions: (1) there is an inverse relationship between equality and societal wealth;[41] (2) utility is derived from personal wealth; and (3) there is a declining marginal utility of wealth. Of these three, Baker identifies the first and third as "critical" assumptions.[42] The first assumption defines the alternative states of the world that Baker poses in an illustration and their implications for equality:

TABLE 1

PERSONS	POSSIBLE WEALTH DISTRIBUTIONS		
	A	B	C
X	10	8	4
Y	9	6	4
Z	1	2	4
Totals	20	16	12

Under the first assumption, state of the world A is the least egalitarian and C the most egalitarian. The third assumption, at the analytical core of Baker's approach, determines which state of the world is utility-maximizing. This assumption, that wealth has declining marginal utility, is based on the belief that "[p]eople place a higher value on their first dollar than their second, on the second dollar than on their third." In other words, a "poor man would thus value an extra dollar more than would a rich man." This assumption is crucial to an egalitarian argument because it eliminates state of the world A as necessarily utility-maximizing, which it would be if every increment of wealth (20 in the case of A, as opposed to 16 in B and 12 in C) were valued equally.[43]

In taking his position on the declining marginal utility of wealth and interpersonal comparisons, Baker had struck at the core of neoclassical economics. Lionel Robbins had argued that rejecting interpersonal comparisons of utility was required to position neoclassical economics as an exact science. Utilitarian implications for an outsider attack on law and neoclassical economics, and derivatively the Calabresi-Posner research program, would soon be developed in Baker's "The Ideology of the Economic Analysis of Law."[44] Baker's central claim in the article was that "welfare economics as *currently* used by legal writers provides an ideological, and frequently objectionable, basis for policy judgment."[45] The ideology is reflected in two biases in law and neoclassical economics, which (1) "[f]avors the claimant of the right whose use is productive over one whose use is consumptive"; and (2) "[f]avors the rich claimant whose use is consumptive over the poor claimant whose use is consumptive."[46]

The source of this ideology centered on the neoclassical stance that value is measured by the consumer's willingness to pay and that, as Posner phrased it, " 'willingness to pay is . . . a function of the existing distribution of wealth in a society.' "[47] This belief runs against utilitarian arguments for redistributing wealth. It is not surprising then that Baker, a proponent of egalitarian utilitarianism, should have become one of the harshest critics of law and neoclassical economics. Baker takes his generalized argument for egalitarian utilitarianism and uses it to attack the maximization of wealth as a normative goal in legal-economic theory. Wealth maximization stood as the fundamental policy basis for law and neoclassical economics. Much more will be said about Posner's defense of wealth maximization in due course.

Baker notes the utilitarian aspect of Posner's wealth maximization norm. Of the A, B, and C choices listed in "Utility and Rights," Posner would choose A over either B or C because it creates the greatest level of wealth. The basis for this choice is that Posner, in the neoclassical tradition, rejects the "critical assumption" that rough ("typical") interpersonal comparisons of utility can be made. Baker's critique of this position tracks his argument in "Utility and Rights." His case for an egalitarian distribution on utilitarian grounds only rests on assumptions regarding average or "typical" interpersonal comparisons: "a transfer of money from a wealthy man to a poor one is *likely* to increase the sum of the two men's utilities."[48]

Baker's critique is significant not only for its analytic cogency but also because it reflected the arguments leveled against law and neoclassical economics by others in the critical legal studies movement. A historical summation of critical legal studies raises particular challenges. Even members of the CLS movement admit to its amorphous nature. It does not adhere to the same methodological rigidity of a discipline such as law and neoclassical economics. However, there are some affinities that members of the movement share (most particularly a commitment to a leftist politics). Importantly for our purposes, there is a distinct strand of CLS with affinities to an emerging branch of legal-economic theory that will be labeled "law and distribution economics." This strand, which may loosely be described as neo-instrumentalist, is shaped by the neopragmatist ethos. Again, the claim is not that individual CLS scholars grappled with particular neopragmatist philosophers, but that philosophical neopragmatism shaped the intellectual terrain. Moreover, like their predecessors in legal academe, the legal realists, members of the CLS movement had an important critical element (which supplemented and at times diverged from instrumentalist dictates). This critical element was just as likely to be influenced by such continental or postmodern figures as Jean-Paul Sartre, Jacques Derrida, and Michel Foucault as by neopragmatist philosophers.

The invitation letter to the CLS organizing conference, written in 1977 by Mark Tushnet (for the organizing committee), described CLS as consisting of two complementary strands. The first was described as "social scientific" and inspired by Max Weber. The purpose of this strand was to demystify the formal structures ("logic") of law and "reveal their latent social structures." The other, "critical," approach (which was described as derivative of the first) focused on the "ideological character of legal doctrine" and viewed law as an "instrument of social, economic and political domination."[49] These two strands of CLS, roughly mapped the beliefs of two of its founders, David Trubek (social scientific) and Duncan Kennedy (critical). Trubek had been a faculty member at the Yale Law School and one of Kennedy's professors. This link is important in the trajectory of legal-economic thought because Trubek was associated in the late 1960s and early 1970s with the "Law and Modernization" program at Yale, essentially a version of the legal realists' social science movement.[50] Both Trubek and Kennedy became disaffected with the use of social science as an instrument of progress. Kennedy turned to the technique of "critique," described by John Schlegel as "critical Marxism," that would have the more profound impact on legal-economic thought.[51]

A central theme voiced by CLS adherents is that law by its very nature is a political enterprise. There are no non-controversial norms that provide an objective basis for legal decision making. Of course, various sets of practices and modes of argument generally accepted under the rubric of legal reasoning do constrain practitioners. Indeed, legal theory is one of the instruments in the legal reasoning toolkit. However, the uses of those instruments, and indeed the instruments themselves, are not neutral or objective. Ironically, the CLS movement developed in the legal academy shortly after law and neoclassical economics ascended to the citadel of legal-economic theory. Since law and neoclassical economics stood as the principal legal theory purporting to legitimate the objectivity of law, claimed to be scientific (nonpolitical) and had conservative-to-moderate policy implications, it became an obvious target for CLS.

Nowhere was the critique more succinctly distilled than in Morton Horwitz's "Law and Economics: Science or Politics?"[52] Horwitz was another founder of the CLS movement and an eminent historian. Looking back historically at the trajectory of law and neoclassical economics, he prophetically (though somewhat polemically) concluded, "Once its practitioners become overt apologists for grossly unequal Distribution of Wealth, it is obviously only a matter of time before they are *pluralistically* assigned to the class of one of many 'ideologies' from which one may pick and choose."[53] Horwitz's insight that law and neoclassical economics is fated to be one of many theoretical choices deserves emphasis. The dissolution of law and neoclassical economics and the future development of legal theory would bear out his conclusion. We will return to this point later.

Law and neoclassical economics would have to undergo further critique before its final dissolution. While Baker had laid the groundwork for this critique, Duncan Kennedy put it in full relief, combining an attack on the indeterminacy of the neoclassical concept of efficiency and a progressive questioning of its pretensions to agnosticism regarding the distribution of wealth. It was this latter criticism that became part and parcel of law and distribution economics, a vision of legal-economic theory that places distributional concerns at the center of analysis.

The confrontation between the legal-economic vision of law and neoclassical economics on the one hand and law and distribution economics on the other culminated in 1980 with the publication by the *Hofstra Law Review* of a symposium entitled "Efficiency as a Legal Concern." The symposium might just as well have been entitled "The Law and Distribution Economics Challenge." (Horwitz's "Science or Politics?" was published as part of the follow-up "response" to the symposium.) It pitted Posner as the representative of law and neoclassical economics against, among others, Calabresi, Baker, Kennedy, Jules Coleman, Ronald Dworkin, and Frank Michelman, all of whom argued for the centrality of distributional concerns in some form. It is noteworthy that the attack on law and neoclassical economics came not only from those associated with CLS, considered the radical fringe of the legal academy, but also from liberals such as Calabresi, Dworkin, and Coleman. It suggests that a liberal-left consensus had formed to press the point that distributional considerations should be part of legal-economic theory.

We can take Baker's response to his fellow symposium participants in "Starting Points in Economic Analysis of Law" as a guide to the law and distribution economics stance.[54] As would be expected, Baker attacked Posner's support of the status quo distribution in a manner reminiscent of his earlier critiques. Baker organized his criticism around the importance of starting points in determining what constituted the maximization of wealth and around the related question of which legal rules to choose under an efficiency criterion:[55] "Any use of wealth maximization presupposes both prior normative judgments in order to make it determinate . . . and possibly related normative judgments in order to justify its use. . . . [Posner fails] to defend or define starting points and other commentators have emphasized his related failure to provide a normative grounding."[56] These "other commentators" included Calabresi, Dworkin, Coleman, Kennedy, and Michelman. Calabresi obviously mounted his critique as a pro-redistribution (liberal) member of the law and neoclassical economics community. Coleman's background is that of an analytic philosopher, and Dworkin is a political philosopher who centers his analysis on rights. While Calabresi, Coleman, and Dworkin have much to say regarding the distribution issue, I will first focus on Baker, Kennedy, and Michelman as representatives of the CLS movement and later return to Calabresi in an effort to highlight the convergence (and differences) of the CLS and liberal positions.

Discussing Kennedy and Michelman, Baker notes that "[f]or one who feels that law-and-economics writing keeps saying the same things over and over without making any conceptual progress, the article by Professors Kennedy and Michelman will be pleasantly refreshing."[57] Despite expressing some minor disappointment with portions of the Kennedy's and Michelman's thesis, Baker argues that their analysis (mirroring his) "clearly demonstrates the importance of starting points." Specifically, Kennedy and Michelman show that any discussion of starting points must begin with a "good deal of specific factual information" and, implicitly, that "efficiency still leads nowhere until one makes further value judgments, until one relies on a background of normative theory."[58] Baker does not disavow efficiency analysis in legal-economic theory. His reluctance to jettison efficiency illustrates that the law and distribution economics paradigm *does not* eliminate neoclassical economic analysis as a mode of intellectual exploration. Law and distribution economics interrogates the professed agnosticism of law and neoclassical economics toward distribution, displacing it with distribution consciousness.

The "starting point problem is fundamental in the legal context because the givens or starting points are typically the subject of the legal dispute."[59] With this in mind, Baker puts forth a positive theory to rival Posner's positive theory of law as wealth maximizing. Baker's theory, based on a "simplistic class analysis," is that "those with power to choose rules will, when possible, choose as their givens or starting points those preferences and distributions that further ruling class interests." Baker "treats law as a realm of political struggle, of value conflict, and of ethical development and realization."[60] In his statement we see a blending of the analytic critique of law and neoclassical economics (based on starting points) and the conception of law as a site of political contestation (a hallmark of CLS theory).

Starting points could serve a central organizing function for normative analysis in law and distribution economics. However, "[w]hile many of the symposium's contributors usefully focused on the dependence of economic analysis on starting points and normative theory . . . there were few attempts to offer descriptions of any adequate normative theory."[61] Baker made reference to his earlier works as not being specifically directed to law and distribution economics but possibly pointing toward a normative theory for the paradigm: (1) "an egalitarian political process and not an economic market . . . provides the proper basis for defining or determining value to the extent that value notions are used in necessarily collective decisions such as the choice of legal rule"; (2) "[r]espect for people's autonomy requires that the collective recognize arenas of liberty where individual choice is free from collective control"; and (3) "utilitarianism is generally an appropriate policy criterion" because it respects the individual and leads to a "fulfillment of people's preferences."[62] Baker unmasks the indeterminacy of efficiency analysis and its failure to acknowledge the crucial role that the initial distribution of wealth plays in determining efficient outcomes. As such, his analysis fits well with a CLS position. However, his allusions to an "adequate normative theory" for resolving this dilemma would more than likely cause some disquiet in the movement.

The article by Kennedy and Michelman referenced by Baker is largely an exercise in demonstrating the indeterminacy of efficiency analysis.[63] The authors ingeniously deconstruct efficiency arguments to reveal that on the basis of the efficiency criterion one cannot as a matter of "economic science" prefer private property (the law and neoclassical economics prescription) to a society based on anarchy (lack of any state-enforced property rights) or a system of forced sharing (redistribution of wealth). While Kennedy and Michelman suggest that efficient outcomes depend on the initial distribution of income, and while it may be inferred from their other writings that they intend to illustrate the viability of a forced sharing regime based on need as an overarching norm, the arguments are not sharply delineated.

In a later piece, Kennedy would go on to level the most devastating CLS critique of law and neoclassical economics' distribution agnosticism and the clearest articulation to date of the law and distribution position. I will take this up later because it was largely a response to subsequent attempts by those associated with law and neoclassical economics to confront law and distribution adherents on their own terms. One suspects that the reason why law and neoclassical economics scholars felt the need to address the distribution issue is that the assault came not only from self-proclaimed leftists (followers of CLS) but also from moderates and liberals (including those formerly associated with law and neoclassical economics) such as Calabresi. Thence the further development of Calabresi's views on the subject is noteworthy.

In a lecture in 1981 entitled "The New Economic Analysis of Law: Scholarship, Sophistry, or Self-Indulgence?," Calabresi raised issues very similar to Baker's.[64] Calabresi reiterated that until we know more about starting points, we can say little about what constitutes wealth. These starting points are the "definers of wealth": "what wealth *is* depends on what people want, and what people want depends on the allocation of starting points."[65] This observation parallels Baker's assault on law and neoclassical economics because the "[neoclassical] economist knows this and defines 'wealth maximization' only *given an initial distribution of wealth*." However, lawyers (including lawyer-economists) must understand that "any change in law changes this initial distribution" and thus "is allowed no such luxury."[66]

Utilitarianism has the benefit of allowing us, if we could define happiness, to set up a scheme of starting points "so as to maximize happiness." According to Calabresi, "[t]he same unfortunately is not true for the strong claim made by Professor Posner and *his* school."[67] What is this strong claim? It is nothing more than the formerly "axiomatic" policy of which Calabresi now states, "there is nothing in itself desirable in reducing the sum of accident and safety cost if the result is to burden the wrong party."[68] The "wrong party" is determined by an analytically and politically defensible theory of distribution. But what is this theory of distribution? Calabresi admits to failing to spell out such a theory and to the extent that he and others produced "[a]rticle upon article and book upon book . . . in the last twenty years . . . based on [the] Calabresian proposition [(the Calabresi-Posner research program)]," the program constituted "no more than a reflection of the scholars' own values."[69] This was "self-indulgence."

The problem posed by Baker of devising an "adequate normative theory" for law and distribution economics remained unsolved. To get beyond self-indulgence, again citing Baker's "Starting Points," the call is to at least begin a conversation about utilitarianism as an overarching distributional theory: "An example of a philosophical theory that, to the extent adopted, gives rise to distributional insights that need factual assumptions to apply is, of course, utilitarianism."[70] These utilitarian assumptions are ones about which "[e]conomists traditionally have said: 'Nothing,' but they have said it for rather odd reasons."[71] The principal odd justification is the refusal to make interpersonal comparisons of utility. Calabresi breaks with this tradition for many of the same reasons as Baker: "If we *can* say that by and large marginal utility declines, and that by and large most members of a species get roughly similar pleasure from (i.e. desire similarly) the generality of goods (however much they differ as to particular goods), then if we accept the utilitarian philosophical premiss, we have a very powerful distributional theory indeed."[72]

But how does one operationalize such a theory? According to Baker, "utilitarianism is generally an appropriate policy criterion"[73] and might serve as a critique of distribution agnosticism but be problematic as jurisprudence or as a philosopher's rationale.[74] We get a sense of how law and distribution economics can, and cannot, address distributional considerations from Calabresi's "First Party, Third Party, and Product Liability Systems: Can Economic Analysis of Law Tell Us Anything about Them?"[75]

Calabresi restates his critique of distribution agnosticism based on the failure to set forth a suitable theory of starting points but also notes that "[w]hile this argument would imply that economic analysis does not and cannot carry the day, it does not mean that the values that economic analysis tends to further can be ignored." Particularly, "[a]voidance of waste [(efficiency)] *is* part of a common notion of justice."[76] Calabresi goes through an analysis of winners and losers under various tort law regimes; his principal distributional guide is avoidance of a system that disadvantages the "poor and the aged." This criterion is not based on any a priori philosophical justification but on the "rather strong indications of *society's* distributional preferences in this area."[77] Calabresi favors a system that furthers the goal of benefiting the poor and aged because "all systems would be equally good as far as economic efficiency is concerned."[78] So while "Posnerians would suggest that we cannot say anything at all"[79] regarding distribution, Calabresi uses distribution as a jurisprudential tool in conjunction with efficiency.

However, it is not possible to make strong Truth (philosophical) claims regarding distribution, because it is "difficult to define the overarching distributional preferences of a polity."[80] (Is this a retreat from the utilitarian position?) "[A]bsent a notion of starting points, we cannot say anything about distribution."[81] The law and distribution economics starting-points critique of law and neoclassical economics, given democratic sensibilities, turns on itself when attempts are made to apply utilitarianism. Calabresi's resolution to this impasse is that "it may not be so hard to identify . . . [distribution] preferences in a specific area."[82]

Thus what we are looking for are particular "indications of society's distribution preferences."[83] This political conception of legal-economic theory, combined with the "analytic structure" of law and distribution economics (utilitarianism),[84] is called "middle theorizing."[85] This sort of theorizing in its best moments "allows us to see far better what is at stake in the choice among the systems discussed," thus helping our "authorized decision makers [to] choose among systems of accident law intelligently."[86] Consequently all practitioners of law and economics (law and distribution economics, law and neoclassical economics) must recognize the limits of theory (science) and take their place in that "area of middle theorizing that defines much of American legal scholarship."[87] It is an area, after analytic criticisms and general intellectual shifts, in which even Posner would settle.

With the publication in 1979 of "Utilitarianism, Economics, and Legal Theory" Posner began constructing the philosophical argument for law and neoclassical economics that would directly lead to the heated debates of 1980.[88] Not surprisingly, in light of the specter of egalitarian utilitarianism and criticisms of utilitarianism as a philosophical position, Posner began his construction by attempting to disassociate law and neoclassical economics from utilitarianism: "the economic norm I shall call 'wealth maximization' provides a firmer basis for a normative theory of law than does utilitarianism."[89] Posner wished to distinguish adherents of law and neoclassical economics from "practitioners of 'welfare economics' (the commonest contemporary appellation for economics as a normative discipline) [who] regard their activity as applied utilitarianism"[90]—law and distribution economics.[91]

The contours of wealth maximization are succinctly stated: "Wealth is the value in dollars . . . of everything in society. It is measured by what people are willing to pay for something or, if they already own it, what they demand in money to give it up. The only kind of preference that counts in a system of wealth maximization is thus one that is backed up by money."[92] The import of linking law and neoclassical economics to wealth, as opposed to utility, was principally moral. For Posner, utilitarianism suffered the fatal flaw of having no principled boundaries for defining whose happiness should count in our social calculus. Thus utilitarianism has to "give capacity for enjoyment, self-indulgence, and other hedonistic and epicurean values at least equal emphasis with diligence, honesty, etc." Wealth maximization, however, pays homage to the "productive" and "encourages and rewards the traditional values ('Calvinist' or 'Protestant')."[93]

Although Posner also sets forth analytic (logical) shortcomings in utilitarianism, his ultimate evaluative criteria in arguing for wealth maximization are nontechnical. They include whether (1) "the theory yields precepts sharply contrary to widely shared ethical intuitions" and (2) "a society which adopted the theory would not survive in competition with societies following competing theories." Posner begins to form a pragmatist defense. Wealth maximization "accommodates, with elegant simplicity, the competing impulses of our moral nature." In this regard, wealth maximization could serve as an objective, consensus basis of adjudication. Of course it is also an ideological ethic. Harkening back to Adam Smith, and evoking F. A. Hayek and Milton Friedman, Posner describes the maximization of wealth as a " 'capitalistic conception of justice.' "[94]

Posner made attempts to clarify his defense of wealth maximization in the immediate wake of "Utilitarianism," once by contributing to the symposium convened in 1980.[95] However, it is in 1985 that we begin to see the

pragmatic, political conception of law and neoclassical economics crystal-
lize. In "Wealth Maximization Revisited," Posner welcomes the opportunity to "reconsider" his position on wealth maximization.[96] He begins by
providing numerical illustrations (involving the sale of a house on his
part and a car by someone else) of the relationship between willingness to
pay, exchange, and the law and neoclassical economics concept of wealth.
Significantly, he recognizes that "both examples ignore a fundamental
problem—how it is that I initially came to have the house, and he the car."[97]
With the formation of law and distribution economics, the "fundamental
problem" of starting points must be dealt with. Distribution agnosticism is
no longer an option.

Posner rejects the law and distribution economics prescription to the
distribution issue, interpersonal comparisons of utility: "The refusal of
modern economists to make 'interpersonal comparisons of utility' means
in effect that they use wealth rather than happiness as the criterion for an
efficient allocation of resources."[98] In staking out this position, Posner
directly addresses the egalitarian utilitarianism of law and distribution
economics. His attack mixes moralism with consequentialism. In contrast
to the law and distribution economics position that the "poor" are more
deserving based on the declining marginal utility of wealth, Posner, harkening back to "Utilitarianism," raises the specter of a utilitarian world where
the "pleasure-loving scamp" and "sadist" make claims for redistribution
against the "productive and hard-working and self restrained." Wealth
maximization, by contrast, favors the "productive side of human activity,"[99]
confirming Baker's analysis of "bias" in law and neoclassical economics.[100]
Yes, Posner does look askance at "the consuming, the appetitive,"[101] in stark
contrast with Calabresi's concern for the elderly and poor.

Posner recognizes that favoring production over consumption is a political choice and that to "defend wealth maximization rigorously [(analytically)], it would of course be necessary to assign some ethical value to productivity." He attempts to evade this dilemma by stating that it "would not
be difficult but will not be attempted here."[102] Posner admits the problematic nature of this assertion: "Ethical arguments do not convince doubters
but rather provide rationalizations for ethical positions taken on emotional grounds. Indeed, more ethical arguments have been won on the
battlefield than in the lecture hall. . . . Perhaps—speaking descriptively
and in the long run—might is responsible for most opinions of what is

right."[103] This fortunately is not an invitation for a brawl between adherents of law and distribution economics and adherents of law and neoclassical economics. However, it is an admission that "scientific" arguments ("rationalizations") for law and neoclassical economics will not carry the day: "you cannot prove, deductively or inductively, that social decisions ought to conform to some ethical theory."[104] No, we cannot rely on a philosopher's rationale—the quest for scientific objectivity has come to an end.

If analysis, of either the deductive or the inductive sort, cannot provide us with "Truth" and certainty, what are we left with? Posner pushes forward his pragmatist response. His *starting point* is that "very few people who live in wealthy societies would like to live in poor ones."[105] This observation goes a long way toward supporting an ethic that is consistent with wealth creation (production), such as wealth maximization. However, even wealth maximization is "an incomplete guide to social decision-making" precisely because, among other reasons, it cannot tell us when *some* redistribution—not the "free-wheeling redistributions of utilitarian society"—is called for. Thus the pragmatist solution is to allow "redistributions that conform to the altruistic feelings that most people harbor or that otherwise serve the interest of the *productive people* in the society."[106]

Posner realizes that "it is a *political* philosophy" that he is expounding.[107] Ultimately we hear echoes of Calabresi ("First Party, Third Party, and Product Liability Systems") in that "[g]iven the absence of anything approaching a consensus on the optimum distribution of wealth . . . it is very hard to see how courts could adopt a redistributive ethic to guide their decisions." Jurisprudence is confined to an expression of the "fundamental values of our political culture."[108]

Posner would expand on this concept of jurisprudence and philosophical (or anti-philosophical?) defense of law and neoclassical economics in *The Problems of Jurisprudence* (1990).[109] He began by taking a general jurisprudential stance. The history of jurisprudence according to Posner is marked by two distinct groups: adherents of natural law ("true believers") and adherents of positivism ("skeptics"). *The Problems of Jurisprudence* was "devoted to exploring the basic issues debated by the two groups and the issues that grow out of those issues." As for Posner, he would steer a middle course and argue "against formalism, against overarching conceptions of justice such as 'corrective justice,' 'natural law,' *and 'wealth maximization'*—though not against modest versions of these normative systems—but also against 'strong' legal positivism."[110] In other words, Posner staked out a position of philosophical pragmatism (middle theorizing).

Posner's philosophical pragmatism questions the capacity to reach conclusive "Truth." It argues for the "critical as distinct from the constructive use of logic; for the idea that the judge's proper aim in difficult cases is a reasonable result rather than a demonstrably right one." Significantly, Posner also "argues for objectivity as a cultural and political rather than epistemic attribute of legal decisions."[111] If this pragmatist stand seems in tension with my previous account of how the law and neoclassical economics enterprise was founded on analytic precepts, it is. And it is the reason why Posner's pragmatist turn helps mark the dissolution of law and neoclassical economics, at least as formerly (formally) constituted. This does not mean that the formal (analytic) structure of law and neoclassical economics is dismantled, but that its claim to preeminence (epistemic objectivity) must be staked out on grounds other than science ("constructive use of logic").

With the reprise of formalism in the neoclassical era, wealth maximization was defended on the basis of "science" because utilitarianism would violate the verifiability norm—scientists cannot make interpersonal comparisons of utility. In conjunction with the analytic blow dealt to this position by law and distribution economics, the decline of analytic philosophy and the classical conception of science undercut its scientific pretensions as well. With the assault on scientism, claims to objectivity based on science no longer rang true. *The Problems of Jurisprudence* deals with this dilemma by "recasting the wealth-maximization approach to law in pragmatic terms."[112]

The pragmatic justification for law and neoclassical economics was "cultural and political." For judges, maximizing wealth is a "relatively uncontroversial policy, and most judges steer from controversy." Historically, it is "no accident, therefore, that many common law doctrines assumed their modern form in the nineteenth century, when laissez-faire ideology, which resembles wealth maximization, had a strong hold on the Anglo-American imagination."[113] We are still captives of our classical past. Yet the key for Posner is not ideology but rather "prosperity." A pragmatic jurisprudence attempts to fashion rules that further social welfare; prosperity is a proxy for social welfare and can be measured in terms of wealth maximization, thus providing the justification for law and neoclassical economics.

But this rationale does not address the law and distribution economics arguments that the distribution of wealth is also a central consideration in measuring social welfare. No longer able to evade or counter the arguments of law and distribution economics with plausible analytic defenses, Posner extends his pragmatic account. First, "judges can, despite appearances, do little to redistribute wealth."[114] If this were the only argument offered by Posner, it would indeed look more instrumental than one based on philosophical pragmatism. However, there is a broader sociohistorical (pragmatist) justification for maximizing wealth: "We look around the world and see that in general people who live in societies in which markets are allowed to function more or less freely not only are wealthier than people in other societies but have more political rights, more liberty and dignity, are more content (as evidenced, for example, by their being less prone to emigrate)—so that wealth maximization may be the most direct route to a variety of moral ends. The recent history of England, France, and Turkey, of Japan and Southeast Asia, of East versus West Germany and North versus South Korea, of China and Taiwan, of Chile, of the Soviet Union, Poland, and Hungary, and of Cuba and Argentina provides striking support for this thesis."[115] There are several steps and historical parallels in Posner's argument that merit attention.

Of course, it seems a stretch to perfunctorily dismiss redistributive claims on the basis of, at best, vague contrasts in "prosperity" across countries.[116] This ad hoc comparison of economic systems based on prosperity is reminiscent of F. A. Hayek's argument in *The Road to Serfdom*: socialism, or the welfare state, leads to totalitarianism (the Soviet Union or Nazi Germany). In Posner's view the "mounting evidence that capitalism is more efficient than socialism gives us an additional reason for believing [neoclassical] economic theory."[117] This of course elides the definition of what constitutes a capitalist or socialist economy, which Posner realizes: "My pragmatic judgment is, moreover, a qualified one. All modern societies depart from the precepts of wealth maximization [(capitalism)]. The unanswered question is how the conditions in these societies would change if the public sector could somehow be cut all the way down to the modest dimensions of the night watchman state that the precepts of wealth maximization seem to imply. . . . Until it is answered, we should be cautious in pushing wealth maximization; incrementalism should be our watchword."[118] Returning to the puzzle that Baker posited in "Utility and Rights," could Posner's vague, qualified distinctions help us choose between states A and B? Is Germany (which has a relatively large welfare state) less "prosperous" than the United States? Who determines what constitutes prosperity? Judge Posner? The "productive people"? The poor? These questions illustrate that Posner must provide a theoretical foundation to buttress his pragmatist account.

The foundation is revealed in Posner's *Overcoming Law*,[119] which he calls the "fullest articulation to date" of his "overall theoretical stance."[120] The three pillars of this stance are pragmatism, neoclassical economics, and liberalism: "[A] taste for fact, a respect for social science, an eclectic curiosity, a desire to be practical, a belief in individualism, and an openness to new perspectives . . . —all interrelated with *a certain kind* of *pragmatism*, alternatively of a certain kind of *economics* and a certain kind of *liberalism* —can make legal theory an effective instrument for understanding and improving law."[121] The key to Posner's "theoretical stance" is equating pragmatism with *neoclassical* economics and *classical* liberalism. In fact, the circularity of his arguments makes one wonder whether classical liberalism is indeed doing the heavy lifting, with neoclassical economics acting as a surrogate and pragmatism put forward as a philosophical (or antiphilosophical) antidote.

It is the type of justification required in an intellectual environment where "doubts about the pragmatic worth of philosophy even touch analytic philosophy":[122] "The pragmatist thinks the analytic philosopher . . . too prone to equate disagreement with error by exaggerating the domain of logic and thus prematurely opposing views. . . . Logical positivists believe that all propositions can be sorted into three bins: tautological, empirically verifiable, and nonsensical. Pragmatists think this is too simple an epistemology, because it leaves no room for nontautological propositions that can be neither verified nor disbelieved."[123] The "*real* antithesis to pragmatism is the kind of rationalism, fairly termed Platonic, that claims to use purely analytic methods to reason to the truth about contested metaphysical and ethical claims."[124] This rejection of *analytic* science could mean the death of law and neoclassical economics

As in *The Problems of Jurisprudence*, Posner recognized his dilemma in rescuing law and neoclassical economics as a viable enterprise: "[w]hen a pragmatic approach is taken to law . . . the results are damaging to the *amour propre* of the legal profession. . . . A certain [(neoclassical)] conception of economics withers as well. But the enterprise of 'law and economics' does not . . . because it epitomizes the operation in law of the ethic of scientific inquiry, pragmatically understood."[125] But despite the virtue of being an "instrumental science par excellence," law and neoclassical economics has "normative as well as positive baggage, such as efficiency and wealth maximization."[126] Thus the mere equation of neoclassical economics with pragmatism—particularly in light of criticisms from adherents of law and distribution economics—does not get Posner very far. Enter classical liberalism.

Posner articulates his most powerful and forthright vision of the politics underlying law and neoclassical economics: "At some point even one strongly committed to the economic approach to law will have to take a stand on issues of political and moral philosophy. I take my stand with the John Stuart Mill of *On Liberty* (1859), the classic statement of classical liberalism. *On Liberty* argues that every person is entitled to the maximum liberty—both personal and economic—consistent with liberty of every other person in the society."[127] Of course it is noteworthy that Posner does not rely upon the John Stuart Mill of *Utilitarianism*, the Mill that inspires the adherents of law and distribution. Posner's political "stand" is the linchpin in his argument for the supremacy of law and neoclassical economics over law and distribution economics. There is a symbiosis between liberty and neoclassical economics: "Liberalism also has an intimate *practical* relation to economics. Competitive markets, being arenas of self-regarding behavior, are in classical liberal theory off limits to government interference."[128]

Is Posner's a foundational case for liberalism and thus one in violation of his own pragmatist stance? Not for Posner. In a manner again reminiscent of Hayek, he argues for liberalism on historical (empirical and pragmatic) grounds: "[t]he history of the twentieth century is rich with evidence that communal alternatives to liberalism, whether *fascistic* or *socialistic*, are monstrous, nonviable, or both."[129] But history does not end the debate between law and neoclassical economics and law and distribution economics, because the "history lesson is also blurred by the fact that modern 'liberal' states are suffused with socialist elements."[130] Ultimately Posner cannot stake out either a pragmatic or an analytic claim for the supremacy of law and neoclassical economics over law and distribution economics, or other disciplines for that matter. This is why we must in the end reconcile ourselves to its dissolution—left with the "fundamental values of our political culture."[131] Faced with the specter of dissolution through politics, can we find sufficient *analytic* resilience in the neoclassical paradigm to constitute a resolution?

Steven Shavell put forth an ingenious attempt at a resolution. Although ensconced inside both the law school and economics department of Harvard University since 1980, he was formally trained as an economist and began his career in 1974 in the economics department.[132] Significantly, in light of the heated debates of 1980, his endeavor at resolution would begin in 1981, soon after his appointment to the law school. Shavell sought to resolve the debate over efficiency and distribution not by declaring distributional agnosticism but by placing distributional concerns in their proper institutional forum. Specifically distributional concerns should be dealt with through the income tax system, leaving efficiency as the principal concern of the common law legal system—much as Posner would have it. The institutional division of goals proposed by Shavell constitutes a resolution because it presents an analytic, as opposed to Posner's pragmatist, defense that leaves the law and neoclassical economics enterprise intact while responding to the equity concerns raised by law and distribution economics. While Shavell approached the subject with an impressive degree of technical acumen and focus, the basic stance that distributional issues should be consigned to the taxation and spending policies of central government has become the standard position in law and neoclassical economics texts.[133]

Shavell's central insight in "A Note on Efficiency vs. Distributional Equity in Legal Rulemaking: Should Distributional Equity Matter Given Optimal Income Taxation"?[134] is that "an attempt at redistribution through the choice over legal rules would involve the same sort of [disincentive] problem as exists under the income tax."[135] That is, although redistribution effected by the income tax system creates disincentive problems, turning to the legal system only exacerbates them. Shavell's original contribution is his proof that if we replace an inefficient liability rule (because of distributional considerations) with an efficient one and appropriately modify the income tax schedule, "everyone can be made strictly better off."[136] Thence there is *never* an occasion to favor inefficient liability rules to address distributional concerns. Efficiency reigns.

The results of the proof are tempered by the "qualification" that "if the income tax would not be altered on adoption of new liability rules, then in strict *logic* [(analytic)] the argument given for use of efficient rules does not apply."[137] Distribution agnosticism is an untenable position post law and distribution economics. However, Shavell seemed to have solved the distribution problem with his argument for redistribution through income taxation. Legal academics dealing with common law rules need not concern themselves.

Teaming up with Louis Kaplow, Shavell presented his thesis to legal academe some thirteen years later in "Why the Legal System Is Less Efficient Than the Income Tax in Redistributing Income."[138] In the article Kaplow and Shavell lament, "[i]t does not appear . . . that the point [from "Efficiency vs. Distribution"] is understood in legal academia."[139] In particular, Guido Calabresi and Duncan Kennedy (the law and distribution camp) misunderstood the point.[140] Kaplow and Shavell reiterate the theoretical insight that "using legal rules to redistribute income distorts work incentives fully as much as the income tax system," producing a double distortion effect because doing so "creates inefficiencies in the activities regulated by the legal rules."[141] To bring the message to the masses (legal academia), Kaplow and Shavell do an "informal demonstration" of the "Efficiency vs. Distribution" model.

The demonstration pays considerable attention to institutional dynamics, recognizing that an adequate response to distributional concerns raised by shifting to efficient legal rules requires a functioning "democracy." The "qualification" to the theory pushes us back to politics, an area that Kaplow and Shavell "do not seek to address." They in effect substitute political agnosticism for distribution agnosticism: "[c]ombined with [the] article's efficiency argument, [this] suggest[s] that normative economic analysis of legal rules should be primarily concerned with efficiency rather than the distribution of income."[142]

Kaplow and Shavell have extended their position in *Fairness versus Welfare*, in which they argue for "welfare economics" rather than "fairness" as the criterion for legal theory. Their argument is centered on the supremacy of welfare economics, defined as a mode of analysis that "depends solely on individuals' well-being."[143] They specifically disavow wealth maximization and efficiency as norms, claiming that both have been associated with economic analysis because of popular misconception.[144]

In a short subsection describing the role of distribution concerns in welfare economics, Kaplow and Shavell make a statement that parallels the law and distribution view: "redistributing income from the rich to the poor will tend to raise social welfare."[145] This is precisely the point made by Baker. They thus go beyond pushing distributional considerations to the realm of the "democratic process" to recognize that redistribution may be required as part of the politics of law and economics. However, Kaplow and Shavell again point to the tax system rather than legal rules as the basic tool for fashioning desired redistribution.

Kaplow's and Shavell's attempt at a resolution illustrates that adherents of law and neoclassical economics can no longer ignore distributional considerations. Yet Kaplow and Shavell attempt to privilege law and neoclassical economics over other interdisciplinary approaches that have fairness as their justification. The most intriguing aspect of their argument is that it explicitly takes into account the macroeconomic picture, by acknowledging the role of central government and looking to the tax system as a means to redistribute wealth. Historically, legal-economic theorists had limited their consideration of the effects of legal rules to the microeconomic sphere. The broader picture of the economy was taken as given, without any necessary relevance to how we might consider choosing among legal policy options. During the classical period the hold of laissez-faire ideology was so strong that there was a presumed requirement for any legal rule to comport with it. There was no need to consider the distributive consequences of legal rules because the distribution of wealth was part of the natural order of things. This held true both on the macroeconomic level (where the idea of taxation for redistributive purposes was unheard of) and at the level of legal-economic theory.

Even the dissenting voices of the legal realists failed to make any links to macroeconomic policy. Why? Again, despite their progressive leanings, they were not equipped with a theoretical argument to counter classical orthodoxy. While institutionalist economists expressed progressive sentiments and did have an effect on issues such as labor policy, particularly workers' compensation, they had little to say regarding macroeconomic policy. Moreover, what institutionalists did have to say could easily be dismissed by classical adherents as displaying theoretical naïveté.

The definitive theoretical argument against laissez-faire would have to wait for the advent of Keynesian economics. This was a welcomed event among institutionalists, who supported Keynes's conclusion that government intervention could benefit the economy and believed that their instinct toward focusing on institutions as the principal focus of analysis was buttressed by his approach, which was infused with qualitative insights (despite Keynes's significant mathematical prowess and the analytical elegance of his theory).[146]

John Maynard Keynes is generally considered the most influential economist of the twentieth century. He began writing seriously on the topic of macroeconomic theory in *A Treatise on Money*, published in 1930. However, it was the publication in 1937 of *The General Theory of Employment, Interest, and Money* that would truly revolutionize economic thinking. Postwar macroeconomic thought was dominated by Keynesian economics, making the insurgence of neoclassical theorists such as Hayek, Robbins, Knight, and Coase all the more impressive. Hayek's *The Road to Serfdom*, as well as his more technical writings, may be viewed as written in an effort to stem the Keynesian tide.

The technical details of Keynes's argument in *The General Theory* are rather obtuse and not germane in an account of legal-economic thought. However, the basic policy thrust of *The General Theory* is highly relevant. Keynes argued that under certain conditions (when unemployment or underinvestment prevailed) government intervention (particularly in the form of deficit spending) was the preferred policy prescription, notwithstanding the bias against government intervention in classical doctrine. While Keynes's principal target was the ills of unemployment and inadequate investment, he was also concerned with what he perceived to be the maldistribution of wealth.

Keynes set forth the political position that would underpin his theoretical oeuvre in his essay *The End of Laissez-Faire* (1926).[147] As the title suggests, Keynes took issue with the individualism and laissez-faire economic doctrine that had ruled economic and philosophical thought since the writings of Adam Smith. Keynes saw Smith's vision as crystallized in the argument by economists that "by the working of natural laws individuals pursuing their own interests with enlightenment in conditions of freedom always tend to promote the general interests at the same time!" He cited Smith as the major proponent of the proposition and credits him with having provided the "scientific proof" of its validity.[148] Smith's analytical argument was combined with general political and philosophical leanings to form a powerful consensus against government intervention in the marketplace. This was so even though many economists described as laissez-faire adherents, such as Alfred Marshall, did recognize instances when there was room for government intervention.[149]

The principal area where economists agreed that government intervention was called for was that in which private and social costs diverged. Pigou is an excellent exemplar of the consensus position. As discussed earlier, he favored government intervention in cases where polluters did not fully internalize the costs of their operations—microeconomic intervention. On the other hand, though a mentor of Keynes early on and generally sympathetic toward redistributionist policies, Pigou adamantly believed that the market would solve the unemployment problem without government interference—macroeconomic intervention.[150]

For the most part, in accord with Lionel Robbins's dictates for an "economic science," economists did not favor government intervention to remedy the inequitable distribution of wealth. According to Keynes, "they have begun by assuming a state of affairs where the ideal distribution of productive resources can be brought about through individuals acting independently by the method of trial and error."[151] Keynes introduced an amusing way to view the issue, analogizing the wealthy to long-necked giraffes that have an evolutionary advantage and thus "overfeed" while poor, short-necked giraffes suffer from malnutrition.[152] The question that Keynes posed was whether this outcome was fair if we are equally concerned about all giraffes.

Keynes's solution to the problem was not Marxian socialism, which he viewed as scientifically discredited, but sufficient government intervention in capitalist economies to save capitalism from itself. In this way, Keynes can be described as a "conservative" reformer.[153] He can be described as a technical reformer as well, distinguishing "those services which are *technically social* from those which are *technically individual*."[154] As social problems to be tackled he listed inequalities of wealth, unemployment, and the uncertainties of business decision making. He would take up these problems, particularly unemployment, in *The General Theory*.

The basic argument in *The General Theory* is that the free market will not necessarily act as a self-correcting system in times of unemployment. The classical view, championed by Smith and later others, was that in times of unemployment wages would decline and the unemployed would be hired at these reduced wages. Keynes leveled a series of technical criticisms at this and other assumptions of classical economics that underlay the philosophical critique in *The End of Laissez-Faire*. While many of these technical arguments had been in circulation before 1937, it was Keynes's synthesis and rhetorical flourish that brought the argument into full intellectual relief.[155] Keynesian economics also came about at precisely the time when economic depression and chronic unemployment had so mired the American economy that classical theory defied economic reality. Many policy makers were of the opinion that "something" (in the form of government intervention) had to be done to save capitalism from itself, and Keynes provided the theoretical justification for why it needed to be done.[156] This sentiment later developed into the Keynesian consensus that dominated macroeconomic thinking from the 1930s through the 1960s, when neoclassical economic theory began to reassert itself.

Even with the rise of neoclassical thought, which dovetailed with the law and neoclassical economics movement in legal-economic theory, the level of government intervention in the economy is now significantly greater than it was pre-Keynes. We see this pragmatic reality reflected in Posner's acquiescence that even the democratic societies he so admires have deviated from the stark precepts of laissez-faire ideology, and have a level of state intervention in the marketplace that Posner is hesitant to deviate from (because it seems to work). Posner in effect is making a broader argument that reflects the narrower point regarding taxation put forward by Kaplow and Shavell. A redistributive taxation scheme is part of the post-Keynes general political-economic backdrop. Kaplow's and Shavell's point on this matter is indisputable.

The politics of this post-Keynesian synthesis is decidedly centrist. Indeed, it very much reflects the political sentiment of its original author, Keynes. While Keynes railed against the dominance of free-market ideology in *The End of Laissez-Faire*, he was very much a moderate. This much is evident in *The General Theory*. In the final chapter, entitled "Concluding Notes on the Social Philosophy towards Which the General Theory Might Lead," Keynes notes the progressive implications of his theory but also recognizes that "in some other respects the foregoing theory is moderately conservative in its implications."[157] Keynes believed that the level of government intervention suggested in *The General Theory*, including policies directed at the redistribution of wealth, could "be introduced without a break in the traditions of society."[158] The "traditional advantages of individualism," including "efficiency" and "personal liberty," must be nurtured, lest we deteriorate into some form of a "totalitarian state."[159] Keynes, the liberal, was just as much concerned as his intellectual foe, Friedrich Hayek, the conservative, about the specter of communism. He therefore believed in a level of redistribution sufficient to remedy the "arbitrary and inequitable distribution of wealth and income" but no more, since there is "social and psychological justification for significant inequalities of wealth."[160] This very much sums up the postwar political consensus.

The question for legal-economic theorists is whether distributive considerations should be taken into account in legal policy as well as the macroeconomic structure. Kaplow and Shavell attempt to elide this issue by placing taxation policy under the rubric of "welfare economics" and in effect grafting it on to legal-economic theory.[161] The response of law and distribution economics to this proposed grafting of common law rules and taxation policy came in the form of Duncan Kennedy's "Law and Economics from the Perspective of Critical Legal Studies."[162] The explicit purpose of the essay was to put forward the critical legal studies (law and distribution economics) critique of the standard solution (taxation) to the distribution problem.

This critique can be viewed as a leftist intervention. The Keynesian position fit nicely with the moderately conservative to moderately liberal politics of mainstream legal-economic thought as represented initially by Posner and Calabresi. While Calabresi, given his liberal leanings, always had some predisposition toward redistribution, it was not of the "free-wheeling" sort championed under the umbrella of CLS. Thus although Keynesian economics can be viewed as opening up mainstream intellectual space for a discourse on the redistribution of wealth, the CLS intervention suggests a level of redistribution beyond the Keynesian consensus. Though any sort of labeling does not readily capture the CLS position, it may be summarized as "realist socialism" in some respects.

Part of Kennedy's critique was based on the indeterminacy of efficiency rules, an argument that can be traced back to "Are Property and Contract Efficient?" Kennedy combines this "technical" argument with a number of "practical" observations that call into question the proposed resolution by Kaplow and Shavell. First, it seems highly implausible that the legislative body would keep track of, and base taxation policy on, common law decision making. Second, in the "real world" courts do not act solely upon efficiency-based considerations but do indeed take into account what Shavell and Kaplow define as "fairness" (rights, morality, the "public interest," and so on). Of course Shavell and Kaplow would simply reply that the courts are misguided, but the reality of praxis cannot be assumed away. Finally, judges are political—law is politics. They construct legal rules to adhere to their personal distributive preferences (liberal judges favoring redistribution from the wealthy to the poor and conservative jurists favoring redistribution to the wealthy, whom they consider the most productive members of society).[163] This does not mean that judges are unrestrained in what they do. Precedent, institutional limitations, the prevailing ideological climate, and a host of other restraints are ever-present. This is why there is some level of predictability in law.

Kennedy argued that the free market, regulatory structure, and tax system are all interdependent parts of the economic order. Therefore the neoclassical position (attempting to carve out space for the common law in the realm of the free market) is implausible.[164] Citing Baker's article "Starting Points in Economics of Law," Kennedy states that it is inevitable for us to "rely on rights, morality, the public interest, in short on politics, philosophy and ideology" to frame legal-economic theory. Yet there is still room for legal-economic theorists to do efficiency analysis.[165] The difference is that unlike in the proposal put forward by Kaplow and Shavell, efficiency has to take its place alongside the plurality of other visions of legal theory. Kennedy explicitly attempts to open up intellectual space not only for his leftist vision of large-scale redistribution of wealth but for rightist arguments in favor of further concentration of wealth. These possibilities are set off against the moderate, mainstream of legal academe, which he describes as a constellation of "liberals and conservatives" who support a program based on "moderation, statism, and rationalism."[166] The locus of moderate policy tradeoffs between efficiency and equity is the "central government, which alone can regulate the whole economy to counteract market failures, and which alone can devise tax and transfer (statism)."[167] This is a perfect synopsis of the Keynesian synthesis (although Kennedy makes no reference to Keynes), which though it may not have held up in terms of Keynes's technical arguments is still the dominant political location in American politics. In this light, CLS goes beyond a critique of law and neoclassical economics as the dominant stream of legal-economic thought. It is exemplary of our times, in which scientism is in decline, to borrow Kennedy's formulation: "[There is a] general cultural conflict between advocates of hard methods, and soft methods. The crits have seen hard methods, in technical legal analysis as well as in economic analysis of law, not as bad in themselves, but as a vehicle for technocratic imperialism, at the expense of participatory modes of decision making. It is not that hard methods fall to a global critique that simply invalidates them. It is rather that case by case internal critique can often show that their pretensions and their prestige are unwarranted. This seemed clearly to be the case for the [neoclassical] economic analysis of law."[168]

Yes. Law and neoclassical economics' ascendancy, on the wings of claims to scientific status, foreshadowed the resurgent intellectual ferment in the legal academy. Its dissolution took place at an intellectual moment, as illustrated in Posner's recent pragmatist turn, which marks the waning of scientism. With this dissolution and the move toward *instrumental* science, if the debate within contemporary legal-economic theory (law and neoclassical economics versus law and distribution economics) is illustrative, we may find a more forthright discussion of politics throughout legal academe. The implication is that the "technocratic imperialism" that has marked legal-economic theory will be replaced by a pluralistic vision that favors "participatory modes" of intellectual discourse. If this is the case, then legal-economic theory will indeed take its place with the rest of the legal academy in reconciling itself to a moment of what Guido Calabresi described as "middle theorizing."

GAZING INTO THE FUTURE AND OUR POSTMODERN TIMES

■ To this point the discussion has been focused on the trajectory of legal-economic theory. I would now like to broaden the scope and muse upon what the history and current resting place of legal-economic theory may tell us about the future of legal theory generally. But first we must begin by filling in the story of our postmodern situation.

Throughout the development of physics scientists have been able to accomplish Herculean technological tasks, such as constructing "smart" bombs and inventing hand-held computers. However, physicists have not been able to discover the ultimate truth about the universe. There are some who believe we have reached the limits of human knowledge regarding the structure of the universe. That belief has led to the inevitable declaration, "The End of Science." Of course, in recent times there has been a virtual cottage industry in "End of . . ." predictions: "The End of History," "The End of Progress," "The End of Science." With regard to science, and other fields of endeavor as well, from the vantage point of the philosophy of science it is more appropriate to think of the current phase of history as marking the intense questioning of a particular type of scientific quest—the search for *the Truth* (a universal Truth that has application irrespective of time or location, in contrast to a pragmatist notion of "truth" that is contingent and particular). The quest for Truth animated the scientific revolution in the seventeenth century and the ideology of scientism that has consumed western intellectual thought on a number of levels—including legal-economic theory.

The noted physicist David Bohm has championed a fundamental

reconsideration of how we think about science. Bohm argues that the mechanistic view, our Newtonian and Cartesian legacy, still dominates scientific thinking. However, given that the basic assumption behind this view—that appearance reflects reality—is false, we are in effect tilting at windmills. At a minimum, physicists are beginning to question the quest for certainty. Another prominent physicist, Steven Weinberg, has stated that "[a] lot of philosophy of science going back to the Greeks has been poisoned by the quest for certainty, which seems to me a false search."[1]

Bohm has argued that science is an inexhaustible enterprise in which once we determine what seems to be an appearance of reality, we then move to a different level of perception and appearance—reality shifts. The leap from a Newtonian perspective to theories of relativity to a quantum view is a perfect example of this phenomenon. Bohm believes that we would be well served if we thought in terms of merging art and science: "This division of art and science is temporary. . . . It didn't exist in the past, and there's no reason why it should go on in the future." The idea is that just as art has as its essence an attempt to deal with perception, so does science.[2]

John Horgan's popular *The End of Science: Facing the Limits of Knowledge in the Twilight of the Scientific Age* has asked whether "science" has reached its limits and discovered that the holy grail of science, "the answer," is out of its reach.[3] The answer is the ever-elusive theory that provides the solution to the mysteries of existence: the theory that Einstein searched for in vain. It would be the ultimate theory of scientific Truth. Much of theoretical physics (under the rubric of theories with such exotic names as superstring theory, M-theory, grand unified theory, and quantum cosmology) in the last few decades has been devoted to developing the sort of "theory of everything" that captured Einstein's imagination.

Commenting on Horgan's thesis in *The End of Science*, two prominent physicists, R. B. Laughlin and David Pines, have quipped that the book might more aptly be entitled "The End of Reductionism." They describe reductionism, echoing Weinberg, as the "ideal of the ancient Greeks, an approach to the natural world that has been fabulously successful in bettering the lot of mankind and continues in many people's minds to be the central paradigm of physics."[4] It was Descartes who laid out the modern philosophical statement for reductionism. Laughlin and Pines argue that certain physical phenomena are not susceptible to reductionist accounts.[5] To their minds, "in most respects the reductionist ideal has reached its limits as a guiding principle. Rather than a Theory of Everything we appear to face a hierarchy of Theories of Things."[6] They propose that we are not seeing the end of science or even the end of theoretical physics but that more emphasis should be placed on experimentalism. This suggestion seems in many ways to be a call to revive the type of scientific quest implicit in Bacon's methodological musings. The tension regarding what it means to do "science," which was initially highlighted in Descartes's and Bacon's philosophical formulations of modern science, continues. However, the state of physics has raised a more fundamental question highlighted by Laughlin, Pines, Horgan, Weinberg, and Bohm: "What is knowable in the deepest sense of the term"?[7]

Posing this question does not amount to adopting some fanciful post-modern notion that there are no scientific truths. Newton's theory of gravitation, in its limited application, is right. As Sheldon Glashow has aptly put it, Newton's laws are "fine for predicting the trajectories of ICBMS or the times of eclipses."[8] Quantum mechanics works. It is partly responsible for such technological innovations as television, lasers, computers, and electron microscopes.[9] Francis Bacon would be pleased. Nonetheless, a heavy blow has been dealt to the ideology of scientism. Richard Feynman, winner of the Nobel Prize in physics, bemoaned that the fundamental rules governing the physical world had been revealed to us, yet "the Answer" remained elusive. He feared that science would no longer be able to stave off the incursions of philosophers.[10] However, the end of scientism has come from within. Without reconciling ourselves to some form of relativism, how do we cope with the possibility of multiple versions of truth? One solution is perspectivism.

The most popular harbinger of perspectivism in philosophy is Richard Rorty, who in *Philosophy and the Mirror of Nature* critiques the Kantian philosophical tradition.[11] He describes this as the tradition obsessed with constructing a totalizing theory of knowledge so as to bring all of human inquiry under the umbrella of science (scientism). At no time was this quest more evident than when logical positivists sought to construct a philosophy that would "unify" the sciences, the philosophical version of a theory of everything. Rorty chronicles the collapse of this effort, with a particular focus on Quine and Sellars, and what he takes to be the "end" of the philosophical project. His critique is particularly telling because he at one time was well ensconced as a member of the analytic movement.

Rorty is faced with the same dilemma that plagues any proponent of an "end of" thesis. Where do we go from here? We can take his effort as an example of one philosophical approach to the question. A problem with trying to construct a synopsis of Rorty's position is that he has published widely, and his position has not necessarily been consistent. I will focus my attention on *Philosophy and the Mirror of Nature*, one of his most important and influential works. In it Rorty suggests that the future of philosophy is in "hermeneutics." He is not putting forward hermeneutics as another form of epistemology, but as "an expression of hope that the cultural space left by the demise of epistemology will not be filled."[12] Rorty's hermeneutics would eviscerate the modernist requirement of a common, commensurable language. Instead we would be left to encounter a multiplicity of languages that we do not attempt to translate but with which we engage in dialogue. Rorty's critique of commensurability borrows heavily from Thomas Kuhn's *The Structure of Scientific Revolutions*.

Rorty views the concept of rationality as being culturally contingent. However, he is still fond of what he refers to as our Enlightenment inheritance. The hermeneutics that he proposes, under the rubric of "edification," is described as a commitment to finding "new, better, more interesting, more fruitful ways of speaking."[13] These ways of speaking may come from multiple perspectives, including "poetic" activity. Harkening back to William James, Rorty holds on to the concept of "objectivity," defined as "conformity to the norms of justification (for assertions and for actions) we find about us."[14]

While Rorty's vision of hermeneutics may seem far afield from science debates, there are some parallels between his vision and what scientists have been forced to do as scientists in the post-quantum era. Just as the science debates have not cut off, without consideration, what might be thought of as "abnormal" inquiry (the theory of a ten-dimensional universe in string theory, for example), Rorty would not have our general quest for knowledge be limited to the "normal" (that which conforms to the norms around us).[15] Let us keep the conversation going.

The perspectivist turn in philosophy has made itself manifest in the debates over the end of science. Ian Hacking, in his presentation to the 25th

Nobel Conference, entitled "The End of Science? Attack and Defense," offered an intriguing answer to the question "Where do we go from here?" Hacking, in his essay "Disunified Science," begins by making it clear that he is not a skeptic when it comes to science and is dismissive of what he refers to as the "rage against reason." However, he does share the skeptical desire to "prune" the ideology of scientism. 6 For Hacking, scientism revolves around assertions that there is "one ultimate reality, one ultimate truth, one road to the truth (the scientific method), one sound mode of reasoning, [and] one national way of speaking."[17] Hacking believes that this ideology has come under legitimate critique as far back as initial criticisms of Bacon and Galileo. However, he refuses to accept that scientific discovery is not an objective enterprise or that we have reached the end of science. He takes as a prescient fact, though it is obviously disputable, that science is almost universally accepted as a good thing.[18] To hearken back to Rorty, science is a part of our Enlightenment inheritance that we might want to keep around. The problem is to dethrone it from the all-encompassing position it has assumed since Bacon and Descartes.

Hacking argues that the real problem is not science but the hold that the concept of "unity" has on the western mind. The West has been obsessed with the notion that there is a singular *Answer* or *Truth*. Hacking proposes that we substitute this concept of "singleness" with one of "harmonious integration."[19] The alternative vision of harmonious integration, which is analogous to Rorty's concept of conversation, has concrete implications. For example, Hacking describes the biology department at the University of California, Berkeley, which at the time was divided into six divisions as opposed to being placed under a single umbrella. The need to have a disunified science is manifest because there is no common scientific language —apparently not even within biology. Hacking extends his thesis even further to argue that there is no common method in science. Quoting A. C. Crombie on the different styles of scientific reasoning in the European tradition, Hacking lists six: (1) mathematical or axiomatic reasoning; (2) experimental reasoning; (3) hypothetical modeling; (4) ordering by comparison and taxonomy; (5) statistical analysis of populations; and (6) historical derivation of genetic development.[20] Of course this disunity in scientific method was evident at the conception of modern science and in the methodological divide between Bacon and Descartes. Perhaps the idea of unification was always a myth.

Given the plurality of voices in science, there must be some way of bridging the divide between enterprises that have the family resemblance of being a science. For bridging Hacking introduces the concept of "unifiers" ("tools, practices and bodies of knowledge that span science").[21] One example of a unifier is mathematics, a "language" that spans a variety of scientific disciplines. Hacking also cites computation and even scientific instruments as scientific unifiers. He is admittedly tentative in his discussion of unifiers, but he does present an interesting conception of how competing theories might hang together in some sort of stable relationship: "Stability results from a sort of self-authentication resulting from the mutual adjustment of theory, apparatus, data and much more. We get stability across radical change partly because a great many lesser scientific revolutions do not result in discarding a body of knowledge but in supplementing it with new kinds of instruments, creating a new category of data for which radically new theory is demanded. . . . Here we see a new use for Kuhn's idea of incommensurability."[22] Hacking gives an interesting example of the type of analysis suggested under his theory. One can look at a table as a solid mass of wood or as a collection of atoms with huge spaces between the particles, held together by electromagnetism and giving the appearance of being solid. How can this be, if there is only one table? Yes, but there are different perspectives from which to analyze that table. Our job is to connect these perspectives.

Hacking concludes by linking his view of a disunited science with general cultural movements. He recognizes that in our postmodern times there is increasing disunity in a variety of intellectual fields. Yet somehow there is a myth, dating back to the seventeenth century, that the sciences are unified. Those who resist the pull of disunity in an effort to prove the rightness of their position have too often held up this myth. This is a mistake. However, the position on the other side that given the disunity of science we can declare its end is also mistaken. Again, as discussed earlier, what it marks is the end of a conception of science as omnipotent and infallible. At the dawn of modernity Sir Isaac Newton had planted the cultural seed that *all* phenomena (both physical and social) were knowable in a reductionist sense. While the implications of Darwinism gave some pause, the history of science, particularly physics until the twentieth century, seemed to confirm the modernist quest. The current state of physics casts doubt on this quest.

Richard Bernstein in *Beyond Objectivism and Relativism: Science, Hermeneutics, and Praxis* puts forward the thesis that contemporary philosophy has settled at a position offering hermeneutics as an alternative to objectivism and relativism.[23] He defines objectivism as the belief that there is an ahistorical (or foundational) matrix upon which we can draw to measure truth claims.[24] Relativism, on the other hand, stands for the position that all truths are relative to cultural and temporal settings.[25] Bernstein argues that hermeneutics is prevalent in natural and social science philosophies as a mechanism for avoiding the dichotomy between objectivism and relativism. It has become a part of our cultural landscape much as formalism, pragmatism, and the analytic turn had done during prior historical epochs. This marker of our times may be cast under a number of rubrics: neopragmatism, postmodernism, hermeneutics, and so on.

Bernstein takes Richard Rorty, Hans-Georg Gadamer, Jürgen Habermas, and Hannah Arendt as exemplifying the hermeneutic turn. All four offer up some form of dialogic method as an antidote to what Bernstein refers to as our "Cartesian anxiety." The Cartesian anxiety is traced back to Descartes's *Meditations*, in which he set out the "*locus classicus* in modern philosophy for the metaphor for the 'foundation' and for the conviction that the philosopher's quest is to search for an Archimedean point upon which we can ground our knowledge."[25] All four philosophers reject this view and the ideology of scientism to which it led. A hermeneutic view resists the pull toward seeking a fixed Truth, acknowledging that in the world we inhabit there can be multiple perspectives on truth.

Of course this could be a recipe for a relativist quagmire, with warring sides positioned in opposition and no ultimate arbiter of truth. However, hermeneutics paves a different path. The process to truth is found in dialogue. For dialogue to take place, certain conditions must be met. There must be an ability to communicate under ground rules for persuasion. Rationality is not abandoned, but the idea that there is an a priori touchstone (or algorithm) to determine results is rejected. In its place there should be rational persuasion. Thus hermeneutics emphasizes the practical aspects of dialogue: evidence, data, reasons, and arguments.[27] Thomas Kuhn, in an essay following *The Structure of Scientific Revolutions*, suggested analogous criteria for guiding conversations regarding scientific validity: accuracy, consistency, scope, simplicity, and fruitfulness.[28] He also emphasized that deliberations best take place through the "collective judgment of scientists."[29] In order for deliberations to have any bearing, all participants must be open to the discovery process. This process includes entertaining different views regarding what it means to be rational.[30] Even in terms of process, the dialogic model is diametrically opposed to the Cartesian view. In a Cartesian world the lone thinker plays the role of "philosopher king," turning inward to uncover truth. By definition, the dialogic view posits a community of thinkers undertaking a mutually beneficial exchange. It is much the same as what Charles Sanders Peirce had envisioned.

This does not mean that there will always be consensus, or that one must abandon one's views to engage in the process.[31] Yet it is essential to recognize one's preconceptions and prejudices when engaging in the conversation.[32] Such a recognition is a key to openness. While there is no resting point (the conversation is continuing), there is a point where action is taken given our best practical judgments at the time—as William James would have it.

What impact will the hermeneutic turn have on legal-economic theory? With the rise of law and distribution economics, I suppose that one might declare the "End of Law and Neoclassical Economics." However, as with physics, this would seem a bit premature, since from all indications law and neoclassical economics continues to hold a central place in American legal theory. The disunity revealed by the rise of law and distribution economics may be analogized to the disunity in biology highlighted by Hacking. Today methodological disunity is the rule, not the exception, in legal-economic theory. A leading introductory text for law and economics courses, Avery Katz's *Foundations of the Economic Approach to Law* (in addition to highlighting what amounts to the law and distribution brand of economic analysis), covers methodological approaches emphasizing strategic behavior, risk, information, and bounded rationality.[33] In addition, there is a notable movement to broaden the scope of legal-economic theory under the rubric of socioeconomics.

Socioeconomics was given its own section within the Association of American Law Schools (AALS) in 1996 in no small part as a reaction to law and neoclassical economics. It was preceded by the Society for the Advancement of Socio-Economics, which was founded in 1989. Socioeconomics is explicitly interdisciplinary. The founding document for the section declares that socioeconomics draws upon "economics, sociology, political science, psychology, anthropology, biology, and other social and natural sciences, philosophy, history, law, management and other disciplines."[34] Its methodological openness is evident in the position that it "respects both inductive and deductive reasoning."[35] While socioeconomics continues to lay claim to the mantle of science, it is openly declared to be a "positive and normative science" and explicitly rejects scientism— socioeconomics "seeks to be self-aware of its normative implications rather than maintaining the mantle of an exclusively positive science." It is explicitly "paradigm conscious," taking a page from Thomas Kuhn and acknowledging that values are implicit in paradigms.[36] There is also a degree of disciplinary openness in socioeconomics that seems well suited to hermeneutical dialogue: "socio-economics does not entail a commitment to any one paradigm or ideological position, but is *open* to a range of thinking."[37]

This openness is tied to paradigm consciousness because such consciousness allows participants in a dialogue to recognize their own prejudices in a way that Richard Bernstein emphasized. A founder of socioeconomics, Robert Ashford, has written that "the socioeconomic approach provides an inclusive, intellectual foundation on which a diverse array of disciplines, and schools of thought within disciplines, can contribute to understanding, and on which a broad spectrum of people can beneficially participate with mutual respect for their disparate methodologies."[38] However, there are "rules of the road": "[Socioeconomics'] paradigm neutrality reflects a willingness to examine conflicting paradigms from a mutually agreed frame of reference, such as the extent to which particular paradigms are (1) based on reasonable, workable, testable assumptions; (2) internally consistent; and (3) useful in describing past events and predicting and influencing future events."[39] Socioeconomics fits well within the neopragmatist schema. In an address entitled "Toward a New Pragmatism" to the Socio-Economics Section of AALS in 1993, James Kenneth Galbraith declared that in the view of socioeconomists social problems are "not to be solved by a great mind working alone" but "developed in conversation and correspondence, in discussion and debate." He identified this view of knowledge production as synonymous with American pragmatism.[40] Substantively, regarding what I have described as the central issue in legal-economic thought, economic distribution, Ashford sees it as "implicit in the socio-economic approach . . . that the distribution of wealth, opportunities, and risk can matter significantly both normatively and positively."[41] Thus socioeconomics incorporates the basic tenets of law and distribution economics.

The socioeconomics movement reflects a larger trend of proliferating economic perspectives. This phenomenon has been well chronicled in Nicholas Mercuro's and Steven Medema's *Economics and the Law: From Posner to Post-Modernism.* Mercuro and Medema have identified several schools of thought that are either subsumed under law and economics or have some implications for the field: the Chicago school, the New Haven school, public choice theory, neo-institutional economics, and critical legal studies.[42] Law and economics specialties include behavioral economics, feminist theory as it relates to economic analysis, humanitarian approaches to economics, economics and psychiatry, and a critical race theory approach to economic issues.[43] Each of these approaches critiques and builds on the market assumptions of neoclassical economics.

Today it is almost a necessity for any top-flight law school to have at least some faculty conversant in law and economics (broadly defined), and in good part it is difficult to teach even the most basic of law school subjects without some rudimentary knowledge of legal-economic theory. However, there is no longer the viable claim to the epistemological superiority of law and neoclassical economics that marked Posner's earlier pronouncements. The hegemony of legal-economic thought has come to an end, and the field is also more diverse internally.

What does this portend for legal theory generally? Stephen Feldman has noted a significant feature of recent trends in legal theory: unlike in earlier times, theorists have "failed to agree widely on the worth of any overarching jurisprudential approach."[44] The result has been the "diverse and uncertain attitudes that currently prevail in the legal academy."[45] As discussed earlier, Richard Posner has come to realize that in our postmodern times there can no longer be any a priori claim to Truth. In *Overcoming Law* he concedes that since "all perspectives are . . . partial," he is obligated to recognize the contemporary perspectivism in American legal theory.[46] Covering the terrain of legal theory, Posner manages to have something to say about such divergent fields as law and neoclassical economics, feminist theory, law and literature, critical race theory, and "left-wing" (CLS) legal history. It is revealing that he sees the need to at least address the proliferation of ideas in postmodern American legal theory.

We can take as an example of his project Posner's discussion of critical race theory. It would be hard to imagine a legal theory farther removed from Posner's brand of legal-economic theory and more alien to the ideology of scientism. Derrick Bell, an African American law professor with a civil rights background, pioneered critical race theory. There are historical connections to critical legal studies, but critical race theory emphasizes different themes. It takes as its central proposition the importance of race in American law. However, there are no a priori rules grounding deductive analysis and no requirement that analysis be done by induction of any particular sort. Indeed, one of the prominent methods in critical race scholarship is storytelling.

Posner's point of departure is *The Alchemy of Race and Rights*[47] by Patricia Williams, a prominent critical race scholar and a leading exponent of the storytelling genre. Posner describes the book as taking a "black feminist perspective" in an effort to critique "law's pretense to objectivity and impersonality."[48] He identifies Williams's storytelling method as a novel form, but notes that she is not alone in American legal theory in her use of literary methods. The subtitle, "Diary of a Law Professor," reveals Williams's purpose as chronicling the law and society through her gaze. At points, Posner praises Williams, citing her "powerful gift for narration" and comparing her favorably to Tom Wolfe.[49] However, Posner is also very critical.

The criticism has as its foundation certain assumptions about the nature of legal reasoning even in the postmodern era. Posner is particularly taken aback at what he sees as Williams's failure to deal with facts. This first instance arises in Williams's description of a young white store clerk in New York City who refuses her entry, ostensibly because the store is closed. In her narrative Williams assumes that the store was open, since it was one o'clock in the afternoon on a weekend before Christmas. Posner asks: Was the store in fact closed? He is critical that apparently "she [Williams]—a lawyer—did not attempt to verify the point."[50]

Posner notes that by her own account Williams is using the storytelling genre in "reconceptualizing from 'objective truth' to rhetorical event" to provide a "more nuanced sense of legal and social responsibility." However, since Williams is doing legal theory, Posner will hold her to what he views as the proper ground rules to engage the conversation and admonishes her to find out "what *really* was going on in that white teenager's mind when he told her the store was closed."[51] What of Posner's pragmatism? He responds, "Pragmatists may be dubious about truth with a capital T, but they respect those lowercase truths that we call facts."[52]

Posner takes up several examples where he believes that Williams has failed to meet the standard of factual truth. Again Williams, I suppose unlike Tom Wolfe, is a "lawyer and an academic" and must play by the "rules of the scholarly game."[53] Here Posner has assumed the position of high priest of legal reasoning. Pierre Schlag, in his provocative text *The Enchantment of Reason*, identifies a tension between legal reasoning as "central command" and legal reasoning as "big tent" that bedevils Posner.[54] All too often one resolves the tension, as Posner does, by forcing those under the tent to adhere to a certain definition of reason. However, to Posner's credit, he recognizes that his criticisms of Williams may "turn out to be one-sided, misleading, and tendentious." He understands his opinion as being "only one voice in an ongoing *conversation* and can leave it to others to rectify any omissions or imbalance in [his] contribution."[55] This call for a pluralist conversation is surprisingly similar to the type alluded to under the umbrella of cls by Duncan Kennedy.

Posner seems genuinely concerned when he directly addresses the substantive implications of doing narrative legal scholarship, as opposed to playing his game of factual "gotcha." He argues, "A more basic point is that the internal perspective—the putting oneself in the other person's shoes—that is achieved by the exercise of empathetic imagination lacks normative significance."[56] Here Posner is really attempting to engage Williams on her own terms. This does not necessarily mean that there will be agreement. He believes that viewing the world from the "internal perspective" can cloud judgment and is not necessarily edifying. Posner also faults Williams for lacking clarity. The argument is not that Williams has made factual misrepresentations, but that Posner honestly cannot understand what Williams means by certain statements. In a "big tent" regime where we take differing ideas seriously and are attempting to bridge the gaps between disparate approaches, this type of constructive criticism is necessary for genuine dialogue. Posner ends by recognizing that "the very one-sidedness of [Williams's] presentation, however questionable by the *conventional standards* of scholarship . . . has value in providing insight into the psychology and rhetoric of many blacks"[57]—nonscientific endeavors, including literary ones, do have the potential for contributing to our perception of the world.[58] In this light Posner seems to forthrightly be struggling with the problem of perspectivism in legal theory. However, in "overcoming law" Posner still values the "methods of science," even though he does not have any metaphysical "faith in the power of science . . . as the deliverer of final truths."[59] The evolution of Posner's views on science marks a telling moment in the intellectual history of American legal theory (not only legal-economic theory)—given his standing among legal theorists, his previous (and continued) association with the law and neoclassical economics movement, and his current position as a U.S. Circuit Court Judge. It may be a moment of hope.

Posner's position recalls Calabresi's concept of "middle theorizing." Both reflect the general rise of neopragmatism in American legal theory. Schlag identifies neopragmatist legal theorists who he argues represent a range of perspectives such as Margaret Jane Radin (politically progressive), Dan Farber (doctrinal instrumentalist), Joe Singer (Sartrean existentialist), and Posner. He accuses all these legal pragmatists, as well as others who fall into the category, of paying lip service to perspectivism, only to pull back once they reach the precipice. For Schlag, what makes this failure of conviction all the more disconcerting is that the result of legal pragmatism is a hodgepodge of policy prescriptions, ultimately (as illustrated by Posner) in the service of the theorist's initial leanings.[60] While linking pragmatist theory with any particular substantive point of view is problematic, and there is the danger that it might be called upon in the service of a "hidden agenda," the proliferation of perspectives that are generated seems fitting in our postmodern setting. If anything, the range of positions, when viewed from the outside (of legal theory) looking in, only highlights the disunity of legal theory. Perhaps there really is a "big tent."

Hacking's model of disunity may be the most apt for postmodern legal theory. The point was made earlier that leading American law schools now find it necessary to have scholars on the faculty who specialize in law and economics. Although the representation model certainly may not be fully manifest in practice, there does seem to be a tendency to at least entertain representation from other fields of legal theory.

The annual meeting of AALS provides an interesting peek at what can be referred to as "representational disunity." Each year the AALS officers choose a theme for a conference that hosts over a thousand law professors. For example, the theme for the January 2005 meeting was "Engaged Scholarship." The theme serves as a provisional unifier for the conference. However, if you asked most of the participants about the theme, they would look at you with puzzlement. The real energy of the meeting is in the sections, made up of professors who have some shared interest. Frequently the interest is substantive. For example, there are sections on torts and compensation, law and religion, maritime law, indigenous nations and peoples, and legal history—to name only a few. However, there are also sections centered on theoretical interests such as the previously discussed socioeconomics section, as well as sections devoted to social science, law and neoclassical economics (referred to as law and economics), and jurisprudence.

Except during plenary sessions, the meetings of the various sections convene during overlapping time periods, creating a chaotic sense of section members scurrying to their corners to caucus about their own little slice of the law or legal theory. However, while the sections centered on theory may not be particularly malleable with regard to varying perspectives, one does notice differing theoretical perspectives being highlighted from year to year in the substantive sections. Perhaps the shared interest in a substantive topic, tax law for example, works as a Hackian unifier. Therefore, the tax section might take a critical race theory perspective on tax policy in one year and employ empirical analysis in another. It is also common for panelists in any given session to approach a topic from divergent perspectives. Indeed, it seems to be an unwritten rule that there must be a mixed representation of views. It makes the panel more "interesting."

Representational disunity could reflect what legal theory may look like in our postmodern times—with no overarching theory dominating discourse or laying claim to Truth by dint of a superior method (such as science). This state of affairs will only come to pass if we heed the hermeneutic admonition to maintain a sense of openness and a willingness to keep the conversation going. There has to be true pluralism.

David Bohm, donning his hat as a social commentator rather than a theoretical physicist, has written an extensive treatise, *On Dialogue*, outlining a method of communication.[61] One of his key ideas is that dialogue cannot take place if one party tries to convince others of the Truth of his or her ideas. This sort of communication leads to an inability to listen and "blocks" dialogue. Bohm sees lack of communication as crucial because it has shaped our current patterns of collective thought (the constellation of ideas that govern our perceptions of reality). Collective thought is part of what Duncan Kennedy has referred to as our "consciousness."[62] It might more aptly be characterized as our unconsciousness. (Pierre Schlag describes this as "unthought.")[63] While it determines the way we live our lives and has serious material consequences, it is rarely confronted directly.

This historical account of legal-economic theory is an attempt at a confrontation, forcing us to recognize scientism as part of legal-economic theory's unconscious. A large part of it has been addressed toward the substantive content of legal-economic thought (particularly the issue of distribution of wealth). However, the content is inextricable from the process. It has not been a process of dialogue, but an exercise in ideological struggle. By establishing the modern quest for knowledge as one of Truth seeking, our seventeenth-century forebears set the stage for combat over whose Truth would prevail because there was little room to recognize the multiplicity of truths (perspectivism). While the historiography in this book has portrayed a landscape of hegemonic thought at various periods in American legal-economic theory, in fact there were always dissenting voices. But because of the modernist ethos and the ideology of scientism, those voices were all too often drowned out under the cover of science and the claim to objectivity.

With the twenty-first century ushering in a new conception of truth and uncertainty, perhaps a pattern of dialogue and openness, much as suggested by Michel de Montaigne in response to the impending rise of science at the end of the sixteenth century, will prevail in a climate in which scientism is waning. John Dewey summed up the basis for this prospect in the statement: "All materials of experience are equally real; that is, all are existential; each has a right to be dealt with in terms of its own special characteristics and its own problems."[64] This may be a utopian vision. It could be that power dynamics in the legal academy and the larger culture will thwart any movement toward dialogue. On the other hand, in a country whose population is becoming increasingly diverse, the pluralistic movement in legal academe may be inevitable. Only time will tell.

Nevertheless, the rise of fundamentalist movements in the United States and across the globe highlights the risks we run if we take relativist claims too seriously. This is a danger that even Richard Rorty, echoing Posner, would recognize: "the ideals of the Enlightenment not only are our most precious cultural heritage, but are in danger of disappearance as totalitarian states swallow up more and more of humanity."[65] The specter of religious fundamentalism may indeed renew the search for secular certainty in law. Law may be called upon to stem the tide of a "religious zealousness" that some view as the new totalitarianism. Today the choice between secular liberalism and religious fundamentalism may be framed as starkly as Hayek framed that of communism versus capitalism. To my mind it is a false choice. A truly liberal (pluralistic) society would have room for the practice of fundamentalism as well as other forms of expression. (Of course, there is still the question of whether fundamentalists are willing to share the stage of expression.)

Privileging any form of knowledge or expression as holding out anything akin to absolute Truth is problematic and risks devolving into a secular form of fundamentalism. In good part, science has been the basis of a secular fundamentalism in western culture since the seventeenth century. This is not to say that we can no longer reach justified beliefs regarding what form social practice should take. I would not even object to descriptions of such beliefs as "objective" or constituting the "truth." However, in our historical moment, the implications of what it means to satisfy the criteria of objectivity or truth are radically altered. This much is implicit given the current state of science.

In contemplating the quest for a theory of everything, David Lindley remarked, "[p]erhaps physicists will one day find a theory of such compelling beauty that its truth cannot be denied; truth will be beauty and beauty will be truth."[66] Such a theory would meet the Cartesian requirement of a "conception which an unclouded and attentive mind gives us, so readily and distinctly that we are wholly freed from doubt" of its validity.[67] At that point, according to Lindley, science will constitute a "story that makes sense within its own terms, offers explanations for everything we can see around us, but can be neither tested or disproved"—myth. In other words, science will be a form of religion. In many ways this would be a logical resting place for science, since the hope for a simple picture of the world owes much to the tenets of our "great" religions.[68] What will hopefully differentiate science is that scientists will always be in search of empirical verification, and if that remains an impossible chore (which I hazard to guess it will be for most "big" questions) there will be at least some level of uncertainty regarding the myth even as the search for (and conversation regarding) truth marches forward.

"Truth" marks a point at which we are justified in taking action based on our belief. Even in the course of taking action, we must still remain open to further dialogue regarding the course of future events. This openness is not a form of *noblesse oblige* on our part, but a realization that objectivity is measured by existing norms. I trust that this book has provided a graphic illustration of the point. Of course, norms will continue to include the traditional notions of objectivity (including "science"), but perhaps there will also be an openness to forms of expression not previously allowed and to an explicit consideration of political consequences. A "big tent" should be the rule, not the exception. The idea is not to paralyze us or have us fall into the quicksand of relativism, but to make us all a bit less certain of ourselves. Perhaps such *uncertainty* would be our most effective unifier.

ONE BIRTH OF AMERICAN LEGAL-ECONOMIC THEORY

1   Stephen Toulmin, *Cosmopolis: The Hidden Agenda of Modernity* (Chicago: University of Chicago Press, 1990), 23.

2   Stephen Feldman, in his thoughtful account of American legal theory, had divided its intellectual history into premodern, modern, and postmodern periods, with substages in each period. While his periodization differs from mine, particularly his identification of premodernism, this can be attributed to a difference in the focus of our two projects. Feldman has a broader focus than the one taken in this book, and the themes that he emphasizes dictate a more complex periodization. My focus on science justifies the association of early American thought with modernism. See Stephen Feldman, *American Legal Thought from Premodernism to Postmodernism: An Intellectual Voyage* (Oxford: Oxford University Press, 2002). In addition, "classical legal thought" is often dated post Civil War. Morton Howritz, *The Transformation of American Law, 1870–1960* (Cambridge: Harvard University Press, 1992); Duncan Kennedy, "Toward an Historical Understanding of Legal Consciousness: The Case of Classical Legal Thought in America, 1850–1940," 3 *Research in Law and Sociology* 3 (1980). While the years after the Civil War may have marked the zenith of classical jurisprudence, the intellectual origins of classical legal theory can be traced to a much earlier period. In addition, marking the pre–Civil War origins of classical legal theory helps to clarify its connection to classical economics.

3   Richard H. Popkin, *The History of Skepticism from Erasmus to Spinoza* (Berkeley: University of California Press, 1979).

4   Michael de Montaigne, *Essays* (1580), trans. Donald M. Frame, in *The Complete Essays of Montaigne* (Stanford: Stanford University Press, 1957).

5   René Descartes, *The Meditations* (1641; New York: Penguin, 1968, trans. with an introd. by F. E. Sutcliffe).

6   Descartes consciously positioned *Meditations* as a tract against Aristotle. In a letter to a friend, Marin Marsenne, he wrote: "I hope that readers will gradually get used to my principles [as set forth in *Meditations*] and recognize their truth, before they notice that they destroy the principles of Aristotle." Quote excerpted from Tom Sorell, *Descartes: A Very Short Introduction* (Oxford: Oxford University Press, 1987).

7   John Cottingham, *Descartes* (New York: Routledge, 1986), 14–15.

8   René Descartes, "Rules for Direction of Our Native Intelligence," *The Philosophical Works of Descartes*, trans. Elizabeth Haldane and G. R. T. Ross (Cambridge: Cambridge University Press, 1972).

9   René Descartes, *Discourse on the Method* (1637; New York: Penguin Classics, 1968, trans. with an introd. by F. E. Sutcliffe).

10   Ibid., 80.

11   Ibid., 90.

12   Rule XI, 33.

13   Rule III, 7.

14   Ibid.

15   Thomas Kuhn, "Mathematical versus Experimental Traditions in the Development of Physical Science," *The Essential Tension* (Chicago: University of Chicago Press, 1977), 30–65.

16   Francis Bacon, *Novum Organum*, I aphorism 92 at 102 (1620; Chicago: Open Court, 1994, ed. and trans. Peter Urback and John Gibson) (all references are to this edition, with the Roman numeral referring to book I or II of the *Novum*).

17   Ibid., I aphorism 86 at 96.

18   Ibid., I aphorism 8 at 45.

19   Ibid., I aphorism 17 at 47.

20   Ibid., I aphorism 25 at 50.

21   Ibid., I aphorism 50 at 60.

22   Ibid., I aphorism 54 at 62.

23   Ibid., I aphorism 63 at 68.

24   Laurence Lampert, *Nietzsche and Modern Times: A Study of Bacon, Descartes, and Nietzsche* (New Haven: Yale University Press, 1993).

25   *Novum Organum*, I aphorism 68 at 77.

26   Ibid., I aphorism 95 at 105.

27   John Henry notes that the idea of magic in the sixteenth century is very
      much different from the one that is conjured up in our contemporary
      imagination. As Henry describes it, the magical tradition did not involve
      stunts such as levitation but "the professed aim of using knowledge of nature
      for practical benefit." John Henry, *Knowledge Is Power: How Magic, the
      Government and an Apocalyptic Vision Inspired Francis Bacon to Create Mod-
      ern Science* (Cambridge: Icon, 2003), 61.

28   Ibid., 136.

29   This description of Newtonian mechanics is based in large part on Nathan
      Spielberg's and Byron Anderson's *Seven Ideas That Shook the Universe* (New
      York: Wiley Science, 1987).

30   John Dewey, *The Quest for Certainty: A Study of the Relation of Knowledge
      and Action* (New York: Minton, Balch, 1929), 209.

31   The following rendition of Newtonian physics comes largely from Stephen
      Mason, *A History of the Sciences* (New York: Simon and Schuster, 1962) (orig.
      published 1956 as *Main Currents of Scientific Thought*).

32   Henry, *Knowledge Is Power*, 159–60.

33   Mason, *A History of the Sciences*, 207; for a general discussion see 205–7.

34   Toulmin, *Cosmopolis*.

35   The idea that "thought" is collective (societal) as opposed to individual is
      borrowed from David Bohm. David Bohm, *On Dialogue* (New York: Rout-
      ledge, 1996), 48–60.

36   Hoeflich, "Law and Geometry: Legal Science from Leibniz to Langdell," 30
      American Journal of Legal History 95 (1986).

37   Ibid.

38   *Black's Law Dictionary* (1983).

39   Roger Berkowitz, *The Gift of Science: Leibniz and the Modern Legal Tradition*
      (Cambridge: Harvard University Press, 2005), 17–27.

40   Ibid., 19.

41   Sir William Blackstone, *Blackstone's Commentaries on the Laws of England*
      (1756–69; London: Cavendish, 2001, ed. Wayne Morrison).

42   Daniel Boorstin, *The Mysterious Science of the Law* (Chicago: University of
      Chicago Press, 1941).

43   Blackstone, *Commentaries*, 1:7 (Introduction, titled *On the Study of the Law*).

44   Ibid., 1:42.

45 Ibid., 1:30.

46 Boorstin, *The Mysterious Science of the Law*, 12.

47 Blackstone, *Commentaries*, 1:24.

48 Ibid., 1:24–25.

49 Boorstin, *The Mysterious Science of the Law*, 167–86.

50 Blackstone, *Commentaries*, 1:30–31.

51 Ibid., 30.

52 Dewey, *The Quest for Certainty*, 212.

53 Richard Cosgrove has noted that Blackstone's jurisprudence had broad implications for dealing with a wide range of social problems and examined the general foundations of English social structure—including its economic foundations. In this regard Blackstone is likened to Adam Smith. See Richard A. Cosgrove, *Scholars of the Law: English Jurisprudence from Blackstone to Hart* (New York: NYU Press, 1996), 46–49.

54 Blackstone, *Commentaries*, 1:31.

55 Toulmin, *Cosmopolis*, 128.

56 Perry Miller, *The Life of the Mind in America: From the Revolution to the Civil War* (New York: Harcourt, Brace and World, 1965), 109.

57 Ibid., 105 (quoting letter from Thomas Jefferson to Edmond Randolph, August 1799).

58 Ibid., 99–102.

59 Ibid., 3–35, 73–95.

60 See Dennis Nolan, "Sir William Blackstone and the New American Republic: A Study of Intellectual Impact," 51 *New York University Law Review* 731 (1976); Stephen Feldman, *American Legal Thought from Premodernism to Postmodernism*, 50–52 (discussing reception of Blackstone in America).

61 Nolan, "Sir William Blackstone and the New American Republic," 737.

62 Ibid., 756–59.

63 Miller, *The Life of the Mind in America*, 117–85.

64 Nolan, "Sir William Blackstone and the New American Republic," 764–67.

65 David Hoffman, *A Course of Legal Study: Addressed to Students and the Profession Generally* (New York: Amo, 1836).

66 Howard Schweber, "The 'Science' of Legal Science: The Model of the Natural

Sciences in Nineteenth-Century American Legal Education," 17 *Law and History Review* 421 (1999).

67   Hoffman, *A Course of Legal Study*, 55.

68   Ibid., 64–65.

69   David Hoffman, "The Civil Law," 8 *American Jurist* 203, 203 (1832).

70   Ibid., 205.

71   Ibid., 207.

72   William Warren Bailey, "Early Legal Education in the United States: Natural Law Theory and Law as a Moral Science," 48 *Journal of Legal Studies* 311 (1998). Howard Schweber has described this movement as "Protestant Baconianism." Schweber, "The 'Science' of Legal Science," 441–55.

73   Hoeflich, "Law and Geometry," 112.

74   Miller, *The Life of the Mind in America*, 117.

75   Ibid., 159.

76   For a discussion of the anti-egalitarian sentiment of the "founding fathers" see Feldman, *American Legal Thought from Premodernism to Postmodernism*, 57–65.

77   *Lochner v. New York*, 25 Supreme Court Reporter 539, 543 (1904).

78   Kennedy, "Toward an Historical Understanding of Legal Consciousness," 5.

79   Blackstone, *Commentaries*, 1:29.

80   Betty Jo Dobbs and Margaret Jacob, *Newton and the Culture of Newtonianism* (New York: Humanity, 1998), 69.

81   Adam Smith, *The Wealth of Nations*, book I, chapter 8, 167 (1776; New York: Penguin, 1999, ed. Andrew Skinner) (emphasis mine).

82   Ibid., 169.

83   Ibid., 180.

84   Ibid., 181.

85   Andrew Skinner, Introduction, Smith, *The Wealth of Nations*, 81.

86   John van Wyhe, "Science vs. Religion, or Are My Gods Better Than Your Gods? The Controversies over Combe's *Constitution of Man*, 1826–60," *Intellectual News* 11–12 (2003): 24.

87   John Austin, *Province of Jurisprudence Determined* (New York: Burt Franklin, 1970), cviii–cix.

88   Cosgrove, *Scholars of the Law*, 21.

89   Austin, *Province of Jurisprudence Determined*, 162–63.

90   Ibid., 164.

91   Ibid., 232.

92   Jeremy Bentham, *A Fragment on Government* (1776; Cambridge: Cambridge University Press, 1988).

93   Ibid., 4, 7.

94   Ibid., 13. Richard Cosgrove has argued that Bentham and others overstated Blackstone's anti-reform tendencies. See Cosgrove, *Scholars of the Law*, 37–42.

95   Bentham, *A Fragment on Government*, 3.

96   Elie Halevy, *The Growth of Philosophic Racialism* (1833; London: Faber and Faber, 1934, trans. Mary Morris).

97   Bentham, *A Fragment on Government*, 4.

98   Ibid., 26.

99   Ibid., 28 (emphasis in original).

100   Thomas Horne, *Property Rights and Poverty Political Argument in Britain, 1605–1834* (Chapel Hill: University of North Carolina Press, 1990), 142–59.

101   Ibid.

102   John Stuart Mill, *The Logic of the Moral Sciences* (1843; Lasalle, Ill.: Open Court Classics, 1987), 32.

103   Ibid., 34.

104   Ibid., 55. Mill referred to this science as "ethology."

105   Ibid., 57.

106   Ibid., 73.

107   Ibid., 80.

108   Ibid., 88.

109   Ibid., 135.

110   Ibid., 140.

111   Ibid., 142.

112   J. S. Mill, *Utilitarianism* (1863; New York: Meridian, 1962, ed. Mary Warnock), 251.

113   Ibid., 257.

114   John Stuart Mill, *Autobiography* (1873; New York: Penguin, 1989).

115   Mill, *Utilitarianism*, 266.

116   John Stuart Mill, *Principles of Political Economy* (1848; Cambridge: Hacket, 2004, ed. Stephen Nathanson), 3.

117   Ibid., 85.

118   Ibid., 110.

119   Ibid., 92.

120   Ibid., 280.

121   Ibid., 292.

122   Ibid., 295.

123   "Address by C. Langdell to the Harvard Law School Association, 1866," Arthur E. Sutherland, *The Law at Harvard: A History of Ideas and Men, 1817–1967* (Cambridge: Belknap, 1967), 175. See Thomas Grey, "Langdell's Orthodoxy," 45 *University of Pittsburgh Law Review* 1, 5 (1983) (emphasizing the role of science in Langdell's conception of law).

124   See Grey, "Langdell's Orthodoxy," 28–30; Anthony Sebok, *Legal Positivism in American Jurisprudence* (New York: Cambridge University Press, 1998), 92–96. Howard Schweber has characterized Langdell as straddling two competing scientific models: Protestant Baconianism and Darwinism. Schweber, "The 'Science' of Legal Science," 457.

125   Nolan, "Sir William Blackstone and the New American Republic," 763–64.

126   See Feldman, *American Legal Thought from Premodernism to Postmodernism*, 91–93 (discussing Langdell as marking a transition from classical reliance on natural law to legal realists' positivism). See also Sebok, *Legal Positivism in American Jurisprudence*, discussing the importance of inductivism to Langdell's legal theory.

127   For a discussion of Langdell's "unsophisticated scientism" and its reification of normative principles embedded in the common law see Patrick Kelley, "Holmes, Langdell and Formalism," 15 *Ratio Juris* 26 (March 2002).

128   See Grey, "Langdell's Orthodoxy," drawing links between Langdell's blend of inductivism and deductivism and J. S. Mill's *Logic*.

129   Feldman, *American Legal Thought from Premodernism to Postmodernism*, 94, 100 (noting that Langdellian legal analysis was "remarkably Cartesian in style" and relied upon claims to scientific certainty to inspire confidence).

130   Grey, "Langdell's Orthodoxy," 19.

131   Sebok, *Legal Positivism in American Jurisprudence*.

132   Ibid., 87–90 (discussing the false accusation that Langdell was a believer in natural law).

TWO PRAGMATIC RECONSTRUCTION

1   For a general discussion of the impact of Darwinian thought in America see Richard Hofstadter, *Social Darwinism in American Thought, 1870–1915* (Philadelphia: University of Pennsylvania Press, 1944).

2   Scott Gordon, "Darwinism and Social Thought," *Darwin in Retrospect*, ed. H. H. J. Nesbitt (Toronto: Ryerson, 1960).

3   Darwinism and its relationship to nineteenth-century notions of progress are discussed by Scott Gordon in "Darwinism and Social Thought," 49. For a general discussion of the idea of progress in nineteenth-century America as well as its relationship to Darwinism theory see Stephen Feldman, *American Legal Thought from Modernism to Postmodernism: An Intellectual Voyage* (Oxford: Oxford University Press, 2000), 74–77, 85.

4   Gordon, "Darwinism and Social Thought," 49.

5   Paul Croce, *Science and Religion in the Era of William James* (Chapel Hill: University of North Carolina Press, 1995), 90.

6   Betty Dobbs and Margaret Jacob, *Newton and the Culture of Newtonianism* (Atlantic Highlands, N.J.: Humanities Press, 1995), 20–27.

7   Ibid., 88.

8   David Hull has argued that the noted nineteenth-century philosophers John Herschel, William Whewell, and John Stuart Mill all disagreed with Darwin to varying degrees and for differing reasons. David Hull, "Charles Darwin and Nineteenth-Century Philosophies of Science," *Foundations of Scientific Method: The Nineteenth Century*, ed. Ronald Giere and Richard Westfall (Bloomington: Indiana University Press, 1973), 115.

9   Ibid., 121

10   See Louis Menand, *The Metaphysical Club: A Story of Ideas in America* (New York: Farrar, Straus and Giroux, 2001); Philip Wiener, "The Background of Pragmatism: Peirce's Metaphysical Club," *Evolution and the Founders of Pragmatism* (Cambridge: Harvard University Press, 1949), 18–30.

11   Menand, *The Metaphysical Club*, 201. Wright, Green, Holmes, and Peirce studied at Harvard in the Department of Intellectual and Moral Philosophy in the 1850s. John P. Murphy, *Pragmatism: From Peirce to Davidson* (Boulder: Westview, 1990), 7.

12 Wiener, "The Background of Pragmatism," 31.

13 Louis Menand notes that the club began to break apart (at least formally) as early as the summer of 1872. Menand, *The Metaphysical Club*, 226.

14 These four ideas are enumerated by Philip Wiener as the philosophical legacy of pragmatism. "The Background of Pragmatism," 190. In addition, Wiener lists secular democratic individualism as part of the pragmatist legacy. While I agree with Wiener's inclusion of democratic individualism as part of the pragmatist legacy, it was not a central theme in legal-economic theory. Richard Bernstein has enumerated five similar pragmatist threads: (1) anti-foundationalism; (2) thoroughgoing fallibalism; (3) the nurturing of a critical community of inquirers; (4) awareness of and sensitivity to radical contingency; and (5) plurality. Richard Bernstein, "Pragmatisms, Pluralism, and the Healing of Wounds," *The New Constellation: The Ethical-Political Horizons of Modernity/Postmodernity* (Cambridge: MIT Press, 1992) (Presidential Address to Eighty-Fourth Annual Eastern Division Meeting of the American Philosophical Association, 1988).

15 Wiener, "The Background of Pragmatism," 194.

16 Ibid., 198. Whether the context is historical, linguistic and symbolic, or social depends upon what the objects dealt with are relative to.

17 Ibid., 198–99.

18 Ibid., 200.

19 Ibid., 200–201.

20 Hull, "Charles Darwin and Nineteenth-Century Philosophies of Science," 129.

21 Menand, *The Metaphysical Club*, 207.

22 The term "empiricism" has many meanings in philosophy. As used in this discussion it refers to the empiricism of Charles Peirce and John Dewey.

23 Much of the discussion of these principles is derived from chapter 9 of Wiener, "The Background of Pragmatism."

24 Charles Peirce, "Questions Concerning Certain Faculties Claimed for Man," *Collected Papers* 5 (1934): 135.

25 Ibid., 149.

26 Peirce's empiricism, as well as Dewey's, marked a decided break from the European empirical tradition, which stressed that experience (empirical observation) stemmed from the domain of sense as opposed to the external world. John E. Smith, "The Reconception of Experience in Peirce, James and

Dewey," *America's Philosophical Vision* (Chicago: University of Chicago Press, 1992), 17–35.

27 Peirce, "Questions Concerning Certain Faculties Claimed for Man," 159.

28 Ibid., 162.

29 Ibid., 152.

30 Ibid., 183.

31 Charles Peirce, "Some Consequences of Four Incapacities," *Collected Papers* 5 (1934): 156.

32 Ibid., 156–57.

33 Ibid., 157.

34 Ibid.

35 Croce, *Science and Religion in the Era of William James.*

36 For an excellent rendition of the intellectual environment surrounding James at the time see ibid.

37 William James, *Pragmatism: A New Name for Some Old Ways of Thinking* (1907; Cambridge: Harvard University Press, 1975, introd. by A. J. Ayer).

38 Ibid., 12.

39 Ibid., 13–14.

40 Ibid., 20.

41 Ibid., 31.

42 Ibid., 31.

43 Ibid.

44 Menand, *The Metaphysical Club*, 217–18.

45 James, *Pragmatism*, 33.

46 Ibid., 39.

47 Ibid., 57.

48 Ibid., 116.

49 Ibid., 123.

50 See Morton Horwitz, *The Transformation of American Law, 1870–1960: The Crisis of Legal Orthodoxy* (Cambridge: Harvard University Press, 1992), 54. (Green's importance lies not in his direct influence on legal doctrine but in how his perceptions influenced others.)

51 Wiener, "The Background of Pragmatism," 154.

52   Menand, *The Metaphysical Club*, 225.

53   4 *American Law Review* 201 (1870), repr. in Nicholas St. John Green, *Essays and Notes on the Law of Tort and Crime*, ed. J. Frank (Menasha, Wis.: George Banta, 1933), 1. See Horwitz, *The Transformation of American Law*, 51–54 (discussing how Green's theoretical perspective constituted a precursor to an all-out assault on causation by legal realists).

54   Green, *Essays and Notes on the Law of Tort and Crime*.

55   Ibid., 10.

56   Professor Horwitz attributes the American courts' adoption of certainty in causation not so much to a misunderstanding of Bacon's maxim but to an attempt to undercut any redistributionist consequences of tort. Horwitz, *The Transformation of American Law*, 51.

57   Green, *Essays and Notes on the Law of Tort and Crime*, 11.

58   Ibid.

59   Ibid.

60   Ibid., 15–16 (emphasis added).

61   Ibid., 16 (emphasis added).

62   Ibid., 15.

63   Ibid., 16–17.

64   Wiener, "The Background of Pragmatism," 161.

65   Oliver Wendell Holmes, "Natural Law," 32 *Harvard Law Review* 40 (1918).

66   Anthony Sebok, *Legal Positivism in American Jurisprudence* (Cambridge: Cambridge University Press, 1998), 65.

67   Oliver Wendell Holmes to Harold Laski, 1 June 1922, *Holmes-Laski Letters*, ed. Mark DeWolfe Howe (New York: Atheneum, 1963), 1:329.

68   Morton White, *Social Thought in America: The Revolt against Formalism* (New York: Viking, 1949), 11–12.

69   Sebok, *Legal Positivism in American Jurisprudence*, 63–65.

70   Oliver Wendell Holmes, "The Path of the Law," 10 *Harvard Law Review* 457 (1897), repr. in *The Mind and Faith of Justice Holmes: His Speeches, Essays, Letters and Judicial Opinions* (Boston: Little, Brown, 1943), 71, 86.

71   Menand, *The Metaphysical Club*, 217 (quoting from letter of Holmes to Frederick Pollock, 30 August 1929).

72   Ibid., 341–44.

73   Oliver Wendell Holmes, "Law in Science and Science in Law," 12 *Harvard Law Review* 443 (1898), repr. in *The Collected Works of Justice Holmes* (Chicago: University of Chicago Press, 1998), 3:406.

75   Ibid., 407.

76   Ibid., 413.

77   Ibid., 418.

78   Ibid., 420.

79   Oliver Wendell Holmes, *The Common Law* (1881; New York: Dover, 1991, introd. by Sheldon Novick), 36.

80   Holmes, *The Common Law*, 35.

81   Ibid.

82   Ibid.

83   7 *American Law Review* 652 (1873), repr. in *The Collected Works of Justice Holmes*, 1:326.

84   Ibid., 327.

85   Ibid., 330.

86   Sebok, *Legal Positivism in American Jurisprudence*, 63–64.

87   Holmes, *The Common Law*, 94.

88   Ibid., 16.

89   Ibid., 95.

90   Ibid., 96.

91   For a discussion of John Stuart Mill's influence on Holmes see Patrick Kelley, "Oliver Wendell Holmes, Utilitarian Jurisprudence, and the Positivism of John Stuart Mill," 30 *The American Journal of Jurisprudence* 189 (1985); H. L. Pohlman, *Justice Oliver Wendell Holmes and Utilitarian Jurisprudence* (Cambridge: Harvard University Press, 1984).

92   G. Edward White, *Justice Oliver Wendell Holmes: Law and the Inner Self* (New York: Oxford University Press, 1993), 152; White, *Social Thought in America*; Henry Steele Commager, *The American Mind* (New Haven: Yale University Press, 1950), 374–90.

93   Oliver Wendell Holmes, "The Path of the Law," 71, 88.

94   Ibid., 88.

95   Ibid., 86.

96   Ibid., 79.

97 Ibid., 85.

98 Ibid., 79.

99 Ibid., 81.

100 Ibid., 81.

101 Ibid.

102 Ibid.

103 Ibid., 81–82.

104 *Lochner v. New York*, 25 Supreme Court Reporter 539, 546–47 (1904).

105 Holmes, "The Path of the Law," 82.

106 Ibid., 83.

107 For a general discussion of formalism as imbedded in late-nineteenth-century judicial thought see G. Edward White, "From Sociological Jurisprudence to Realism: Jurisprudence and Social Change in Early Twentieth Century America," 58 *Virginia Law Review* 999, 1001 (1972).

108 Holmes, "The Path of the Law," 80.

109 Dewey studied mathematical logic with Peirce at Johns Hopkins as a graduate student. Robert Westbrook, *John Dewey and American Democracy* (Ithaca: Cornell University Press, 1991), 20.

110 Ibid., 321, 341.

111 Holmes remarked to Frederick Pollock that *Experience and Nature* seemed to him "after several readings to have a feeling of intimacy with the inside of the cosmos that I found unequaled." *Holmes-Pollock: The Correspondence of Mr. Justice Holmes and Sir Frederick Pollock, 1874–1932*, ed. Mark DeWolf Howe (Cambridge: Harvard University Press 1941), 2:287. Holmes goes on to say: "me thought God would have spoken had He been inarticulate but keenly desirous to tell you how it was." Ibid. In addition, Holmes wrote to Harold Laski that reading *Experience and Nature* for the third time was one of the greatest things he had experienced on earth and that "if reduced to not more than two pages it would be the profoundest *aperçu* of the universe" that he had ever read. Ibid., 261. Part of Holmes's attraction to *Experience and Nature* may have been due to Dewey's having spoken admiringly of Holmes in the latter pages of the book. See Thomas C. Grey, "Holmes and Legal Pragmatism," 41 *Stanford Law Review* 787, 869 (suggesting that Holmes may have been motivated by self-indulgence in praising Dewey).

112 John Dewey, *Experience and Nature* (1925; New York: Dover, 1958), 1a.

113 Ibid.

114   Ibid.

115   Ibid., 2a.

116   Ibid., 4a.

117   Ibid., 3; see also ibid., 15 (describing dichotomy of mind and matter as dominant in philosophy and as being derived from Descartes).

118   Ibid., 3.

119   Ibid., 6.

120   Ibid., 6.

121   Ibid., 6.

122   Ibid., 7.

123   Ibid., 10.

124   Ibid., 11.

125   Ibid., 11.

126   Ibid., 22.

127   Ibid., 27.

128   Ibid., 398.

129   Ibid., 411. For an excellent discussion of the relevance of Dewey to social reform, particularly in contrast to Rorty's pragmatism, see Larry Hickman, "Liberal Irony and Social Reform," *Philosophy and the Reconstruction of Culture: Pragmatic Essays after Dewey*, ed. John Stuhr (Albany: State University of New York Press, 1993), 223.

130   Dewey, *Experience and Nature*, 412.

131   In making this historical point, I do not mean to suggest that this was the only possible implication of Dewey's framework ("social reform"). The open-textured nature of Dewey's formulation is susceptible to other, more conservative, political interpretation.

132   Dewey, *Experience and Nature*, 408.

133   Ibid., 409. Obviously, given Dewey's political call for social reform, this was not to be political detachment but rather analytical detachment allowing one to clearly survey the social terrain in order to better achieve one's political objective.

134   Ibid., 381. Dewey's belief in the connection between philosophy and the social sciences, as well as the belief that social scientists held regarding the relevance of philosophy, is illustrated by the inclusion of a chapter on the role of philosophy in social science research as part of a collection of essays

on the subject. John Dewey, "Philosophy," *Research in the Social Sciences: Its Fundamental Methods and Objectives*, ed. Wilson Gee (New York: Macmillan, 1929), 240. *Research in the Social Sciences* included essays on sociology, economics, anthropology, statistics, psychology, jurisprudence, history, and political science, as well as philosophy. Among its contributors were Roscoe Pound and Charles Beard.

135   Dewey, *Experience and Nature*, 433.

136   John Dewey, "The New Social Science," *Characters and Events*, ed. Joseph Ratner (New York: H. Holt, 1929), 2:736.

137   Ibid.

138   Ibid., 737.

139   Ibid.

140   Ibid., 738.

141   Dewey specifically stated that his solution did "not involve absolute state ownership and absolute state control, but rather a kind of conjoined supervision and regulation." Dewey, "The Elements of Social Reorganization," *Characters and Events*, 2:746, 759.

142   Ibid.

143   Ibid., 747.

144   Ibid., 749.

145   Clarence Ayres, "The Co-ordinates of Institutionalism," 41 *American Economic Review* 47 (1951). Ayres, one of the leading institutionalists, was trained as a philosopher under John Dewey. William Breit, "Institutional Economics as an Ideological Movement," *Philosophy, History and Social Action*, ed. Sidney Hook, William O'Neil, and Roger O'Toole (Boston: D. Reidel, 1988), 119, 128. This point is also illustrated by the fact that Dewey, along with the institutional economists Wesley Claire Mitchell and Thorstein Veblen, helped to found the New School for Social Research in 1919. Westbrook, *John Dewey and American Democracy*, 278. In addition, Dewey served along with Veblen as an editor of the *Dial*. Ibid., 233.

146   John R. Commons, *Institutional Economics: Its Place in Political Economy* (New York: Macmillan, 1934), 1:150. For a discussion of the similarity between the method of scientific inquiry undertaken by Thorstein Veblen (another leading institutionalist) and Charles Sanders Peirce see Alan Dyer, "Veblen on Scientific Creativity: The Influence of Charles S. Peirce," 20 *Journal of Economic Issues* 21 (1986).

147   In discussing the extent to which other disciplines influenced economic

thought in the 1920s, Robert Dorfman has stated that "significant cross influence derived from the widespread adoption of the programmatic approach to social studies." Robert Dorfman, *The Economic Mind in American Civilization*, vols. 4–5, *1918–1933* (New York: Viking, 1946–59), 125. Commager in *The American Mind* lists three attributes of the "new economic thought" (institutionalism) in the early twentieth century: (1) "recognition that economics was an inductive and pragmatic science"; (2) "appreciation of the relevance of ethical as well as scientific considerations"; and (3) "acknowledgement of the necessity of state intervention in the economic processes." Commager, *The American Mind*, 235.

148   Paul T. Homan, *Contemporary Economic Thought* (New York: Harper and Brothers, 1928), 414.

149   Dorfman has summarized the contributions of Veblen, Mitchell, and Commons as follows: "Thorstein Veblen, by his systematic view of the consequences of business processes upon society, furnished the theoretical stimulus of the developments of the thirties; Wesley C. Mitchell supplied statistical materials. But it was the earlier activity of Commons . . . [that] provided the New Dealers with a considerable number of practical instrumentalities and devices." Dorfman, *The Economic Mind in American Civilization*, 398.

150   Veblen was an editor and contributor to the *Dial* along with Dewey and took part in founding the New School of Social Research. Dorfman, *The Economic Mind in American Civilization*, 353.

151   White, *Social Thought in America*. (White also included Charles Beard and James Harvey as having led the revolt against formalism.)

152   Thorstein Veblen, *Absentee Ownership* (1923; New York: Viking, 1954), 83.

153   Ibid., 86.

154   Ibid., 89.

155   Thorstein Veblen, *The Theory of Business Enterprise* (1904; New York: August M. Kelley, 1965), 28–29.

156   Ibid., 29. Veblen did recognize that there were instances in which businessmen would take a more philanthropic perspective. Ibid., 42.

157   Ibid., 52.

158   Ibid., 52–53.

159   Ibid., 55.

160   Veblen, *Absentee Ownership*, 96.

161   Ibid.

162 Commager notes that the report of the Industrial Commission of 1902, which was the basis of much of Veblen's argument in *The Theory of Business Enterprise*, also contributed to the education of Commons. Commager, *The American Mind*, 243.

163 Commons, *Institutional Economics*, 2:844.

164 See Roy Lubove, *The Struggle for Social Security: 1900–1935* (Pittsburgh: University of Pittsburgh Press, 1968), 25 (arguing that social insurance was not a serious topic of debate in America before the founding of the AALL).

165 The AALL was conceived at an organizing meeting of the American Economics Association in 1905. Theda Skocpol, *Protecting Soldiers and Mothers: The Political Origins of Social Policy in the United States* (Cambridge: Belknap, 1992), 172.

166 See e.g. George Priest, "The Invention of Enterprise Liability: A Critical History of the Intellectual Foundations of Modern Tort Law," 14 *Journal of Legal Studies* 461, 465–70 (1985) (discussing connection between workers' compensation movement and strict products liability).

167 See Skocpol, *Protecting Soldiers and Mothers*, 186.

168 Lubove, *The Struggle for Social Security*, 32 (quoting from Commons letter).

169 Lubove, *The Struggle for Social Security*, 31. Theda Skocpol has labeled Seager the principal exemplar of the "AALL's overall-programmatic vision." Skocpol, *Protecting Soldiers and Mothers*, 194.

170 Henry Seager, *Social Insurance: A Program for Reform* (New York: Macmillan, 1910).

171 See generally Horwitz, *The Transformation of American Law*, 183.

172 Seager, *Social Insurance*, 5.

173 Ibid., 174.

174 Ibid., 19.

175 Ibid., 15.

176 Ibid., 16.

177 Ibid.

178 Ibid., 18–19.

179 Ibid., 5.

180 Richard Ely, *Property and Contract in Their Relations to the Distribution of Wealth* (1914; Port Washington, N.Y.: Kennikat, 1971), 1:25.

181 Ibid., 33.

182　Ibid., 12.

183　Seager, *Social Insurance*, 55.

184　Ibid., 55.

185　Ibid., 56.

186　The connection between Seager and Mitchell, as well as Mitchell's respect for Seager as an economist, is evidenced by Mitchell's eulogy for Seager in the *Journal of the American Statistical Association*. Wesley Mitchell, "Henry Rogers Seager: 1870–1930," 26 *Journal of the American Statistical Association* 83 (March 1931). In the eulogy Mitchell specifically recognized Seager's work on the Wainwright Commission to study employers' liability and the publication of *Social Insurance*, which was an outgrowth of the commission's work. In this light, Mitchell recognized Seager as "a thorough realist, always ready to face the facts however complicated or discouraging, but equally intent upon clear thinking." Ibid., 84.

187　Seager, *Social Insurance*, 58.

188　Ibid., 58–59.

189　Ibid., 59.

190　Ibid., 60.

191　Ibid.

192　Horwitz, *The Transformation of American Law*, 169; White, *Social Thought in America*, 64.

193　Holmes, "The Path of the Law," 83.

194　For a discussion of the connection between institutionalists and legal realists in national labor reform see Daniel Ernst, "Common Laborers, Industrial Pluralists, Legal Realists, and the Law of Industrial Disputes," 11 *Law and History Review* 59 (1993).

195　See Horwitz, *The Transformation of American Law*, 200–202; Edward Purcell, *The Crisis in Democratic Theory* (Lexington: University Press of Kentucky, 1973).

196　Laski had positive things to say about his interactions with Veblen. Joseph Dorfman, *Thorstein Veblen and His America* (New York: Viking, 1934), 450–51.

197　Thomas Bender, "E. R. A. Seligman and the Vocation of Social Science," *Intellect and Public Life: Essays on the Social History of Academic Intellectuals in the United States* (Baltimore: John Hopkins University Press, 1993), 49, 74. There were several other prominent intellectuals on the initial faculty, including Charles Beard, Harvey Robinson, Elsie Clews Parsons, Emily James Putnam, and Graham Wallas. Ibid.

198   See e.g. Isaac Kramnick and Barry Sheerman, *Harold Laski: A Life on the Left* (New York: Allen Lane/Penguin, 1993).

199   Harold Laski, "The Basis of Vicarious Liability," 26 *Yale Law Journal* 105 (1916).

200   Ibid., 111–12.

201   Ibid., 134.

202   Ibid., 113.

203   Ibid., 112. Laski also makes a direct reference to "social context" later in the article in discussing the need to view the world in "social context" when examining issues of liberty. Ibid., 130. For a contemporary discussion of "context" in legal theory see Martha Minow and Elizabeth V. Spellman, "In Context," *Pragmatism in Law and Society* (Boulder: Westview, 1991), 247.

204   *Holmes-Laski Letters*, 1:394–95 (Holmes agreeing with Laski that Charles Peirce was overrated). See also ibid., 18 (Holmes discouraging Laski from too loosely associating legal thought with pragmatism).

205   Laski, "The Basis of Vicarious Liability," 112.

206   Ibid., 123.

207   *Holmes-Laski Letters*, 2:451–52.

208   See White, *Social Thought in America*, 92–96; Horwitz, *The Transformation of American Law*, 61.

209   1 *Texas Law Review* 423 (1923).

210   Ibid., 429. See Nicholas St. John Green *Essays and Notes on the Law of Tort and Crime*, 15–16 for reference to "probable consequences."

211   L. Green, "Are Negligence and Proximate Cause Determinable by the Same Test?," 429, 434. See N. Green, *Essays and Notes on the Law of Tort and Crime*, 16, for reference to "experience."

212   L. Green, "Are Negligence and Proximate Cause Determinable by the Same Test?," 437.

213   Ibid., 443.

214   For a discussion of Llewellyn's contribution to strict products liability, though not emphasizing the influence of pragmatism and institutionalism on his thinking, see Note, "Karl Llewellyn and the Intellectual Foundations of Enterprise Liability," 97 *Yale Law Journal* 1131 (1988).

215   Ibid., 1134.

216   Karl Llewellyn, *Cases and Materials on the Law of Sales* 341 (1930). The
       reference to *McPherson* illustrates the essential role of a temporal view to the
       transformation of tort law. Cardozo, in seeking to undermine the doctrine
       of privity in tort law, states: "Precedent drawn from the days of travel by
       stagecoach do not fit the conditions of travel to-day. The principle that
       danger must be imminent does not change, but the things subject to the
       principle do change. They are whatever the needs of life in a developing
       civilization require them to be." *MacPherson v. Buick Motor Co.*, 111 N.E. Rpt.
       1050, 1053 (N.Y. 1916).

217   Karl Llewellyn, "Law and the Modern Mind: A Symposium," 31 *Columbia
       Law Review* 82, 91 (1931).

218   Karl Llewellyn, "On Warranty of Quality, and Society," 36 *Columbia Law
       Review* 699 (1936); Karl Llewellyn, "On Warranty of Quality, and Society: II,"
       37 *Columbia Law Review* 341 (1937).

219   Llewellyn, "On Warranty of Quality, and Society," 699 note *.

220   Ibid., 710.

221   Llewellyn, "On Warranty of Quality, and Society II," 402–3 (emphasis in
       original).

222   Ibid., 404 (emphasis in original).

223   Ibid., 407.

224   Llewellyn, "On Warranty I," 713.

225   Ibid., 732.

226   Ibid., 704 note 14.

227   Ibid., 713. Llewellyn cited specifically to Hamilton's article on caveat emptor.
       Walton Hamilton, "The Ancient Maxim Caveat Emptor," 40 *Yale Law Jour-
       nal* 1133 (1931). See also Llewellyn, "On Warranty II," 370 (Llewellyn reference
       to Hamilton's torts materials.)

228   Ben Seligman, *Main Currents in Modern Economics* (1962; New Brunswick:
       Transaction, 1990), 158.

229   Karl Llewellyn, "The Effects of Legal Institutions upon Economics," 15 *Amer-
       ican Economic Review* 665 (1925). Llewellyn states that he is "particularly con-
       scious of indebtedness to Sumner, Holmes, Veblen, Commons, and Pound;
       but the borrowings are legion and often unconscious." Ibid., 665.

230   Ibid.

231   Ibid., 682.

232 When setting out what he meant by "institution" in the social science context, Llewellyn would respond by citing to Walton Hamilton: "Institution is a verbal symbol which for want of a better describes a cluster of social usages. It connotes a way of thought or action of some prevalence and permanence which is embedded in the habit of a group or the customs of a people. In ordinary speech it is another word for procedure, convention or arrangement." Walton Hamilton, "Institution," *Encyclopedia of the Social Sciences*, ed. Edwin R. Seligman (New York: Macmillan, 1935), 8:84.

233 Benjamin Cardozo, *The Nature of the Judicial Process* (New Haven: Yale University Press, 1921).

234 There is a direct reference to William James in regard to the construction of personal truth as a part of everyone's makeup. Ibid., 12.

235 Ibid., 102.

236 Ibid.

237 Cardozo explicitly identifies and disavows "formalism" at two points in *The Nature of the Judicial Process*. Ibid., 66, 100.

238 Ibid., 31.

239 Ibid., 65–66.

240 Ibid., 100, 104–5, 137.

241 Ibid., 81.

242 See Priest, "The Invention of Enterprise Liability," 461.

243 Fleming James, "Tort Law in Midstream: Its Challenge to the Judicial Process," 8 *Buffalo Law Review* 315 (1958–59).

244 Professor Priest astutely notes that "James' influence . . . cannot be attributed to the novelty or persuasiveness of his theories." Priest, "The Invention of Enterprise Liability," 470.

245 James, "Tort Law in Midstream," 295.

246 There were other prominent legal scholars who echoed James's dissatisfaction with conceptualist thinking. For example, Leon Green levied a similar assault on conceptualist abstractions. Green believed that legal doctrine should be dynamic and not static. The basis of his belief, as it applied to tort law, was his humanitarianism. White, *Social Thought in America*, 75.

247 James, "Tort Law in Midstream," 338.

248 Ibid., 339.

249 Fowler Harper and Fleming James, *The Law of Torts* (Boston: Little, Brown, 1956), vol. 2.

250   Ibid., 759–84.

251   Ibid., 759. There is a spate of social insurance literature referenced in the chapter. Ibid. Although many references are to Harper's and James's treatise, James had already set forth his central theoretical claims in earlier work. See e.g. Fleming James, "Accident Liability: Some Wartime Developments," 55 *Yale Law Journal* 365 (1946); "Contribution among Joint Tortfeasors: A Pragmatic Criticism," 54 *Harvard Law Review* 1156 (1941); "Last Clear Chance: A Transitional Doctrine," 47 *Yale Law Journal* 704 (1938).

252   Harper and James, *The Law of Torts*, 759.

253   Professor Priest has also recognized the workers' compensation movement as an important antecedent to strict products liability. Priest, "The Invention of Enterprise Liability," 465–70.

254   Harper and James, *The Law of Torts*, 762.

255   Ibid. (emphasis added).

256   Ibid., 763 note 7.

257   James, "Tort Law in Midstream," 328–33.

258   See generally Henry Spiegel, *The Growth of Economic Thought* (Englewood Cliffs, N.J.: Prentice-Hall, 1971); Seligman, *Main Currents in Modern Economics.*

259   Fowler Harper, Fleming James, and Oscar Gray, *The Law of Torts*, 2d edn (Boston: Little, Brown, 1986), 23:132–33 note 7. Calabresi used this text in his torts course at Yale Law School.

260   Ibid.

261   John Schlegel, "American Legal Realism and Empirical Social Science," 28 *Buffalo Law Review* 459, 533 (1979).

262   *Report by the Committee to Study Compensation for Automobile Accidents to the Columbia University Council for Research in the Social Sciences* (Philadelphia: International Printing, 1932).

263   Schlegel, "American Legal Realism and Empirical Social Science," 521.

264   Ibid. Corstvet studied at the London School of Economics in 1923–24. Ibid., 521 note 304. During those years Harold Laski was a professor of political science at the LSE. Isaac Kramnick and Barry Sheerman, *Harold Laski*, 46. However, there is no evidence that Corstvet studied under Laski.

265   Emma Corstvet, "The Uncompensated Accident and Its Consequences," 3 *Law and Contemporary Problems* 466 (1936).

266 Ibid., 466.

267 Ibid.

268 Ibid., 467.

269 *Report by the Committee to Study Compensation for Automobile Accidents,* 76–90.

270 Ibid., 92.

271 James, "Tort Law at Midstream," 328 (emphasis added).

272 Harper, James, and Gray, *The Law of Torts,* 132.

273 Harper and James, *The Law of Torts,* 762–63 (emphasis added). In a later edition the reference to the "most efficient way to deal with accident loss" was replaced with the following sentence: "*Humanitarian objectives* of society can best be met by finding ways to deal with accident loss that will ordinarily assure accident victims substantial compensation to cover at least their economic loss, and will distribute the losses involved over society as a whole or some very large segment of it." Harper, James, and Gray, *The Law of Torts,* 132 (emphasis added).

274 See White, *Social Thought in America,* 139–79.

275 While legal realist insights infused the policy basis for James's *Restatement* views, the very process of "restating" the law has echoes of Langdellian legal science. See Feldman, *American Legal Thought from Modernism to Postmodernism,* iii.

276 William Prosser, "The Implied Warranty of Merchantable Quality," 27 *Minnesota Law Review* 117 (1943).

277 Ibid., 118, 119.

278 Ibid., 119.

279 Ibid., 122.

280 Ibid., 133.

281 Ibid.

282 Ibid., 123.

283 Ibid., 124.

284 Ibid.

285 Ibid., 125.

286 See Priest, "The Invention of Enterprise Liability," 511–18.

287 Section 402A states:

> (1) One who sells any product in a defective condition unreasonably dangerous to the user or consumer or to his property is subject to liability for physical harm thereby caused to the ultimate consumer, or to his property, if
>
> (a) the seller is engaged in the business of selling such a product, and
>
> (b) it is expected to and does reach the user or consumer without substantial change in the condition in which it is sold.
>
> (2) The rule stated in Subsection (1) applies although
>
> (a) the seller has exercised all possible care in the preparation and sale of his product, and
>
> (b) the user or consumer has not bought the product from or entered into any contractual relation with the seller.

Restatement (Second) of Torts, section 402A (Philadelphia: American Law Institute, 1965).

THREE   NEOCLASSICISM AND THE REPRISE OF FORMALISM

1   "Analytic philosophy" is a term ill suited to precise definition. It is better defined by the ways of doing philosophy followed by those associated with the analytic turn. In this regard, the five historical stages of analytic philosophy proposed by Barry Gross are useful. Gross marks the first stage of development with the early realism and analysis of G. E. Moore and Bertrand Russell. Their concern was with the method of forming precise questions and clear answers. Barry Gross, *Analytic Philosophy: An Historical Introduction* (New York: Pegasus, 1970), 13. The second stage is ushered in by the later work of Russell (1914–19) and the early work of Ludwig Wittgenstein. Gross refers to this stage as adopting the position of logical atomism: "to construct a language whose syntax mirrored the relations of the basic entities of which the world was made." Ibid. The third stage, logical positivism, marked an attempt to dispense with any form of metaphysics, and the "desire to construct a formal language adequate for science." Ibid. Performance of analysis in "natural languages" (ordinary language) marks the fourth stage and is an implicit rejection of stages two and three. Ibid., 14. The final stage is concerned with the problem of untangling the "diversity of language." Ibid. As will be discussed in the text, this chapter focuses on developments in stages two and three, with particular emphasis on the importation of logical positivism onto American soil.

2   Cornel West, *American Evasion of Philosophy: A Genealogy of Pragmatism* (Chicago: University of Chicago Press 1989), 183.

3   Nicholas Rescher has stated the major tenets of analytic philosophy as follows: the enchantments of language, linguistic analysis as a philosophical anodyne, reduction to scientific residues, prioritizing of science, and an end to philosophical theorizing. Nicholas Rescher, *American Philosophy Today and Other Philosophical Studies* (Lanham, Md.: Rowan and Littlefield, 1994), 34–35.

4   Joergen Joergensen, "The Development of Logical Empiricism," *Foundations of the Unity of Science*, vol. 2, ed. Otto Neurath, Rudolf Carnap, and Charles Morris (1939; Chicago: University of Chicago Press, 1970), 845.

5   Einstein's theory of relativity is divided into the special theory and the general theory. The technical distinction between the two is not relevant for this discussion.

6   This discussion is taken from Albert Einstein, *Relativity* (1916; New York: Prometheus, 1995, trans. Robert W. Lawson).

7   Lawrence Sklar, *Philosophy of Physics* (Boulder: Westview, 1992), 13.

8   Einstein, *Relativity*, 9.

9   Ibid.

10   Ibid., 10.

11   Ibid., 25–27.

12   Ibid., 37.

13   Ibid., 35.

14   David Cassidy, *Einstein and Our World* (New York: Prometheus, 1995), 60–62.

15   Ibid., 61.

16   Ibid., 64.

17   This example, and much of the description of the general theory, are taken from David Lindley's *The End of Physics: The Myth of a Unified Theory* (New York: Basic, 1993), 78–90.

18   For a general description of Einstein's influence on the Vienna circle see Cassidy, *Einstein and Our World*, 76–80.

19   See Alan Janik and Stephen Toulmin, *Wittgenstein's Vienna* (New York: Simon and Schuster, 1973), 133.

20   Moritz Schlick, "The Philosophical Significance of the Principle of Relativity," *Moritz Schlick: Philosophical Papers*, vol. 1, *1909–1922*, ed. H. Mulder and B. Vand de Velde-Schlick (Dordrecht: D. Reidel, 1979).

21   Moritz Schlick, "Critical or Empiricist Interpretation," *Moritz Schlick: Philosophical Papers*, 327.

22   Moritz Schlick, "Relativity in Philosophy," *Moritz Schlick: Philosophical Papers*, 345 (emphasis in original).

23   Moritz Schlick, "The Philosophical Significance of the Principle of Relativity," 167.

24   Tom Sorell, *Scientism: Philosophy and the Infatuation with Science* (London: Routledge, 1991), 4 (discussing role of members of Vienna Circle in laying the foundation for scientism).

25   A. J. Ayer, *Language, Truth and Logic* (1936; repr. New York: Dover, 1952).

26   Hao Wang, *Beyond Analytic Philosophy* (Cambridge: MIT Press, 1986), 103.

27   Ayer, *Language, Truth and Logic*, 31 (Preface to 1st edn).

28   Ibid.

29   I am taking this illustration from H. O. Mounce's *Wittgenstein's Tractatus: An Introduction* (Chicago: University of Chicago Press, 1981), 63.

30   Ayer, *Language, Truth and Logic*, 57–58.

31   Ibid., 75.

32   Ibid., 79–80.

33   In later noting the extent to which the theory of ethics revealed in *Language, Truth and Logic* would come under a "fair amount of criticism," Ayer made a point that needs emphasizing: the ethical discussion in *Language, Truth and Logic* does not "entail any of the non-ethical statements which form the remainder of [the book]" and is "valid on its own account." Ayer, *Language, Truth and Logic*, 20 (Introduction to 1946 edition).

34   Ibid., 107. This does not mean that for Ayer there is no place for intellectual, even scientific, investigation regarding ethics. Such an investigation would not constitute an "ethical science" but an inquiry into the "moral habits of a given person or group of people and what causes them to have precisely those habits and feelings." Ibid., 112. In *Language, Truth and Logic* it is proposed that this inquiry takes place in the disciplines of psychology and sociology. Ibid., 112. For an extended discussion of this positivist method of ethical investigation see Moritz Schlick, "What Is the Aim of Ethics?," *Logical Positivism*, ed. A. J. Ayer, trans. David Rynin (New York: Free Press, 1959), 247–63 (orig. published as chapter 1 of Schlick's *Problems of Ethics*, 1939).

35 Wang, *Beyond Analytic Philosophy*, 102.

36 Cornel West, *American Evasion of Philosophy*, 183; Joergensen, *Logical Positivism*; Giovanna Borradori, *The American Philosopher: Conversations with Quine, Davidson, Putnam, Nozick, Danto, Rorty, Cavell, MacIntyre and Kuhn*, trans. Rosanna Crocitto (Madison: University of Wisconsin Press, 1994), 5 (orig. published as *Conversazioni Americane con W. O. Quine, D. Davidson, H. Putnam, R. Nozick, A. C. Danto, R. Rorty, S. Cavell, A. MacIntyre, T. S. Kuhn*, 1991).

37 Borradori, *The American Philosopher*, 4.

38 Carl Schorske, *Fin-de-siècle Vienna: Politics and Culture* (New York: Alfred A. Knopf, 1979), xx.

39 Ibid., xxv. ("[T]he political and intellectual life of post-war America suggested the crisis of a liberal polity as a unifying context for simultaneous transformation in the separate branches of culture.")

40 See Alan Janik and Stephen Toulmin, *Wittgenstein's Vienna*, 242–43 (noting cultural malaise in fin-de-siècle Vienna).

41 Schorske, *Fin-de-siècle Vienna*, xxiii.

42 Ibid.

43 Stephen Feldman, *American Legal Thought from Premodernism to Postmodernism: An Intellectual Voyage* (Oxford: Oxford University Press, 2000), 115.

44 F. A. Hayek, *Hayek on Hayek: An Autobiographical Dialogue*, ed. Stephen Kresge and Leif Wener (Chicago: University of Chicago Press, 1994), 49.

45 Ibid., 1.

46 Ibid., 50.

47 Ronald Coase, "Law and Economics at Chicago," 36 *Journal of Law and Economics* 239, 243–46 (1993). The story as told by Coase is that Hayek, in the wake of the success of *The Road to Serfdom*, had made connections with H. W. Luhnow of the Volker Fund of Kansas City. Ibid., 245. Henry Simons, an economist at the University of Chicago, had ideas of establishing an "Institute of Political Economy" with the aim of bringing together "traditional liberal" or "libertarian" economists. These economists were "not [to] be mainly concerned with formal economic theory" or "engage substantially in empirical research." Ibid., 244. This idea eventually evolved into a project entitled "A Free Market Study" (also referred to as the "Hayek Research Project") housed at the University of Chicago Law School. Ibid., 246. Hayek played a key role in negotiating with the university and the Volker Fund to set up the program, and Aaron Director was put in charge. Ibid.

48   The University of Chicago Press agreed to a publication contract. F. A. Hayek, *The Road to Serfdom* (Chicago: University of Chicago Press, 1944), xvii (Introduction by Milton Friedman).

49   Ibid.

50   Ibid., xlv (Preface to 1944 edn).

51   Ibid., xxviii (Preface to 1956 edn).

52   Ibid., xix (Introduction by Milton Friedman). For a general discussion on the impact of *The Road to Serfdom* on postwar America and how it was instrumental in conservative politics, see Abbott Gleason, *Totalitarianism: The Inner History of the Cold War* (New York: Oxford University Press, 1995), 64–67. Gleason argues that "Hayek's contribution to the British and American understanding of totalitarianism was original in its virtually total emphasis on the economic bases of both democratic freedom and totalitarian freedom" and that *The Road to Serfdom* was "ideally suited to make the debate over totalitarianism a more integral part of arguments between conservative Republicans and liberal Democrats in postwar United States." Ibid., 64. Gleason also cites comments at the time of publication declaring *The Road to Serfdom* " 'one of the most important books of our generation' " and " 'perhaps the most discussed non-fiction work since the war began.' " Ibid., 65. Edmund Whittaker situates *The Road to Serfdom* as an "important" text within the stream of economic thought arguing against government economic planning and stressing individual freedom. Edmund Whittaker, *Schools and Streams of Economic Thought* (Chicago: Rand McNally, 1960), 388. Irving Kristol, a leader in the American neoconservative movement, has made the following statement regarding the influence of *The Road to Serfdom* in America: "Post-World War II conservatism begins to shape with the publication of Hayek's *The Road to Serfdom.*" Irving Kristol, *Neoconservatism: The Autobiography of an Idea* (New York: Free Press, 1995), 378.

53   For an example of the progressive response to *The Road to Serfdom* see "The Road to Serfdom: A Radio Discussion, April 1945," in *Hayek on Hayek*, 108. (Hayek discussing *Serfdom* with Manyard Krueger, the national chair of the Socialist party, and Charles Merriam of the National Resources Planning Board). In June 1945 Hayek debated Harold Laski, a prominent progressive intellectual. Gleason, *Totalitarianism*, 65–66. For a discussion of Laski's role in the intellectual development of strict products liability law see James Hackney, "The Intellectual Origins of American Strict Products Liability: A Case Study in American Parmatic Instrumentalism," 39 *American Journal of Legal History* 443 (1995).

54   Hayek, *The Road to Serfdom*, xxxiv (Preface to 1956 edn).

55   Ibid., xxxiv (Preface to 1956 edn).

56   Ibid., 4.

57   Ibid., 66.

58   Ibid., 41 (emphasis added).

59   Ibid., 41–42.

60   Ibid., 43.

61   An in-depth discussion regarding social costs and neoclassical economics is put forth later. The neoclassical economics focus on social costs preceded Hayek's discussion in *The Road to Serfdom* and is found in the work of A. C. Pigou and Frank Knight, which will be discussed later in this chapter. Suffice it to say that Hayek's discussion of social costs parallels standard neoclassical analysis. Ibid., 43–45.

62   Ibid., 45.

63   Daniel Yergin, *The Commanding Heights: The Battle between Government and the Market That Is Remaking the Modern World* (New York: Simon and Schuster, 1998).

64   Lionel Robbins, *An Essay on the Nature and Significance of Economic Science* (1932; London: Macmillan, 1962). See Ernesto Screpanti and Stefano Zamagni, *An Outline of the History of Economic Thought*, trans. David Field (Oxford: Clarendon, 1993), 97, 270 (discussing how Robbins's contact with Hayek at LSE led to the publication of *An Essay on the Nature and Significance of Economic Science* and the introduction of Austrian ideas in mainstream economics; also discussing how Robbins's conceptual reorganization "helped the neoclassical theoretical system to resume its dominant position"); Ben Seligman, *Main Currents in Modern Economics* (1962; New Brunswick: Transaction, 1990), 520–26 (discussing Robbins's position as a major figure in the neoclassical tradition and *An Essay on the Nature and Significance of Economic Science* as his "major work"); Henry Spiegel, *The Growth of Economic Thought*, rev. and enlarged edn (1971; Durham, Duke University Press, 1983), 528 (describing *An Essay on the Nature and Significance of Economic Science* as "important" and "the leading treatise on economic methods before the advent of macroeconomics"); Everett Johnson Burtt Jr., *Social Perspectives in the History of Economic Theory* (New York: St. Martin's, 1972), 6, 276 (describing *An Essay on the Nature and Significance of Economic Science* as providing the "clearest expression" of the twentieth-century view of economics as " 'pure science' " and as a "highly influential work"); Eric Roll, *A History of Economic Thought*, 3rd edn (Englewood Ciffs, N.J.: Prentice-Hall, 1956), 461 (arguing that the case for a value-free eco-

nomics was "presented most clearly to the English-speaking world" in *An Essay on the Nature and Significance of Economic Science*). That Robbins's work, as well as some of the other fundamental contributions to neoclassical economics theory, appeared before the analytic definition of science became dominant after the Second World War does not negate the importance of its relationship to that definition. (Of course, *An Essay on the Nature and Significance of Economic Science Significance* did appear only some three years before Ayer's *Language, Truth and Language*, which memorialized ideas that were already ensconced in the British intellectual milieu of which Robbins was a part.) The importance of the analytic turn is that it allows a superior claim to science to be made for intellectual products that meet its dictates whether those products took form *before, after,* or *in conjunction with* the turn. Indeed the framework for neoclassical theory had already been constructed in the late nineteenth century. See Dorothy Ross, *The Origins of American Social Science* (Cambridge: Cambridge University Press, 1991), 176 (identifying Carl Menger, Leon Walras, and Stanley Jevons as having independently devised the tools for neoclassical economic theory in the late nineteenth century). In pondering why "the passage from cardinalism to ordinalism [a major neoclassical economics move] occur[red] only during the 1930's if . . . all the necessary presuppositions were already available at the beginning of the century," Ernest Screpanti and Stefano Zanagni, in noting the importance of Robbins's *An Essay on the Nature and Significance of Economic Science*, point to the logical positivist movement as a key explanation:

> There was a widespread opinion, among the economists gathered together by Robbins at the LSE, that the notion of "individual preferences" was epistemologically safer than that of "levels of welfare." Logical positivism had had a dramatic impact on Anglo-American social science, and the entry point in England had been the LSE. At the beginning of the century, positive epistemology had not yet begun to disturb the sleep of the economists. It was not until the philosophical settling achieved by the Vienna Circle that economists, too, began to speak of "observability" as a demarcation criterion between science and fiction, and of neutrality with respect to value judgements as a separation criterion between science and ethics. The notion of "individual preferences" seemed able to dispose of the concept of inobservability of utilities and, the same time, to give a new foundation to the normative character of the interpersonal comparisons which motivate social policies. (Screpanti and Zamagni, *An Outline of the History of Economic Thought,* 270)

65   Robbins, *An Essay on the Nature and Significance of Economic Science,* 16. The

same formulation was integral in Frank Knight's definition of economic science, which will be discussed later in this chapter.

66 Ibid., 4.

67 Ibid., 11.

68 Ibid., 16–17 (emphasis in original).

69 Ibid., 75–78 (emphases added). The idea of preference ordering (indifference curve analysis) is a foundational analytical tool for contemporary neoclassical analysis. For a discussion of how the emphasis on "individual preferences" as opposed to "levels of welfare" fits with the logical positivist view of science, see note 64, above.

70 Screpanti and Zamagni, *An Outline of the History of Economic Thought*, 270.

71 Robbins, *An Essay on the Nature and Significance of Economic Science*, 76.

72 Under the law of diminishing marginal utility, the greater the consumption of a good, the lower the marginal (additional) utility the individual receives from consuming additional units of the good. For example, $10,000 would mean a lot less to me if my net worth were $1,000,000 than if my net worth were only $100. The concept of diminishing marginal utility could be used to argue for the redistribution of wealth as follows. If Person A is worth $100 and Person B is worth $1,000,000, then $10,000 taken from Person B and given to Person A would make society better off, because Person A presumably values the $10,000 to a greater extent. One could continue this analysis and argue for total equality of wealth.

73 Robbins, *An Essay on the Nature and Significance of Economic Science*, 137 (emphasis added).

74 Ibid., 138.

75 See note 72, above, for an illustration related to this point.

76 Robbins, *An Essay on the Nature and Significance of Economic Science*, 139–41 (emphases added). For a detailed discussion on the political significance of not recognizing interpersonal comparisons of utility in economic science, see Lionel Robbins, "Interpersonal Comparisons of Utility: A Comment," 48 *Economic Journal* 635 (1938). In "Interpersonal Comparisons" Robbins regrets that there can be no scientific case for ethical goals such as mitigating economic inequality. Ibid., 637. Robbins does not have a problem with the ends articulated by egalitarians but with the "logical status" of these ends. Ibid., 641. Interpersonal comparisons of utility have no logical status because, unlike other neoclassical postulates, they could not be "verified by observation or introspection, or, least, . . . [be] capable of such verification." Ibid., 637.

77   Yuval Yonay, *The Struggle over the Soul of Economics: Institutionalist and Neoclassical Economiists in America between the Wars* (Princeton: Princeton University Press, 1998).

78   Ibid., 77–99.

79   For an extensive discussion of the values debate see Yonay, *The Struggle over the Soul of Economics*, 150–57.

80   There will be extended discussion later of Robbins's articulation of economic science and Calabresi's and Posner's reconfiguration of tort law theory.

81   A. C. Pigou, *The Economics of Welfare*, 4th edn (1920; London: Macmillan, 1962). See Spiegel, *The Growth of Economic Thought*, 572–74, 806 (recognizing *The Economics of Welfare* as Pigou's most important text, and noting the significance of its having revealed instances where the pursuit of private gain did not benefit the general welfare and of its having used the point to create a "full-fledged system" undergirded by welfare state policies); Seligman, *Main Currents in Modern Economics*, 477–96 (praising *The Economics of Welfare* as an "extraordinary book" responsible for new areas of investigation for economists); Screpanti and Zamagni, *An Outline of the Economic Thought*, 183–85 (situating Pigou as a central figure in formalizing economic thought and arguing that his "most relevant contribution" was the distinction between private and social cost articulated in *The Economics of Welfare*); Robert Lekachman, *A History of Economic Ideas* (New York: Harper and Row, 1959), 386 (stating that "[t]he major work in welfare economics was Pigou's *The Economics of Welfare*"); Whittaker, *Schools and Streams of Economic Thought*, 308–10 (identifying Pigou as a central figure in welfare economics and noting the centrality of *The Economics of Welfare* to his work); Roll, *A History of Economic Thought*, 398, 476 (recognizing Pigou as a founder of welfare economics and labeling Pigou, along with his mentor Alfred Marshall, one of the "chief twentieth century representatives" of the "social reform tradition in English economic thought").

82   This approach dictates a discussion of texts in an author's oeuvre that does not necessarily follow any temporal order. The stress is on thematic ordering as opposed to temporal ordering. This approach, examining how the methodological stance, political position, and position on the specific issue of social costs all intersect, will also be taken in examining Frank Knight. In each case the approach dictates an exploration of specific texts in the author's oeuvre and is justified by the need to search beyond "scientific" texts to illuminate the author's political objectives.

83   Pigou, *The Economics of Welfare*, 4–5 (emphasis added).

84   Ibid., 5.

85 Ibid., 6 (emphasis added).

86 Ibid., 6–7 (emphasis added).

87 Ibid., 7.

88 Ibid., 11.

89 A. C. Pigou, *Socialism versus Capitalism* (1937; London: Macmillan, 1939). In a recent exchange regarding Ronald Coase's dispute with Pigou's analysis in *The Economics of Welfare*, both A. W. Brian Simpson and Coase recognize *Socialism and Capitalism* as a central text in Pigou's oeuvre. A. W. Brian Simpson, "Coase v. Pigou Reexamined," 25 *Journal of Legal Studies* 53, 68–70 (1996); Ronald Coase, "Law and Economics and A. W. Brian Simpson," 25 *Journal of Legal Studies* 103, 113–16 (1996).

90 Pigou, *Socialism versus Capitalism*, 21 (emphasis added).

91 Ibid., 13–14, 17.

92 Pigou, *The Economics of Welfare*, 134–35.

93 Ibid., 135.

94 Ibid., 172.

95 Ibid., 172.

96 Ibid., 183.

97 Ibid., 192.

98 Pigou, *Socialism versus Capitalism*, 138–39.

99 Spiegel, *The Growth of Economic Thought*, 578. For a general discussion of the downfall of Pigouvian economics see Nahid Aslanbeigui, "On the Demise of Pigouvian Economics," 56 *Southern Economic Journal* 616 (1990).

100 Ross, *The Origins of American Social Science*, 420.

101 Seligman, *Main Currents in Modern Economics*, 646.

102 For the importance of *Risk, Uncertainty and Profit* as a theoretical text see Spiegel, *The Growth of Economic Thought*, 642 (identifying it as an important theoretical text in neoclassical theory and Knight as "an intellectual force whose impact was felt by several generations of economists"); Ross, *The Origins of American Social Science*, 420–27 (acknowledging Knight as "one of the most powerful theorists among neoclassical economists" and "founder of the libertarian Chicago school of economics," and *Risk, Uncertainty and Profit* as his "major and still classic theoretical work"); Seligman, *Main Currents in Modern Economics*, 646–65 (arguing that *Risk, Uncertainty and Profit* established Knight as "one of the more important economists on the American scene"); Roll, *A History of Economic Thought*, 439 (recognizing *Risk, Uncer-*

tainty and Profit as the "best exposition of the theory of choice as it emerged at last from the successive refinements of a generation of marginalists").

103   Frank Knight, *Risk, Uncertainty and Profit* (1921; New York: Augustus M. Kelley, 1964), 3. This can be contrasted with Ayer's view that analytical methods help in understanding complex arguments.

104   Ibid., 5–6.

105   Ibid., 5–6.

106   Ibid., 7.

107   Ibid., 7 note 1.

108   Yonay, *The Struggle over the Soul of Economics*, 144.

109   Knight, *Risk, Uncertainty and Profit*, 7–8 n. 1 (emphasis added).

110   Frank Knight, "What Is Truth in Economics?," *On the History and Method of Economics* (Chicago: University of Chicago Press, 1956), 155 (orig. published in 48 *Journal of Political Economy* 1 (1940)).

111   Ibid., 164 (emphasis added).

112   Ibid., 164 (emphasis added).

113   Ibid., 153.

114   Ibid., 169–70 (emphasis added).

115   Frank Knight, "The Role of Principles in Economics and Politics," 41 *American Economic Review* 1 (1951).

116   Ibid., 1, 5.

117   Ibid., 12.

118   Ibid., 7.

119   Ibid., 12 (emphasis added).

120   Ibid., 3.

121   Ibid., 28.

122   Ibid., 20.

123   Frank Knight, "Laissez Faire: Pro and Con," 75 *Journal of Political Economy* 782, 788 note 5 (1967).

124   Ronald Coase, "The Problem of Social Cost," 3 *Journal of Law and Economics* 1 (1960).

125   Frank Knight, "Some Fallacies in the Interpretation of Social Cost," 38 *Quarterly Journal of Economics* 582 (1924).

126 Ibid., 583.

127 Ibid., 583–84 (emphasis in original). As will be discussed later, the entrepreneur played a central part in Knight's formulation of neoclassical economics.

128 Ibid., 586.

129 Ibid. (emphasis added).

130 Ibid., 587.

131 Knight, *Risk, Uncertainty and Profit*, 370 (emphasis added).

132 The choice of the three texts—"The Problem of Social Cost," *The Costs of
Accidents*, and *Economic Analysis of Law*—as core works in law and neoclassical economics discourse mirrors Henry Manne's recognition. Henry Manne,
An Intellectual History of the School of Law, George Mason University (Mono-
graph, Law and Economics Center, George Mason University School of Law,
1993). "The Problem of Social Cost" is widely recognized as a foundational
law and neoclassical economics text. Bailey Kuklin and Jeffrey Stempel,
Foundations of the Law: An Interdisciplinary and Jurisprudential Primer (St.
Paul: West, 1994), 35 (citing "The Problem of Social Cost" as a foundational
text for the "modern Law and Economics movement"); Mark Seidenfeld,
Microeconomics Predicates to Law and Economics (Cincinnati: Anderson,
1996), 91; Robert Rabin, *Perspectives on Tort Law*, 4th ed. (Boston: Little,
Brown), 186 (recognizing "The Problem of Social Cost" as important in
bringing "formal economic theory directly to bear on tort doctrine"); *Law,
Economics and Philosophy: A Critical Introduction with Applications to the
Law of Torts*, ed. Mark Kuperberg and Charles Beitz (Totowa, N.J.: Rowman
and Littlefield, 1983), 4 ("Since most schools of legal thought develop from a
variety of sources, it is usually difficult to identify any individual writer or
work as the foundation of the school. The economic approach to law is an
exception to this generalization, for its origins can be pinpointed exactly:
they lie in Professor Ronald H. Coase's article, 'The Problem of Social Cost,'
which appeared in 1960."). Coase's contribution to neoclassical theory was
recognized by the Nobel Prize in economics in 1991. *The Costs of Accidents*
is generally regarded as having reformulated tort law theory. Kuklin and
Jeffrey, *Foundations of the Law*, 4 (identifying Calabresi as a founder of the
"modern Law and Economics movement"); Rabin, *Perspectives on Tort Law*,
187 ("A leading influence among scholars taking an economics perspective
has been Guido Calabresi, whose book, *The Costs of Accidents*, provides a
comprehensive and systematic economic analysis of the tort system."); Kru-
perberg and Beitz, *Law, Economics and Philosophy*, 7 ("Calabresi's book, *The
Costs of Accidents* (1970), remains a leading example of how the approach
may be applied to a genuinely perplexing issue of tort doctrine—the alloca-

tion of liability for unintended harms."). *Economic Analysis of Law*, while not necessarily providing the novel theoretical insights of Coase's and Calabresi's work, has been recognized as a counterpoint to Calabresi and a text that establishes the foothold of law and neoclassical economics. See Rabin, *Perspectives on Tort Law*, 187 (using *Economic Analysis of Law* as a counter text to *The Costs of Accidents*); Kuklin and Stempel, *Foundations of the Law*, 169 ("L & E did not become firmly established in the legal academy until the publication in 1973 of Richard Posner's *The Economic Analysis of Law*.").

133 Seidenfeld, *Microeconomics Predicates to Law and Economics*, 91.

134 I will refer to the strand of neoclassical economics with a libertarian or laissez-faire bent as "Chicago School" law and neoclassical economics, as distinct from the more progressive school of law and neoclassical economics represented by Guido Calabresi.

135 For a discussion of Coase's criticism of Pigou's analysis in *The Economics of Welfare*, see Simpson, "Coase v. Pigou Reexamined"; Coase, "Law and Economics at Chicago."

136 Edmund W. Kitch, ed., "The Fire of Truth: A Remembrance of Law and Economics at Chicago, 1932–1970," 26 *Journal of Law and Economics* 163 (1983).

137 Ibid., 213, 215. In "The Problem of Social Cost," Coase does not cite Knight for the central proposition commonly referred to as the "Coase Theorem." However, Coase later acknowledged that "The Problem of Social Cost" was a "natural extension of Knight's insight that the institution of property rights would ensure that the excessive investment which Pigou thought private enterprise would make in industries subject to decreasing returns to scale would not in fact happen." Coase, "Law and Economics at Chicago," 250.

138 Coase, "The Problem of Social Cost," 2.

139 The tautological structure of economic arguments based on the assumption of "rational self-interest," including the Coase theorem, has been noted by Paul Samuelson: "Except by fiat of the economic analyst or by his tautological redefining of what constitutes 'nonrational' behavior we cannot rule out a non-Pareto-optimal outcome." Paul Samuelson, *Collected Scientific Papers of Paul A. Samuelson*, ed. Robert C. Merton (Cambridge: MIT Press, 1972), 3:35, 36 note 18.

140 Coase, "The Problem of Social Cost," 18 (emphasis added).

141 A similar observation regarding the lack of an empirical basis for Coase's anti-government leanings has been made by A. W. Brian Simpson. Simpson, "Coase v. Pigou Reexamined," 75, 92–93. Coase disputes that his anti-

government leanings are without empirical grounding. He argues that over the course of his tenure as editor of the *Journal of Law and Economics* the empirical studies on the economic effects of government regulation have led him to the conclusion that such regulation is "bad." Coase, *Law and Economics*, 107–8.

142   The relationship between analysis and libertarianism is implicit in Coase's discussion of Hayek's role at the London School of Economics. In the 1930s it was not the libertarian manifesto *The Road to Serfdom* (which was yet to be published) but Hayek's "encouraging rigour in . . . thinking" that was his contribution to his students. Ronald Coase, "Economics at LSE in the 1930's: A Personal View," *Essays on Economics and Economists* (Chicago: University of Chicago Press, 1994), 208, 209. However, Coase also notes that the effect of Hayek's teaching was to "make students look to private enterprise for solutions to economic problems." Ibid., 214. As for personal influence, Coase states: "[w]ith the arrogance of youth, I myself expounded the Hayekian analysis to the faculty and students at Columbia University in the fall of 1931." Ronald Coase, "How Should Economists Choose?," *Essays on Economics and Economists*, 15, 19.

143   Coase, "The Problem of Social Cost," 33–34.

144   Ibid., 39.

145   Ronald Coase, "Notes on the Problem of Social Cost," *The Firm, the Market and the Law* (Chicago: University of Chicago, 1988), 157, 159.

146   Ibid., 179.

147   Ibid., 189 (emphasis added).

148   Coase, "The Problem of Social Cost," 43. For Coase's part, he believed in the fundamental "truth" of self-interest. Ronald Coase, "Economists and Public Policy," *Essays on Economics and Economists*, 58. This truth formed the core of Coase's belief that "government is attempting to do too much." Ibid., 62. Coase has recently emphasized the political differences between himself and Pigou, and how those differences affect his view of social cost. Coase, *Law and Economics*, 115.

149   Richard Posner, *Economic Analysis of Law* (Boston: Little, Brown, 1972).

150   Thomas Kuhn, *The Structure of Scientific Revolutions*, 2d enlarged edn (Chicago: University of Chicago Press, 1970) (orig. published 1962 in *Foundations of the Unity of Science*, vol. 2). Kuhn notes that textbooks play a key role in perpetuating normal science paradigms. Ibid.

151   Posner, *Economic Analysis of Law*, 1 (emphasis added).

152   Ibid. (emphasis added).

153 Richard Posner, Book review, *The Costs of Accidents*, 37 *University of Chicago Law Review* 636, 637 (1970).

154 Ibid., 637–38 (emphasis added).

155 Posner, *Economic Analysis of Law*, 1 (emphasis added).

156 Ibid.

157 Ibid., 1–3.

158 Ibid., 4.

159 Ibid.

160 Ibid., 4–5.

161 Ibid., 5.

162 Guido Calabresi, *The Costs of Accidents: A Legal and Economic Analysis* (New Haven: Yale University Press, 1970). *The Costs of Accidents* reflected thoughts from several articles by Calabresi dating back to 1961.

163 Robert Rabin gives a brief account of the conceptual break between Fleming James's defense of strict products liability and the need for a reconceptualization post 1960s: "With the two major areas of liability for unintended harm [products liability and no-fault auto compensation] in a state of flux [post 1960s], comprehensive reexamination of the merits of the fault principle was virtually inevitable. A leading influence among scholars taking an economic perspective has been Guido Calabresi." Rabin, *Perspectives on Tort Law*, 187.

164 Calabresi, *The Costs of Accidents*, 5.

165 Ibid., 5.

166 Ibid., 7.

167 Ibid., 20 note 3 (emphasis added).

168 Ibid., 20–21.

169 Ibid., 26 (emphasis added).

170 Ibid., 69.

171 Ibid., 72.

172 Ibid., 70.

173 Ibid., 50 (emphasis added).

174 See text accompanying note 142.

175 For an extended discussion of the role of paternalism and distribution in tort and contract law doctrine, see Duncan Kennedy, "Distributive and Pa-

ternalist Motives in Contract and Tort Law, with Special Reference to Compulsory Terms and Unequal Bargaining Power," 41 *University of Maryland Law Review* 563 (1982).

176   Calabresi, *The Costs of Accidents*, 55.

177   Ibid., 55–56.

178   Ibid., 57–58.

179   Ibid., 24.

180   Ibid.

181   Knight, "Laissez Faire: Pro and Con," 788 note 5.

182   Calabresi, *The Costs of Accidents*, 24. Calabresi's discussion of justice mirrors Knight's arguments that "social justice" is a term which is "hopelessly undefinable" but that there may be agreement regarding "concrete *in*justices."

183   Ibid., 25.

184   Ibid., 25–26.

185   Ibid., 32.

186   Ibid., 28 note 6.

187   Ibid., 39.

188   Ibid., 39–40 (emphasis added). The commonsense notion that a loss to many affects economic well-being less than the same loss to one individual was even acknowledged by Knight. Knight, *Risk, Uncertainty and Profit*, 239. Of course, given the libertarian core of Knight's beliefs, he would not use this commonsense observation to argue for a program of economic redistribution.

189   Calabresi, *The Costs of Accidents*, 43. Calabresi points to Blum and Kalven as conflating the general problem of poverty with compensation in tort law. Ibid., 44 note 11.

190   Ibid., 69.

191   Ibid., 50 (emphasis added).

192   Ibid., 54.

193   *Restatement of the Law, Third: Products Liability* (1998) (published by the American Law Institute). An example of the drift toward negligence is the adoption of a risk-utility (cost-minimization) test in significant areas of products liability law. Ibid., section 2, chapter 1.

194   Posner, Book review, *The Costs of Accidents*, 644.

195   Ibid.

196   Ibid., 646.

197   Kevin Phillips, *The Politics of Rich and Poor: Wealth and the American Electorate in the Reagan Aftermath* (New York: Harper Perennial, 1990), 64–66.

FOUR   DISSOLUTION OF AMERICAN LEGAL-ECONOMIC THEORY

1   "The Fire of Truth: A Remembrance of Law and Economics of Chicago, 1932–1970," 26 *Journal of Law and Economics* 163 (1983). The remembrance chronicles a conversation among a group of the most distinguished members of Chicago School law and economics, including Ronald Coase and Richard Posner.

2   David Cassidy, *Einstein and Our World* (New York: Prometheus, 1995), 60–74.

3   Yaron Ezrahi, "Einstein and the Light of Reason," *Albert Einstein: Historical and Cultural Perspectives*, ed. Gerald Holton and Yehuda Elkana (Mineola, N.Y.: Dover, 1982), 253–78.

4   Maurice Merleau-Ponty, "Einstein and the Crisis of Reason," *Signs* (Evanston: Northwestern University Press, 1964), 192–97.

5   Werner Heisenberg, *Physics and Philosophy: The Revolution in Modern Science* (1958; Amherst, N.Y.: Prometheus, 1999, introd. by F. S. C. Northrop), 47.

6   Ibid., 28–29.

7   David Lindley, *The End of Physics: The Myth of a Unified Theory* (New York: Basic, 1993), 63.

8   Werner Heisenberg, *Physics and Philosophy: The Revolution in Modern Science* (1958; Amherst, N.Y.: Prometheus, 1999, introd. by F. S. C. Northrop), 55.

9   Ibid., 77–81.

10   Ibid., 84–86.

11   Ibid., 92.

12   "A Mystic Universe," *New York Times*, 28 January 1928, 14.

13   John Dewey, *The Quest for Certainty: A Study of the Relation of Knowledge and Action* (New York: Minton, Balch, 1929), 202.

14   Ibid., 204.

15   Max Born and Albert Einstein, *The Born-Einstein Letters* (New York: Walker, 1971), 91.

16   Thomas Kuhn, *The Structure of Scientific Revolutions* (Chicago: University of
      Chicago Press, 2d edn 1970), orig. published 1962 as part of *Foundations of
      the Unity of Science* in *International Encyclopedia of United Science*, 98–99.

17   Thomas Kuhn, *The Essential Tension: Selected Studies in Scientific Tradition
      and Change* (Chicago: University of Chicago Press, 1977), 321.

18   Rudolf Carnap, *The Logical Structure of the World* (Berkeley: University of
      California Press, 1967; orig. published as *Der logische Aufbau der Welt*, 1928).

19   For a discussion of these developments see Christian Delacamagne, *A His-
      tory of Philosophy in the Twentieth Century* (Baltimore: Johns Hopkins Uni-
      versity Press, 1999; orig. published as *Histoire de la philosophie au XXᵉ siècle*,
      1995).

20   Kuhn, *The Structure of Scientific Revolutions*, vi.

21   Willard van Orman Quine, "Two Dogmas of Empiricism," 60 *Philosophical
      Review* 20 (1951), repr. in *From a Logical Point of View*, 2d rev. edn (New York:
      Harper Torchbooks, 1963), 20–46.

22   Hilary Putnam, "Realism with a Human Face," *Realism with a Human Face*,
      ed. J. Conan (Cambridge: Harvard University Press, 1990), 3.

23   Ibid., 4.

24   Ibid.

25   Ibid.

26   Ibid., 16–17.

27   Ibid., 17.

28   Guido Calabresi, *The Costs of Accidents: A Legal and Economic Analysis* (New
      Haven: Yale University Press, 1970), 26. The concept of cost minimization
      would later be defended under the rubric of "wealth maximization" by
      Posner. For the purposes of this chapter, the two concepts may be taken as
      interchangeable.

29   Richard Posner, *Economic Analysis of Law* (Boston: Little, Brown, 1972), 5.

30   Ibid., 216.

31   Guido Calabresi and Jon Hirschoff, "Toward a Test for Strict Liability in
      Tort," 81 *Yale Law Journal* 1055 (1972).

32   Ibid., 1066–67.

33   Ibid., 1077.

34   Ibid., 1078.

35   Ibid.

36 Calabresi has noted this himself in thinking retrospectively about "Toward a Test for Strict Liability in Tort," saying that he finds the "discussion of the relationship of the strict liability and fault-based test to goals other than safety optimization to be inadequate." In addition, "[t]he lumping of other goals under the rubric of distribution is not helpful." Guido Calabresi, "The Most-Cited Articles from *The Yale Law Journal*: Commentary by Guido Calabresi," 100 *Yale Law Journal* 1449, 1501–3 (1991). The extent to which the distribution issue was taking on ever more importance for Calabresi is evident in his "Property Rules, Liability Rules, and Inalienability: One View of the Cathedral," 85 *Harvard Law Review* 1089 (1972), an article written with A. Douglas Melamed in the same year. "Property Rules" emphasizes that distributional concerns "play a crucial role in the setting of entitlements" (1098). It also contains a discussion of the mix between economic efficiency, distributional issues, and other justice considerations in fashioning legal rules.

37 Edwin Baker, "Utility and Rights: Two Justifications for State Action Increasing Inequality," 84 *Yale Law Journal* 39 (1974).

38 Ibid., 39.

39 Invitation letter, Conference on Critical Legal Studies (dated 17 January 1977) (on file with author); Richard Bauman, *Critical Legal Studies: A Guide to the Literature* (Boulder: Westview, 1996).

40 Baker, "Utility and Rights," 40.

41 The justification for this assumption is that inequality provides incentives for productivity and that government intervention to equalize wealth leads to a misallocation of resources. This is the free-market assumption, which Baker adopts. Ibid., 41–43.

42 Ibid., 46.

43 Ibid., 45.

44 Edwin Baker, "The Ideology of the Economic Analysis of Law," 5 *Philosophy and Public Affairs* 3 (1975). Also in 1975, a similar, but less focused, critique of distribution agnosticism in law and neoclassical economics and the refusal to acknowledge interpersonal comparisons of utility was put forward by Richard Markovits, "A Basic Structure for Microeconomic Policy Analysis in Our Worse-Than-Second-Best World: A Proposal and Related Critique of the Chicago Approach to the Study of Law and Economics," 1975 *Wisconsin Law Review* 950, 983–90. Markovits's criticisms are along much the same lines as Baker's but not as fully developed.

45 Ibid., 4 (emphasis mine).

46   Ibid., 9.

47   Ibid., 6.

48   Ibid., 29 (emphasis in original).

49   Invitation letter, Conference on Critical Legal Studies.

50   This account is largely taken from John Schlegel, "Notes toward an Intimate, Opinionated, and Affectionate History of the Conference on Critical Legal Studies," 36 *Stanford Law Review* 391 (1984).

51   Ibid., 397.

52   8 *Hofstra Law Review* 905 (1980).

53   Ibid., 912 (emphasis mine).

54   Edwin Baker, "Starting Points in Economic Analysis of Law," 8 *Hofstra Law Review* 939 (1980).

55   Ibid., 948–51.

56   Ibid., 953.

57   Ibid., 957–58.

58   Ibid., 959.

59   Ibid., 966.

60   Ibid., 968.

61   Ibid.

62   Ibid., 971.

63   Duncan Kennedy and Frank Michelman, "Are Property and Contract Efficient?," 8 *Hofstra Law Review* 711 (1980).

64   Guido Calabresi, "The New Economic Analysis of Law: Scholarship, Sophistry or Self-Indulgence?," 68 *Proceedings of the British Academy* 85 (1982). In framing his alternative program, Calabresi argued that he was "in part" synthesizing arguments that had already been made by him and by Baker, as well as Ronald Dworkin, Anthony Kronman, Jules Coleman, and Richard Markovits (89 note 2).

65   Ibid., 90–91.

66   Ibid., 91 (emphasis in original).

67   Ibid., 92 (emphasis mine).

68   Ibid., 93.

69   Ibid., 97–98.

70   Ibid., 104.

71   Ibid.

72   Ibid. (emphasis in original). These are of course identical to Baker's "critical assumptions," and their defense (on the basis of the "typical," i.e., "by and large") also strongly recalls Baker.

73   Baker, "Starting Points in Economic Analysis of Law," 971.

74   For a critique of egalitarian utilitarianism as either arbitrary or inconclusive see Allen Schwartz, "Products Liability and Judicial Wealth Redistributions," 51 *Indiana Law Review* 558 (1976).

75   Guido Calabresi, "First Party, Third Party, and Product Liability Systems: Can Economic Analysis of Law Tell Us Anything about Them?," 69 *Iowa Law Review* 833 (1984).

76   Ibid., 834.

77   Ibid., 843 (emphasis mine).

78   Ibid., 839–40.

79   Ibid., 843.

80   Ibid.

81   Ibid., 850.

82   Ibid., 843.

83   Ibid.

84   Ibid., 847.

85   Ibid., 851.

86   Ibid., 847.

87   Ibid., 851.

88   Richard Posner, "Utilitarianism, Economics and Legal Theory," 8 *Journal of Legal Studies* 103 (1979).

89   Ibid., 103.

90   Ibid., 105.

91   Among the practitioners of "welfare economics" cited by Posner was A. C. Pigou.

92   Posner, "Utilitarianism, Economics and Legal Theory," 119.

93   Ibid., 122–24.

94   Ibid., 136.

95   Richard Posner, "The Ethical and Political Basis of the Efficiency Norm in Common Law Adjudication," 8 *Hofstra Law Review* 487 (1980). This contribution to the symposium is noteworthy because it represented a final effort to ground wealth maximization on an overarching conceptual basis—consent. I note the devastating criticisms of Posner's consent argument in the same symposium so that the reader will appreciate the futility of his effort. Lucian Bebchuck, "The Pursuit of a Bigger Pie: Can Everyone Expect a Bigger Slice?"; Jules Coleman, "Efficiency, Utility, and Wealth Maximization"; Ronald Dworkin, "Why Efficiency" (all in 8 *Hofstra Law Review* no. 3).

96   Richard Posner, "Wealth Maximization Revisited," 2 *Journal of Law, Ethics and Public Policy* 85 (1985).

97   Posner, "Wealth Maximization Revisited," 86.

98   Ibid., 88. The need to shift the terrain from utilitarianism to wealth, begun in "Utilitarianism, Economics and Legal Theory," might be due to Posner's own recognition that egalitarian assumptions are at least plausible: "[S]uppose, for example, that Bentham and many other utilitarians are right that lacking any real knowledge of the responsiveness of different individuals' happiness to income we should assume that every one is *pretty much alike* [(typical)] in that respect. Then we need only one additional, and as it happens *plausible* assumption—that of diminishing marginal utility of income—to obtain a utilitarian basis for a goal of seeking to equalize incomes." (Posner, "Utilitarianism, Economics and Legal Theory," 115, emphasis mine.)

99   Posner, "Wealth Maximization Revisited," 97.

100   Baker, "The Ideology of the Economic Analysis of Law," 9.

101   Posner, "Wealth Maximization Revisited."

102   Ibid., 98.

103   Ibid., 90.

104   Ibid., 89–90.

105   Ibid., 98.

106   Ibid., 99 (emphasis mine).

107   Ibid., 103 (emphasis in original).

108   Ibid., 104–5.

109   Richard Posner, *The Problems of Jurisprudence* (Cambridge: Harvard University Press, 1990).

110   Ibid., 26 (emphasis mine).

111   Ibid.

112   Ibid., 31.

113   Ibid., 359.

114   Ibid.

115   Ibid., 382–83.

116   Posner does cite secondary sources, but it is difficult to determine their meaning from mere citation. Ibid., 383 note 31.

117   Ibid., 384.

118   Ibid., 387.

119   Richard Posner, *Overcoming Law* (Cambridge: Harvard University Press, 1995).

120   Ibid., ix.

121   Ibid., viii (emphasis mine).

122   Ibid., 8.

123   Ibid., 9.

124   Ibid., 10.

125   Ibid., 15.

126   Ibid., 15, 17.

127   Ibid., 23.

128   Ibid., 24.

129   Ibid., 27 (emphasis mine).

130   Ibid.

131   Posner, "Wealth Maximization Revisited," 105.

132   Shavell was just one of a group of economists who began engaging law and economics in the 1980s. A partial list of this group includes such important figures as Jennifer Arlen, Lucian Bebchuck, John Calfee, Robert Cooter, Richard Craswell, Louis Kaplow, Louis Kornhauser, Susan Rose-Ackerman, and Mario Rizzo. Many in this generation have doctoral degrees in economics and an affiliation with economics departments. They have all participated in the efficiency-distribution debate in some way, with Kornhauser, Bebchuck, and Rizzo making contributions critical of Posner to the *Symposium*.

133   A. Mitchell Polinsky, *An Introduction to Law and Economics*, 2d edn (Boston: Little, Brown, 1989), 119–27; and Richard Posner, *Economic Analysis of Law*, 6th edn (New York: Aspen, 2003).

134   Steven Shavell, "A Note on Efficiency vs. Distribution Equity in Legal Rule-making: Should Distributional Equity Matter Given Optimal Income Taxation?," 71 *American Economics Association Papers and Proceedings* 414 (1981).

135   Ibid., 414.

136   Ibid., 416.

137   Ibid., 417 (emphasis mine).

138   Louis Kaplow and Steven Shavell, "Why the Legal System Is Less Efficient Than the Income Tax in Redistributing Income," 23 *Journal of Legal Studies* 667 (1994).

139   Ibid., 667.

140   Ibid., 667–68 note 3. In addition, they take issue with Anthony Kronman and Jennifer Arlen for not recognizing that the income tax system is the proper vehicle for addressing distributive concerns. Anthony Kronman, "Contract Law and Distributive Justice," 89 *Yale Law Journal* 472 (1978); Jennifer Arlen, "Should Defendants' Wealth Matter?," 21 *Journal of Legal Studies* 413 (1992). The critique of Arlen is particularly noteworthy. Arlen had argued that given the assumption of risk aversion, liability rules should be fashioned to favor the less well off. She adopted the assumption in law and distribution economics that there is a declining marginal utility of wealth: "If individuals are risk averse, then, all other things being equal, a wealthier potential defendant has a lower marginal utility of wealth than does a poorer potential defendant." Ibid., 422. While Arlen framed her analysis in law and neoclassical economics terms of "optimal deference," Kaplow and Shavell criticize her for not disclosing it as the "masked transfer of wealth that it is." They see it as a potentially radical redistributionist argument: "In fact, a complete analysis of her model would lead to the conclusion that the socially ideal outcome involves damages that fully equalize the wealth of the victim and injurer" (State of the world C in Baker, "Utility and Rights"). Kaplow and Shavell do not dispute the analytic soundness of her argument but do dismiss it in stating that "[o]bviously, it would not be socially desirable to take parties' wealth into account in the manner Arlen suggests unless the income tax were unavailable for redistributive purposes." Kaplow and Shavell, "Why the Legal System Is Less Efficient Than the Income Tax in Redistributing Income," 676 note 14. For a further critique of Arlen's thesis, arguing that if actuarially fair insurance is available and income can be redistributed through taxation, liability rules should be set independently of defendant's wealth, see Miceli and Segerson, "Defining Efficient Care: The Role of Income Distribution," 24 *Journal of Legal Studies* 950 (1995). Miceli and Segerson identify the implication of Arlen's thesis and the cause for

Kaplow's and Shavell's concern: "A consequence of this result is that efficiency and distributional considerations cannot be separated in the design of efficient tort rules when the parties are not risk neutral." Ibid., 190.

141 Kaplow and Shavell, "Why the Legal System Is Less Efficient Than the Income Tax in Redistributing Income," 668.

142 Ibid., 675.

143 Kaplow and Shavell, *Fairness versus Welfare* (Cambridge: Harvard Univeristy Press, 2002), 4.

144 Ibid., 5.

145 Ibid., 30.

146 See Yuval Yonay, *The Struggle over the Soul of Economics: Institutionalist and Neoclassical Economists in America between the Wars* (Princeton: Princeton University Press, 1998).

147 John Maynard Keynes, *The End of Laissez-Faire* (London: L. and Virginia Woolf, 1926).

148 Ibid., 10–11.

149 Ibid., 27.

150 E. Ray Canterbery, *A Brief History of Economics: Artful Approaches to the Dismal Science* (Singapore: World Scientific, 2001).

151 Keynes, *The End of Laissez-Faire*, 28.

152 Ibid., 33.

153 Ben Seligman, *Main Currents in Modern Economics* (1962; New Brunswick: Transaction, 1990), 747.

154 Keynes, *The End of Laissez-Faire*, 46.

155 See generally Walter Salant, "The Spread of Keynesian Doctrines and Practices in the United States," *The Political Power of Economic Ideas*, ed. Peter Hall (Princeton: Princeton University Press, 1989); and E. Ray Canterbery, *A Brief History of Economics*, 212–14.

156 Salant, "The Spread of Keynesian Doctrines and Practices in the United States."

157 John Maynard Keynes, *The General Theory of Employment, Interest, and Money* (1936; Amherst, N.Y.: Prometheus, 1997), 377.

158 Ibid., 38.

159 Ibid., 380.

160 Ibid., 372–74.

161 For a similar argument, linking Keynesian economics with utilitarianism, see Seligman, *Main Currents in Modern Economics*, 731.

162 Duncan Kennedy, "Law-and-Economics from the Perspective of Critical Legal Studies," *The New Palgrave Dictionary of Economics and the Law*, ed. Peter Newman (London: Macmillan Reference, 1998).

163 Ibid., 470.

164 Ibid., 472.

165 Ibid.

166 Ibid., 473.

167 Ibid.

168 Ibid.

EPILOGUE   GAZING INTO THE FUTURE

1 Interview in John Horgan, *The End of Science: Facing the Limits of Knowledge in the Twilight of the Scientific Age* (New York: Broadway, 1996), 74.

2 Ibid., 88.

3 Horgan, *The End of Science*.

4 R. B. Laughlin and David Pines, "The Theory of Everything," 97 *PNAS* 28 (2000).

5 Ibid., 29.

6 Ibid., 30.

7 Ibid., 29.

8 Sheldon Lee Glashow, "The Death of Science!?," *The End of Science? Attack and Defense* (Nobel Conference XXV), ed. Richard Elvee (Lanham, Md.: University Press of America, 1992), 23, 29.

9 Michio Kaku and Jennifer Thompson, *Beyond Einstein: The Cosmic Quest for the Theory of Everything* (New York: Anchor, 1995), 40–42.

10 Horgan, *The End of Science*, 90–91.

11 Richard Rorty, *Philosophy and the Mirror of Nature* (Princeton: Princeton University Press, 1979).

12 Ibid., 315.

13 Ibid., 360.

14 Ibid., 361.

15   Ibid., 303.

16   Ian Hacking, "Disunified Science," *The End of Science?*, 33, 34.

17   Ibid., 37.

18   Helge Krogh, *Quantum Generations: A History of Physics in the Twentieth Century* (Princeton: Princeton University Press, 1999), 394–405 (chronicling attacks on science since the 1960s).

19   Hacking, "Disunified Science," 39.

20   Ibid., 46, relying on A. C. Crombie, "Philosophical Presuppositions and Shifting Interpretations of Galileo," *Theory Change, Ancient Axiomatics and Galileo's Methodology*, ed. Jaakko Hintikka, David Gruender, and Evandro Agazzi (Dordrecht: D. Reidel, 1981).

21   Ibid., 47.

22   Ibid., 49.

23   Richard Bernstein, *Beyond Objectivism and Relativism: Science, Hermeneutics, and Praxis* (Philadelphia: University of Pennsylvania Press, 1983).

24   Ibid., 8.

25   Ibid., 8.

26   Ibid., 16.

27   Ibid., 74.

28   Thomas Kuhn, "Objectivity, Value Judgment, and Theory Choice," *The Essential Tension* (Chicago: University of Chicago Press, 1977).

29   Ibid., 320–21.

30   Bernstein, *Beyond Objectivism and Relativism*, 100.

31   Ibid., 203.

32   Ibid., 126.

33   Avery Katz, *Foundations of the Economic Analysis of Law* (New York: Foundation, 1998).

34   Statement, "What Is Socio-Economics?," newsletter, AALS Section on Socio-Economics, 2005.

35   Ibid.

36   Robert Ashford, "Socio-Economics," *Encyclopedia of Law and Society* (forthcoming).

37   Ibid. (emphasis mine).

38   Robert Ashford, "What Is Socioeconomics?," 41 *San Diego Law Review* 5, 8 (2004).

39   Ibid., 7 n. 5.

40   James Kenneth Galbraith, "Toward a New Pragmatism," remarks to the AALS Socio-Economics Sections (available on line at journaloflawandsocioeco nomics.com).

41   Ibid.

42   Nicholas Mercuro and Seven Medema, *Economics and the Law: From Posner to Post-modernism* (Princeton: Princeton University Press, 1997).

43   Cass Sunstein, ed., *Behavioral Law and Economics* (Cambridge: Cambridge University Press, 2000) (collection of essays applying behavioral economics to law); Marianne Farber and Julie Nelson, eds., *Feminist Economics Today* (Chicago: University of Chicago Press, 2003) (collection of essays employing a feminist approach to economic analysis); Regenia Gagnier, *The Insatiability of Human Wants: Economics and Aesthetics in Market Society* (Chicago: University of Chicago Press, 2000) (comparing intellectual shifts in economic and aesthetic theories as a means of critiquing market discourse); Donald McClosky, *The Rhetoric of Economics* (Madison: University of Wisconsin Press, 1985) (deploying literary theory to deconstruct economics texts); Robin Malloy, *Law and Market Economy: Reinterpreting the Values of Law and Economics* (Cambridge: Cambridge University Press, 2000) (taking a humanitarian perspective to reinterpret legal-economic problems addressed under the neoclassical framework); Francesco Parisi and Vernon Smith, eds., *The Law and Economics of Irrational Behavior* (Stanford: Stanford University Press, 2005) (collection of essays using psychology to examine the role of irrationality in economic decision making); Emma Coleman Jordan and Angela Harris, *Economic Justice: Race, Gender, Identity and Economics* (New York: Foundation, 2005) (textbook blending race and economic analysis).

44   Stephen Feldman, *American Legal Thought from Premodernism to Postmodernism: An Intellectual Voyage* (Oxford: Oxford University Press, 2000), 129.

45   Ibid., 157.

46   Richard Posner, *Overcoming Law* (Cambridge: Harvard University Press, 1995), 10.

47   Patricia Williams, *The Alchemy of Race and Rights: Diary of a Law Professor* (Cambridge: Harvard University Press, 1991).

48   Posner, *Overcoming Law*, 368.

49   Ibid., 369, 371.

50   Ibid., 373.

51   Ibid.

52   Ibid., 377.

53   Ibid., 380–81.

54   Pierre Schlag, *The Enchantment of Reason* (Durham: Duke University Press, 1998), 26–29.

55   Posner, *Overcoming Law*, 381 (emphasis mine).

56   Ibid.

57   Ibid., 384 (emphasis mine).

58   See discussion of David Bohm below.

59   Posner, *Overcoming Law*, 395.

60   Schlag, *The Enchantment of Reason*, 81–86.

61   David Bohm, *On Dialogue*, ed. Lee Nichol (New York: Routledge, 1996).

62   Duncan Kennedy, "Toward an Historical Understanding of Legal Consciousness: The Case of Classical Legal Thought in America, 1850–1940," 3 *Research in Law and Sociology* 3 (1980).

63   Schlag, *The Enchantment of Reason*, 69–77.

64   John Dewey, *The Quest for Certainty* (New York: Minton, Balch, 1929), 216.

65   Rorty, *Philosophy and the Mirror of Nature*, 333.

66   David Lindley, *The End of Physics: The Myth of a Unified Theory* (New York: Basic, 1993), 255.

67   René Descartes, *Rules for the Direction of Our Native Intelligence* (1628), rule III, *The Philosophical Works of Descartes*, ed. Elizabeth Haldone and G. R. T. Rosstrans (Cambridge: Cambridge University Press, 1972), 7.

68   Michio Kaku and Jennifer Thompson, *Beyond Einstein*, 129.

Montaigne, Michel de, 2–3, 171
Morey, Edward, 82
"Mystic Universe, A," 125

Natural law, 17–18, 30, 37, 53, 142–43;
    Austin's critique of, 28; defined, 15; in
    English legal doctrine, 16; Holmes's
    disdain for, 51; inductivism and, 20;
    Llewellyn's critique of, 71; wealth dis-
    tribution protected by, 23
Nature of the Judicial Process, The (Car-
    dozo), 72
Nazism, 87–89
Negligence, 49, 53–55, 63, 65–66, 69, 75,
    79, 119
Neoclassical economics: Chicago
    School and, 210 n. 134; as economic
    science, 93; Einstein's influence on,
    89; Hayek's influence on, 89; institu-
    tional economics displaced by, xvii,
    75, 95, 101; legal-economic theory
    and, xv, 166; liberal vs. conservative
    exponents of, 105; logical positivism
    and, 94; Posner's preference for, 109,
    145; rise of, 89; social dislocation and,
    117–18
Neoconservatism (Kristol), 202 n. 52
Neopragmatism, 163; law and distribu-
    tion economics and, 132; legal-
    economic theory and, xv; legal the-
    ory and, 169
"New Economic Analysis of Law"
    (Calabresi), 137–38
New School for Social Research, 68;
    founding of, 189 n. 145
"New Social Science, The" (Dewey), 59
Newton, Isaac: absolute time theory
    and, 12, 82; Baconian and Cartesian
    ideas fused by, 1, 10; cultural recep-
    tion of, 14; deity and, 25, 41; deter-
    minism and, xv; ether and, 82; flat

space hypothesized by, 85; legal the-
    ory and, xv, 15, 24, 74; as modernist,
    62; physical laws and, 11, 39, 41, 55,
    85, 159; quantum theory and, 127;
    seventeenth-century science and,
    xvii; theory of gravity and, 84–85;
    utilitarianism and, 29–30
Nietzsche, Friedrich, 127
"Note on Efficiency vs. Distributional
    Equity in Legal Rulemaking"
    (Shavell), 147–48
Novum Organum (Bacon), 7–9

Objectivity: claims to scientific status
    and, xiv; critiques of, 163; defined,
    xiii–xiv; legal realist challenge to, 67;
    political conception of legal theory
    vs., xiv; praxis of objectivity and, xvi;
    Quine's questioning of, 126–27
"Oliver Wendell Holmes, Utilitarian
    Jurisprudence, and the Positivism of
    John Stuart Mill" (Kelley), 186 n. 91
On Liberty (J. S. Mill), 32, 146
"On Warranty of Quality, and Society"
    (Llewellyn), 70–71
Ordinalism, 94–95
Origin of Species (Darwin), 39–41, 43, 45
Origins of American Social Science, The
    (Ross), 204 n. 64
*Outline of the History of Economic
    Thought* (Screpanti and Zanagni),
    203 n. 64
Overcoming Law (Posner), 145–47, 166

"Path of Law, The" (Holmes), 54–55, 68
Paternalism, 113, 116, 212 n. 175
Peckham, Justice, 23–24, 71
Peirce, Charles, 41–45, 49–50, 57–58,
    60, 163
Perspectives on Tort Law (Rabin), 212 n.
    163

JAMES HACKNEY is a professor of law
at Northeastern University.

Library of Congress Cataloging-in-Publication Data
Hackney, James R., 1964–
Under cover of science : American legal-economic theory
and the quest for objectivity / James R. Hackney Jr.
p. cm.
Includes bibliographical references and index.
ISBN-13: 978-0-8223-3981-6 (cloth : alk. paper)
ISBN-13: 978-0-8223-3998-4 (pbk. : alk. paper)
1. Law—Economic aspects—United States.
2. Torts—Economic aspects—United States.
3. Law and economics. I. Title. K487.E3H33 2007
340'.11—dc22   2006034055